Great Sermons on the Birth, Death, and Resurrection of Christ

Great Sermons on the Birth, Death, and Resurrection of Christ

Edited by

Wilbur M. Smith

VOLUME 2

Jesus' Death

BAKER BOOK HOUSE
Grand Rapids, Michigan 49516

Contents

Appendices

PREFACE

The title of this third volume in the series of Great Sermons is really what might be thought of as a contradiction, for the death of our Lord is such a profound subject, which carries us into the very counsels of the Triune God, an event that has such a vast universal significance that no sermon on any aspect of the death of Christ can rightly be called "great" in comparison with the infinite greatness of the event itself. Nevertheless, I am keeping to the title for the sake of uniformity in this series.

What a tremendous contrast is found in the preëminent place given to the death of Christ, not only in His own teachings, but in the composition of the four Gospels, and in the great doctrinal epistles of the early Apostolic church, as well as the book of Revelation, as contrasted with the comparatively minor significance, or even insignificance, of the death of such a world figure as Napoleon Bonaparte. Here is the way his death is spoken of in the last edition of the *Encyclopedia Britannica*. "He died on the morning of May 5 in his fifty-second year. His body was dressed in his favorite uniform and covered with the cloak he wore at Marengo. He was buried in a lovely spot near a spring, shaded by two weeping willows. He had often walked there. 'Here lies' was on the stone, no name." In other words, the death of Napoleon was about the least important episode of his life, whereas it was the great event in the life of Christ.

Among the innumerable testimonies to the preëminent significance of the death of Christ, may I call attention to one unexpectedly appearing in one of the outstanding surveys of the ancient world that has been produced during this generation. Professor Albert A. Trevor in his *History of Ancient Civilization,* clearly sets forth this indisputable fact in the following concise statement: "In the later years of Tiberius, probably soon after 30 A. D.,

7

occurred in Judaea an event unnoticed by Romans, the crucifixion of Jesus. Yet this seemingly insignificant affair was to become the central event in future Western history, and the despised Galilean was destined to triumph over all the gods and emperors of the Roman world." (*History of Ancient Civilization,* New York, 1939, Vol. 2, p. 467).

The reaction to the Cross of Christ on the part of some world thinkers who have refused to receive the benefits of Christ's atoning work would make an interesting study of its own. Many will recall that our famous essayist, still in his early twenties, R. W. Emerson asked the officers of the Second Church of Concord, Massachusetts, if they would not adopt his idea of eliminating the entire sacrament of the Lord's Supper from their Unitarian services and upon their refusal, he preached his famous sermon on the Lord's Supper, so full of misapprehensions of the New Testament teaching, and offered his resignation, which when accepted, terminated his career as a minister. In this sermon he confessed, "This mode of commemorating Christ is not suitable to me. That is reason enough why I should abandon it. . . . My brethren have considered my views with patience and candor and have recommended unanimously an adherence to the present form. I am clearly of the opinion I ought not to administer it." The words of the now no longer read Robert C. Ingersoll, in reference to the blood of Christ are actually so blasphemous that I would not stain these pages by quoting a single line. (They may be found in the Dresden edition of his *Works,* New York, 1902. I. 457; IV. 258-9).

The bibliographies for each separate text have been constructed with great care and are the result of even more extensive research than was involved in the compilation of the bibliographies for the first two volumes in this series. Actually, I have searched for titles that contained sermons bearing upon the subject of our Lord's death in twenty-one different libraries, from the Pacific to the Atlantic, including this time five libraries in New England, such as Harvard, Yale, Andover, etc. I am more astonished than ever at the poverty of sermonic literature in most of the libraries of our theological seminaries at the present time. My research in New England was done after all the other libraries had been consulted, and out of 105 titles which I hoped to find, only eighteen of them turned up in these five theological libraries.

May I repeat what was said in the earlier volumes, that every sermon mentioned in these bibliographies has been carefully read, and the bibliographic data may be depended upon. I have examined literally hundreds of sermons, which while other bibliographic helps would indicate that they are on one of the texts appearing in this volume, when one actually examines them he finds that they have nothing to do with the death of Christ at all. One simple illustration will suffice. Certainly Revelation 5:9 is one of the great passages on the death of Christ in the New Testament, but the sermon by Dr. Talmage on this text is on the subject, "Music in Heaven," from the opening clause, "they sang a new song."

There is one area of significance in the study of contemporary views of the atoning work of Christ in the Roman Catholic Church which I have not attempted to insert in my bibliographies. Those who are interested may find a great amount of very valuable material in the published *Proceedings of the First Precious Blood Study Week* held at St. Joseph College, Renesselaer, Indiana, August 6-8, 1957. Here will be found scholarly discussions of such subjects as Blood in the Old Testament, the Precious Blood in the Epistle to the Hebrews, the Precious Blood in Art, the Precious Blood a Remedy for Sin, and Devotions to the Precious Blood.

In the volume in this series on the Resurrection of our Lord, I reprinted biographical sketches of those from whom I had also used sermons in the first volume, but in this third volume of the series, I am not reprinting biographical sketches (there would be five of them), because it has been necessary in this volume to include biographical sketches of thirteen authors of sermons whose names did not appear in either of the first two volumes.

I would like to express my deep appreciation to the Editors of

Decision magazine for being allowed the privilege of reprinting Dr. Billy Graham's sermon on the Offense of the Cross, which first appeared in their issue of November, 1961. I cannot close this brief preface without expressing my profound gratitude to the Evangelical Book Club for making each of the first two volumes of the series their leading choice when the volumes appeared.

CHRIST FORESEEING THE CROSS
by
Alexander Maclaren

"From that time forth began Jesus to shew unto His disciples, how that He must go unto Jerusalem, and suffer many things of the elders and chief priests and scribes, and be killed, and be raised again the third day." — Matthew 16:21.

The 'time' referred to in the text was probably a little more than six months before the Crucifixion, when Jesus was just on the point of finally leaving Galilee, and travelling towards Jerusalem. It was an epoch in His ministry. The hostility of the priestly party in the capital had become more pronounced, and simultaneously the fickle enthusiasm of the Galilean crowds, which had been cooled by His discouragement, had died down into apathy. He and His followers are about to leave familiar scenes and faces, and to plunge into perilous and untrodden paths. He is resolved that, if they will 'come after Him,' as He bids them in a subsequent verse, it shall be with their eyes open, and as knowing that to come after Him now means to cut themselves loose from old moorings, and to put out into the storm. Jerusalem is not a triumphal procession to a crown, but a march to a cross.

So, this new epoch in His life is attended with a new development of His teaching. My text sums up the result of many interviews in which, by slow degrees, He sought to put the disciples in possession of this unwelcome truth. It was prepared for by the previous conversation in which His question elicited from Peter, as the mouthpiece of the apostles, the great confession of His Messiahship and Divinity. Settled in their belief of these truths, however imperfect their intellectual grasp of them, they

11

might perhaps be able to receive the mournful mystery of His passion.

I. We have here set forth in the first place our Lord's anticipation of the Cross.

Mark the tone of the language, the minuteness of the detail, the absolute certainty of the prevision. That is not the language of a man who simply is calculating that the course which he is pursuing is likely to end in his martyrdom; but the thing lies there before Him, a definite, fixed certainty; every detail known, the scene, the instruments, the non-participation of these in the final act of His death, His resurrection, and its date, — all manifested and mapped out in His sight, and all absolutely certain.

Now this was by no means the first time that the certainty of the Cross was plain to Christ. It was not even the first time that it had been announced in His teaching. Veiled hints; allusions, brief but pregnant, had been scattered through His earlier ministry — such, for instance, as the enigmatical word at its very beginning, 'Destroy this Temple, and in three days I will raise it up'; or as the profound word to the rabbi that sought Him by night, 'As Moses lifted up the serpent in the wilderness, so must the Son of Man be lifted up'; or as the passing hint, dropped to the people, in symbolic language, about the 'sign of the prophet Jonas'; or as the grief foreshadowed dimly to the apostles, of the withdrawal of the Bridegroom, and their 'fasting in those days.' These hints, and no doubt others not recorded, had cropped to the surface before; and what we have to do with here, is neither the dawning of an expectation in Christ, nor the first utterance of the certainty of the Cross, but simply the beginning of a continuous and unenigmatical teaching of it, as an element in His instructions to His disciples.

So then, we have to recognise the fact that our Lord's prevision of the end — shone, I was going to say, perhaps it might be truer to say, darkened, — all the path along which He had to travel.

I think that people dogmatise a great deal too glibly as to what they know very little about, the interaction of the divine and the human elements in Christ, and on the one side are far too certain in their affirmation that His humanity possessed in some reflected fashion the divine gift of omniscience; and on the other hand, that His manhood, passing through the process of human development, and increasing in wisdom, was necessarily in its earlier stages void of the consciousness of His Messianic mission. I dare not affirm either 'yes' or 'no' about that matter; but this I am sure of, that if ever there was a time in the development of the Manhood of Jesus Christ when He began to know Himself as the Messias, at that same time He began to be certain of the Cross. For His Messianic work required the Cross, and the divine thing that was in Him was born into the world for a double purpose, to minister and to die.

So, dear friends, putting aside mere metaphysics, which are superficial after all, we have to recognise this as the fact, that all through His career there arose before our Lord the certainty of that death, and that it did not assume to Him the aspect which such a prospect might have assumed to others as a possible result of a mission that failed, but it assumed to Him the aspect of the certain result of a work that was accomplished. He began His career with no illusions, such as other teachers, reformers, philanthropists, men that have moved society, have always begun with. Moses might 'suppose his brethren would have understood how that God by His hand would deliver them,' but Christ had no such illusion. He knew from the beginning that He came to be rejected and to die. And so He 'trod life's common way,' with that grim certainty rising ever before Him. I suppose that He did not, as you and I do, forget that death awaits us, and find the non-remembrance of it the condition of much of our energy, but that it was perpetually in His sight.

Now I do not think that we sufficiently dwell upon that fact as an element in the human experience of our Lord. What beauty it gives to His gentleness, to the leisureliness of heart with which He was ready to make everybody's sorrow His own, and to lay a healing and a loving finger upon every wound! With this certainty before Him, there was yet no strain manifest upon His spirit, no self-absorption, no shutting Himself out from other people's burdens because He had so heavy ones of His own to carry; but He was ready for every joy, ready for all sympathy, ready for every help; and if we cannot say that, 'in cheerful godliness,' as I think we may, at least we can say that with solemn joy and untroubled readiness, He journeyed towards that Cross. This Isaac was under no illusions as to who the Lamb for the offering was, but knowing it, He patiently carried the wood and climbed the hill, ready for the Father's will.

II. That brings me to notice the second point here, our Lord's recognition of the necessity of His suffering.

Mark that He does not say that He *shall* suffer. Certainty is not all that He proclaims here, however absolute that certainty might be, but it is '*He must.*' He is speaking not only of the historical fact, but of the need, deep in the nature of things, for His sufferings that were to follow.

And though these were wrought out by His own willing submission on the one hand, and by the unfettered play of the evil passions of the worst of men on the other, yet over all that apparent chaos of unbridled devildom there ruled the unalterable purpose of God; and the 'must' was wrought out through the passions of evil-doers and the voluntary submission of the innocent sufferer; thus setting before us, in the central fact of the history of humanity, viz., the Cross and passion of Jesus Christ, the eminent example of that great mystery how the absolute freedom of the human will, and the responsibility of the guilt of human wrong-doers, are congruous with the fixed purpose of an all-determining and all-ruling Providence.

But that is apart from my purpose. Mark then, that our Lord's recognition of this necessity for His suffering is, on the first and plainest aspect of it, His recognition that His suffering was necessary on the ground of filial obedience. All through His life we hear that 'must' echoing, and His whole spirit bowed to it. As He says Himself, 'The Son can do nothing of Himself.' As was said for Him of old: 'Lo, I come. In the volume of the book it is written of Me, I delight to do Thy will, and Thy law is within My heart.' So the Father's will is the Son's law; and the Father's 'Thou shalt' is answered by the Son's 'I must.'

But yet that necessity grounded on filial obedience was no mere external necessity determined solely by the divine will. God so willed it, because it must be so; that it must be so was not because God so willed it. That is to say, the work to which Christ had set His hand was a work that demanded the Cross, nor could it be accomplished without it. For it was the work of redeeming the world, and required more than a beautiful life, more than a divine gentleness of heart, more than the homely and yet deep wisdom of His teachings, it required the sacrifice that He offered on the Cross.

So, dear friends, Christ's 'must' is but this: 'My work is not accomplished except I die.' And remember that the connection between our Lord's work ond our Lord's death is not that which subsists between the works and the deaths of great teachers, or heroic martyrs, or philanthropists and benefactors, who will gladly pay the price of life in order to carry out their loving or their wise designs. It is no mere appendage to His work, nor the price that He paid for having done it, but it is. His very work in its vital centre.

I pray for you to consider if there is any theory of the meaning and power of the death of Jesus Christ which adequately explains this 'must,' except the one that He died a sacrifice for the sins of the world. On any other hypothesis, as it seems to me, of what His death meant, it is surplusage, over and above His work: not adding much, either to His teaching or to the beauty of His example, and having no absolute stringent necessity impressed upon it. There is one doctrine — that when He died He bare the sins of the whole world — which makes His death a necessity; and I ask you, Is there any other doctrine which does? Take care of a Christianity which would not be much impoverished if the Cross were struck out of it altogether.

There is a deeper question, on which, as I believe, it does not become us to enter, and that is, What is the necessity for the necessity? Why *must* it be that He, who is the Redeemer of the world, must needs be the Sacrifice for the world? We do not know enough about the depths of the divine nature and the divine government to speak very wisely or reverently upon that subject, and I, for one, abjure the attempt, which seems to me to be presumptuous — the attempt to explain why there was needed a sacrifice for sin in order to the forgiveness of sin. If I knew all about God, I could tell you; and nobody, that does not, can. But we can see, as far as concerns us, that, as the history of all religions tells us, for the forgiveness and acceptance of sinful men a pure sacrifice is needed; and that for teaching us the love of God, the hideousness and wages of sin, for our emancipation from evil, for the quieting of our consciences, for a foothold for faith, for an adequate motive of self-surrender and obedience, His sacrificial death is needful. The life and death of Jesus Christ, regarded as God's sacrifice for the world's sin, *does* all this. The life and death of Jesus Christ, regarded in any other aspect, does not do this. Historically speaking, mutilated forms of Christianity, which have not known what to do with the Cross of Christ, have lost their constraining, purifying, and aggressive power. For us sinful men, if we are to be delivered from evil and become sons of God, He *must* suffer many things, and be killed, and rise again the third day.

III. Now note further, how we have been also our Lord's willing acceptance of the necessity.

It is one thing to recognise, and another thing to accept, a needs-be. This 'must' was no unwelcome obligation laid upon Him against His will, but one to which His whole nature responded and which He accepted. No doubt there was in Him the innocent instinctive physical shrinking from death. No doubt the Cross, in so far, was pain and suffering. No doubt we are to trace the reality of a temptation in Peter's rash words which follow, as indicated to us by the severity and almost vehemence of the action with which Christ puts it away. No doubt there is a profound meaning in that answer of His, 'Thou art a *stumbling-block* to Me.' The 'Rock' is turned into a stone of stumbling, and Peter's suggestion appeals to something in Him which responded to it.

That shrinking might be a shrinking of nature, but it was not a recoil of will. The ship may toss in dreadful billows, but the needle points to the pole. The train may rock upon the line, but it never leaves the rails. Christ felt that the Cross was an evil, but that feeling never made Him falter in His determination to bear it. His willing acceptance of the necessity was owing to His full resolve to save the world. He must die because He would redeem, and He would redeem because He could not but love. 'He saved others,' and therefore 'Himself He cannot save.' So the 'must' was not an iron chain that fastened Him to His Cross. Like some of the heroic martyrs of old, who refused to be bound to the funeral pile, He stood there chained to it by nothing but His own will and loving purpose to save the world.

And, brethren, in that loving purpose, each of us may be sure that we had an individual and a personal share. Whatever the interaction between the divinity and the humanity, this at all events is certain, that every soul of man has his distinct and definite place in Christ's knowledge and in Christ's love. Each of us all may be sure that one strand of the cords of love which fastened Him to the Cross was His love for me; and each of us may say — He must die, because 'He loved me, and gave Himself for me.'

IV.   Lastly, notice here our Lord's teaching the necessity of His death.

This announcement was preceded, as I remarked, by that conversation which led to the crystallising of the half-formed convictions of the apostles in a definite creed, 'Thou art the Christ, the Son of the living God.' But that was not all that they needed to know and believe and trust to. That was the first volume of their lesson-book. The second volume was this, that 'Christ must suffer.' And so let us learn the central place which the Cross holds in Christ's teaching. They tell us that the doctrine of Christ as the Sacrifice for the world is not in the Gospels. Where are the eyes that read the Gospels and do not see it? The theory of it is not there; the announcements of it are. And in this latest section of our Lord's ministry, they are fuller and more frequent than in the earlier, for the plain reason which is implied by the preparation through which He passed these disciples, ere He ventured to communicate the mournful and the bewildering fact. There must be, first, the grasp of His Messiahship, and some recognition that He is the Son of God, ere it is possible to go on to speak of the Cross, the full message concerning which could not be spoken until after the Resurrection and the Ascension.

But note, you do not understand Christ's Cross unless you bring to it the faith in Christ's Messiahship and the belief in some measure that He is the Son of God. Neither the pathos nor the power of His death is intelligible if it be simply like other deaths — the dying of a man who is born subject to the law of mortality, and who yields to it by natural process. Unless you and I take upon our lips, though with far deeper meaning, the words with which the heathen centurion gazed upon the dying Christ, and say, 'Truly this was the Son of God!' His Cross is common and trivial and insignificant; but if we can thus speak, then it stands before us as the crown of all God's manifestations in the world, 'the wisdom of God and the power of God.'

And then note, still further, how, without the Cross, these other truths are not the whole gospel. There were disciples then, as there have been disciples since, and as there are today, who were willing to accept, 'Thou art the Christ'; and willing in some sense to say 'Thou art the Son of God,' but stumbled when He said, 'The Son of Man must suffer.' Brethren, I venture to urge that the gospel of the Incarnation, precious as it is, is not the whole gospel, and that the full-orbed truth about Jesus Christ is that He is the Christ, and that He died for our sins, and rose again to live for ever, our Priest and King.

We need a whole Christ. For our soul's salvation, for the quieting of our consciences, the forgiveness of our sins, for new life, for peace, purity, obedience, love, joy, hope, our faith must grasp 'Christ, and Him crucified.' A half Christ is no Christ, and unless we have as sinful men laid hold of the one Sacrifice for sins for ever, which He offered, we do not understand even the preciousness of the half Christ whom we perceive, nor know the full beauty of His example, the depth of His teaching, nor the tenderness of His heart.

I beseech you, ask yourselves, *What* Christ can do for me the things which I need to have done, except 'the Christ that died, yea, rather, that is risen again, who is even at the right hand of God, who also maketh intercession for us'?

BIBLIOGRAPHY

David James Burrell: *The Wondrous Cross,* New York, 1898, pp. 5-17

Alexander Maclaren: *Expositions of Holy Scripture, Matthew IX-XVII,* pp. 333-343

G. Campbell Morgan: *Westminster Pulpit,* Vol. I, 1906, No. 28; Vol. 7, 1912, pp. 89-96

ALEXANDER MACLAREN
(1826-1910)

Different from almost all the other famous preachers whose sermons are appearing in this series of volumes, the father of Alexander Maclaren, David, was not only a business man, but was the pastor of a church where he preached every Lord's Day. Alexander Maclaren was born in Glasgow, February 11, 1826, and underwent an experience of genuine conversion at the age of fourteen, hearing a sermon from Dr. W. Lindsay Alexander, followed by the reading of *The Rise and Progress of Religion* by Doddridge. After graduating from Glasgow University, he entered the Baptist College at Stepney, later known as Regents Park College. In June 1846, he was called to be the pastor of Portland Chapel, Southampton, of which he himself once said, "During the first five years, you could have had a pew all to yourself, and another for your hat." At the age of thirty-two, Maclaren, already famous as a gifted expositor of the Scriptures, was called to Union Chapel, Manchester, July 1858, where he remained for forty-five years, resigning because of health in June, 1903. The new building of Union Chapel seated 1800, and very seldom on Sunday was the church anything else but full.

Maclaren began to write when a young minister, and continued to pour out the very finest kind of work in Biblical exposition down to the very year of his death. His first volume, many people think, was his best, *Sermons Preached in Manchester* (1859). For twenty years he wrote the principal comment on the lesson for the American *Sunday School Times,* the most important single Sunday School paper in America at that time. As many know, Maclaren wrote the volume on Colossians in *The Expositor's Bible,* and the great inimitable volumes on the Psalms in the same series. In 1904, after he had resigned from his pulpit in Manchester, Sir William Robertson Nicoll suggested to him the putting together of all his sermons and other expositions written for various journals, to form what came to be his most memorable work, *Expositions of Holy Scripture,* at which he toiled for five years.

It was, however, for the pulpit that Dr. Maclaren lived and worked. He never let a day pass without translating from the Hebrew a chapter of the Old Testament and a chapter from the Greek New Testament. At the height of his influence, in speaking to a group of young ministers, he confessed, "I began my ministry — and, thank God, I have been able to keep to my aim — I say nothing about attainment — with the determination of concentrating all my available strength on the work, the proper work of the Christian ministry, the pulpit. I believe that the secret of success for all our ministers lies very largely in the simple charm of concentrating their intellectual force on the one work of preaching. I have tried to make my ministry a ministry of exposition of Scripture. I know that it has failed in many respects, but I will say that I have endeavoured from the beginning to the end to make that the characteristic of all my public work. I have tried to preach Jesus Christ, and the Jesus Christ not of the Gospels only, but the Christ of the Gospels and Epistles; He is the same Christ."

Maclaren had no time for the trivialities of life. He would not weary himself with speaking to total strangers after preaching. Committees depressed him, and he attended few of them. He was personally exceedingly shy and for this reason never was given to extensive pastoral visitation. He did not care for public eulogies, and when someone would begin to praise him before his face, he would ask them please to desist. He would never allow himself to read any biographical sketch of his life, or an account of any message he had given. Honors, however, inevitably came to him. He was twice President of the Baptist Union, in 1875, and again in 1901. He was honored by being elected as President of the Baptist World Congress in 1905, when eighty years of age.

Dr. F. B. Meyer, a distinguished expositor himself, once said, "When Dr. Maclaren published his first sermons, he taught all preachers that there was a way of dividing a subject into distinct parts; and when you read his volumes, in the first sentences of every sermon are the lines on which he is going to treat the theme. That method has influenced most modern preachers, and so has

Dr. Maclaren's style of illustrating his subject by analogies drawn from nature and life. To preachers, he has been a model and example which we have all tried to study."

Sir William Robertson Nicoll, in his fascinating volume, *Princes of the Church,* has paid a tribute to Maclaren that I would like to recall for the readers of this volume. "To him preaching was the exposition of the eternal divine thought. Anything else was not preaching. So the Bible was his book. Through his long life he was continually studying it in Hebrew and in Greek. Like Dale, in his latter days he put Westcott's Commentaries above all the rest. Nothing interested him more in recent years than Dr. Moulton's New Testament Grammar, and the translation of the New Testament as affected by the discovery of the Greek papyri. All the wisdom of the world was to him contained in the Bible, but his business was to apply the Bible to life, and he read very widely in general literature. . . . Books of travel attracted him. He was a close student of history, and not ignorant of science. He studied the living book of humanity. His whole effort was to bring Bible truth into effective contact with the human heart. . . . He was a minister of the Word, a minister among the Baptists, faithful to the death, working in the inspiration of the early days to which his heart held firm. In this way he refused almost everything. He was always saying no. Every visitor whom he suspected of a new proposal was received at first with a certain gruffness and suspicion, soon disarmed into smiling gentleness. His first book of sermons was simply dragged out of him. . . . It is difficult to believe that his Expositions of the Bible will be superseded. Will there ever again be such a combination of spiritual insight, of scholarship, of passion, of style, of keen intellectual power? He was clearly a man of genius, and men of genius are very rare. So long as preachers care to teach from the Scriptures they will find their best help and guide in him. That remains, but we who knew him know what has been taken from us as we recall the man, his heart, his voice, his mien, his accent, his accost. We shall not see his like again. We know also that in him as much power was kept back as was brought out. He did his work not merely for the time, but for the time to come. He spoke to those pierced with an anguish, 'whose balsam never grew.' He spoke to the cravings, to the aspirations, to the hopes as well as to the sorrows and the pains of humanity. The generations to come will care little or nothing for our sermons to the times, but they will listen to the sweet, clear voice of the man who preached to the end of Gilead — and Beulah — and the Gates of Day."

Dr. Maclaren died May 5, 1910, at the age of eighty-four.

THE RANSOM
by
Alexander Whyte

"To give His life a ransom for many." — Matthew 20:28

Let us draw near this morning and join ourselves to our Lord
when He is on His way up to the Passover for the last time. And
let us abide near Him this morning till we see the end. And
when we see the end, let us all say for ourselves what Paul said
for himself: "He loved me and gave Himself for me."

1. No sooner had our Lord entered Jerusalem in the begin-
ning of that week than, in His own words, He began "to give
His life a ransom." As long as His time had not yet come, our
Lord took great care of His life. His was the most precious life
on the face of the earth, and He took corresponding care of it.
But now that the work of His life was finished, He began at once
to give His life away. All the beginning and middle of that
Passover week our Lord was preaching all the daytime in the
temple — and then at night He went out and abode in the
Mount that is called the Mount of Olives. All that week, our
Lord preached all day and prayed all night. Now there is nothing
so exhausting as preaching unless it is praying: such preaching,
that is, and such praying as our Lord's preaching and praying
were all that Passover week. Paul in one place speaks about
preaching the "terror of the Lord." And that terrible word best
describes our Lord's last sermons in Jerusalem. It is remarkable
— and there must be a good reason for it — that the only sermons of our Lord that we have anything like a full report of are
His first sermon and His last, — His Sermon on the Mount and
His three days of farewell sermons in the temple. That preacher
was simply throwing his life away who delivered the discourses

that Matthew has preserved in the end of his Gospel. He was walking straight into the jaws of death who stood up in the temple — especially when there was not standing room in its passover-porches, and spoke the parable of "The Wicked Husbandman," and the parable of "The Marriage Feast," and the parable of "The Ten Virgins," and the parable of "The Last Judgment." And then, to make it impossible that His meaning could be missed, He hurled out such bolts of judgment as these: "Woe unto you, Scribes and Pharisees: hypocrites! Woe! Woe! Woe!" For three whole days the terrible Preacher was permitted to anticipate the Last Day; and no man laid hands on Him. And then, all night in the Mount of Olives, our Lord, all that week, was simply squandering away what remained of His life. Unless, indeed, He was in all that ransoming the lost lives of those preachers who tune their pulpits; and who, once they are home from their day's work and have well dined, will not venture out again after either to preach or to pray. The Son of Man gave His life for many ministers, in the temple and in the garden, as well as on the tree.

2. The calmness of mind and the careful deliberation with which our Lord goes about the Last Supper is very affecting and very impressive. The quiet and orderly way in which He gives his instructions about the Supper; the serene and stately way in which He performs His whole part in the Upper Room; the watchful solicitude He shows about the behaviour of the disciples both to Himself and to one another, while all the time His own terrible death was just at the door, — it melts our hearts to see it all. He dwells on the Supper. He lingers over the Supper. He lengthens it out. He takes it up, part after part. He looks back at Moses in Egypt. He looks forward to the marriage-supper of the Lamb. He legislates for the future of His ransomed Church and people. He takes the paschal lamb out of the Supper, and He puts Himself in its place. "Take, eat, this is My body broken for you. This is My blood of the New Testament," said the Lamb of God, "shed for many, for the remission of sins: drink ye all of it. And do this till I come." What a heart-melting

sight! What nobleness! What peace! What beauty of holiness! What boundless love!

3. "Then cometh Jesus with them to a place called Gethsemane, and saith to the disciples, Sit ye there, while I go and pray yonder." Our Lord is in no mood for mockery; but our hearts read their own bitterness into His departing words. He seeks out a seat for the disciples. He seeks out the best, the softest, and the most sheltered seat in the garden. He points them to the place, and He bids them sit down in it. He tells them to keep near one another, and to keep one another company. And before He has got to His place "yonder," they are all fast asleep! *He* has not slept for a week. Night after night He has spent in that same spot, till even Judas "knew the place." More than the city watchmen for the morning He had waited for God in that garden all that week; and He still waits. "Out of the depths have I cried to Thee, O Lord. Out of the belly of hell, O Lord. Then I said, I am cast out of Thy sight. The waters compassed me about even to the soul: the weeds were wrapped about my head." And being in an agony, He prayed more earnestly; and His sweat was as it were great drops of blood falling to the ground. It was the wages of sin. It was the Lord laying on Him the iniquities of us all. It was — every ransomed soul knows what it was. "Yes; it was *my* cup," says every ransomed soul. "I mingled it, I filled it, I have sometimes just tasted it. No wonder He loathed it. No wonder He put it away. No wonder He sweat blood as He drank it. For that cup was *sin*. It was the wages of my sin. It was full of the red wine of the wrath of God against me." And when He rose off His face and left the trampled-down and blood-soaked winepress, He found the disciples still sleeping. And again our hearts mock at us as He says, "Sleep on now, and take your rest."

4. Were you ever false as hell to your best friend? Did you ever take your unsuspecting friend by the hand and say, Welcome! or Farewell? Was there ever a sweet smile on your face, while there was a dagger under your cloak? Did envy, or ambition, or revenge, or some such pure and downright devil ever enter

your heart — till you almost went out and hanged yourself with horror at yourself? Then thou art the man that Jesus Christ ransomed from the halter and from hell when He submitted His cheek to the kiss of the traitor. It is because Jesus Christ has you and so many like you among His disciples that He took so meekly the diabolical embrace of the son of perdition. "It was not an enemy that reproached me: then I could have borne it: neither was it he that hated me that did magnify himself against me: then would I have hid myself from him. But it was thou, a man, mine equal, my guide and mine acquaintance. We took sweet counsel together, and walked into the house of God in company. Yea, mine own familiar friend, in whom I trusted, which did eat of my bread, hath lifted up his heel aaginst me." "For we ourselves were sometimes living in malice and envy, hateful and hating one another. But after that the kindness and love of God our Saviour toward man appeared — not by works of righteousness which we have done, but according to His mercy He saved us, by the washing of regeneration and the renewing of the Holy Ghost: which He shed on us abundantly, through Jesus Christ our Saviour, that being justified by His grace, we should be made heirs according to the hope of eternal life."

5. "Then the band, and the captain and the officers of the Jews, took Jesus and bound Him." It is a very bitter moment to a prisoner when the officers of justice are binding him. I have often thought that the pinioning before execution must be almost more dreadful than the very drop itself. And our Lord felt most acutely the shame and the disgrace of the prison shackles. For once He broke silence and spoke out and remonstrated. "Be ye come out as against a thief?" He turned upon the officers. He had no intention of trying to escape. He had come out to the garden to give Himself up. He had said just the moment before, "I am He: take me; and let these go their way." But the officers were under the instructions of Judas. Their superiors in the city had told them that they were to look to Judas for all their orders that night. And Judas had said to the officers: "Whomsoever I shall kiss, that same is He: take Him

and lead Him away safely: that same is He, hold Him fast."
And they obeyed Judas; they held Him as fast and as safe as
their best prison-cords could hold Him. O officers! officers!
Judas must surely know; but it is impossible that you can know
why it is that your prisoner walks with you so willingly! Did
any of you Roman officers ever hear of "cords of love?" Well,
— it is in the cords of everlasting love that you keep your man
so safely tonight. O officers! officers! if you only knew who that
is you are leading in cords into the city! O Judas, Judas! What
are thy thoughts? O! Better never to have been born!

6. "And all His disciples forsook Him and fled. But Peter
followed Him afar off, unto the high priest's palace, and went in
and sat with the servants to see the end." Did you ever deny a
friend? Did you ever sit still and hear a friend of yours slan-
dered, witnessed against by hired witnesses, and condemned?
Did you ever sit and warm yourself at some man's fire; or more
likely, at some man's wine; and for fear, for cowardice, or for
the sake of the company and the good cheer did you nod and
smile and wink away your absent brother's good name? Look!
redeemed dastard! look at thy dreadful ransom! Look at Jesus
Christ in the hard hands, and under the hired tongues of His
assassins — and Peter, His sworn friend, washing his hands of
all knowledge of the friendless Prisoner! Look! O dog in the
shape of a man! All their sham charges, all their lying witnesses, all their judicial insults and brutalities are clean forgotten
by Peter's Master! He does not hear what they are saying, and
He does not care. A loud voice out in the porch has stabbed our
Lord's heart to death. "I know not the Man! I never saw Him
till tonight!" With oaths and with curses above all the babel —
Peter's loud voice rolls in on his Master: "I know not the Man!"
And the cock crew. And the Lord turned and looked upon
Peter. And Peter went out and wept bitterly. And as the fine
legend has it: Peter never heard a cock crow, day or night, all
his after days, that he did not remember the passover-porch of
Caiaphas the High Priest that year in Jerusalem!

7. You have heard sometimes about hell being let loose. Yes,

but hear this. Come to Caiaphas' palace on the passover night, and look at this. "Then did they spit in His face, and buffeted Him: they blindfolded Him and then they smote Him with the palms of their hands, saying: Prophesy to us, Thou Christ, who is it that smote Thee? And they stripped Him, and put on Him a scarlet robe. And when they had platted a crown of thorns" — I wonder in what sluggard's garden it grew! — "they put it upon His head, and a reed in His right hand; and they bowed the knee before Him and mocked Him, saying: Hail! King of the Jews! And they spit upon Him again, and took the reed out of His hand, and smote Him upon the head. Then Pilate took Jesus and scourged Him. After which they brought Jesus forth wearing the crown of thorns and the purple robe. And when the Chief Priests saw Jesus, they cried out, Crucify Him! crucify Him! Then Pilate delivered Him to them to be crucified." My brethren, — these are dreadful, most dreadful, things. And all the time, God Almighty, the God and Father of Jesus Christ, restrained Himself; He held Himself in, and sat as still as a stone, seeing and hearing all that. The arrest, the trial, the buffeting, the spitting, the jesting and the jeering, the bloody scourging, the crown of thorns, the reed, and the purple robe — Why? In the name of amazement, why did the Judge of all the earth sit still and see all that said and done? Do you know what made Him sit still? Did you ever think about it? And would you like to be told how it could be? God Almighty, my brethren, not only sat still, but He ordained it all; and His Son *endured* it all, — *in order to take away sin.* In order to take away the *curse* of sin, to take away the very existence of sin for ever. You will find the explanation of that terrible night's work, and of the still more terrible morning just about to dawn, — you will find the explanation, the justification, and the complete key to it all *in your own heart.*

Did you ever see yourself to be such a despicable creature that you wondered why all men did not spit upon you? Did you ever wonder that, not friendship and family life only, but very human society itself, did not dissolve, and fall in pieces, such is the meanness, the despicableness, the duplicity, the selfishness, the cruelty, and the diabolical wickedness of the human heart — but above all human hearts, of yours? You will understand the spitting-scene that night when God lets you see your own heart. There was no surplus shame; there was no scorn too much: the contumely was not one iota overdone that night. There was no unnecessary disgrace poured on Christ that night. They are in every congregation, at every Communion Table, and they are the salt and the ornament of it, who say as they sit down at the Table — He hid not His face from shame and from spitting for me! He loved me in my sin and my shame, and He gave Himself for me!

8. If all that will not melt your heart of stone, try the next thing that Pilate and his devils did. For Pilate scourged Him. I will leave the scourging to yourselves to picture, and to ask, What is scourging? Who was it that was that morning scourged? And why was He scourged being innocent? And the crown of thorns, and all the awful scene to the end! O that mine head were waters and mine eyes a fountain of tears!

9. But come out to Calvary at nine o'clock that morning if you would be absolutely glutted with sorrow and with love. All the shame, all the scorn, all the horror, all the agony due to our sin, and undertaken by our Surety — it all met on the Cross. The Cross was the vilest, the cruellest, the most disgraceful, the most diabolical instrument of execution that ever hell had invented and set up on earth. Stand back and let the chiefest sinner in this house come forward. Give him the best place. Whoever sees the crucifixion, let *him* see it. Look, sinner, and see. They lay down the Cross on the ground. They then take the cords off our Lord's pinioned arms, and the painted board off His breast. They then lay Him down on His back on the Cross; they stretch out His arms along the arms of the Cross. They then open out His hands; and with a hammer they drive a great nail of iron through His right hand with the blood spurting up in their faces; and another through His left hand, and another through His feet, placed the one above the other to save the

nails. Five or six strong soldiers then lift up the Cross with its trembling, bleeding Burden, and sink it down with a dash into the stone socket, set in the earth, till all His bones are out of joint. And "They know not what they do!" is all He says. No; *they* know not, but the chief of sinners now looking on, he knows. Paul knew: "He loved me," said Paul, "and gave Himself for me." Cowper knew.

> "There is a fountain filled with blood
>   Drawn from Immanuel's veins;
> And sinners, plunged beneath that flood,
>   Lose all their guilty stains."

We often pray that God would "make the bed" of His dying saints; and He does it. But that was the death-bed God made for His dying Son!

But all that, after all, was the outer porch of death to our Lord. Gethsemane and Caiaphas and Pilate and Herod's palace were but the outer court of the temple. The Cross was the altar; and the sacrifice only began to be fully offered about the sixth hour when there was darkness over all the earth till the ninth hour. It passeth all understanding, and all the power of tongue and pen, what the Son of God suffered in body and soul, during those three dark and silent hours. Only at the ninth hour Jesus cried with a loud voice, "My God, My God: why hast Thou forsaken Me?" And some time after, "It is finished," when He bowed His head and gave up the ghost.

> " 'Tis finished — was His latest voice:
>   These sacred accents o'er,
> He bowed His head, gave up the ghost,
>   And suffered pain no more.
>
> 'Tis finished: The Messiah dies
>   For sins, but not His own:
> The great redemption is complete
>   And Satan's power o'erthrown."

32

"So, after He had taken His garments and was set down again, He said unto them: Know ye what I have done to you?"

Yea, Lord. Thou hast given Thy life a ransom for many. Thou hast loved me and given Thyself for me!

"I am not worthy, holy Lord,
    That Thou shouldst come to me;
Speak but the word; one gracious word
    Can set the sinner free.

I am not worthy; cold and bare
    The lodging of my soul;
How canst Thou deign to enter there?
    Speak, Lord! and make me whole.

I am not worthy; yet, my God,
    How can I say Thee nay, —
Thee, Who didst give Thy flesh and blood
    My ransom price to pay?

O come, in this sweet morning hour
    Feed me with food Divine;
And fill with all Thy love and power
    This worthless heart of mine."

BIBLIOGRAPHY

A. Barry: *The Atonement of Christ*, London, 1871, pp. 39-55

Alexander Maclaren: *Expositions of Holy Scripture, Matthew XVIII — XXVIII*, pp. 71-80

Charles H. Spurgeon: *Metropolitan Tabernacle Pulpit*, Vol. IV, London, 1856, No. 181, pp. 129-136

Alexander Whyte: *With Mercy and With Judgment*, pp. 214-226

For a biographical sketch of Alexander Whyte, see *Great Sermons on the Birth of Christ*, pp. 86-90.

THE BLOOD OF THE NEW TESTAMENT
by
D. L. Moody

"For this is My blood of the New Testament, which is shed for many, for the remission of sins." — Matthew 26:28

I want to take up some passages referring to the subject of the Precious Blood in the New Testament. Soon after we came back from Europe to this country, I received a letter from a lady saying that she had looked forward to our coming back to this country with a great deal of interest, and that her interest remained after we had commenced our services until I came to the lecture on the blood, when she gave up all hope or our doing any good. In closing that letter she said: "Where did Jesus ever teach the perilous and barbarous doctrine that men were to be redeemed by the shedding of His blood? Never! never did Jesus teach that monstrous idea." Let us turn to the fourteenth chapter of Mark, twenty-fourth verse, and we will find: "And He said unto them, This is My Blood of the New Testament, which is shed for many;" and also in Matthew 26:28: "For this is My blood of the New Testament, which is shed for many for the remission of sins." There are a good many passages, but it is not necessary to refer to more. If Christ did not teach it, and also the Apostles — if Christ did not preach it, then I have read my Bible, all these years, wrong. I haven't got the key to the Scriptures; it is a sealed book to me, and if I don't preach it — if I give it up, I've nothing left to preach. Take the blessed doctrine of the blood out of my Bible and my capital is gone, and I've got to take to something else.

I remember when in the old country a young man came to me — a minister came around to me, and said he wanted to talk with me. He said to me: "Mr. Moody, you are either all right and I am all wrong, or else I am right and you are all wrong." "Well, sir," said I, "you have the advantage of me. You have heard me preach, and know what doctrines I hold, whereas I have not heard you, and don't know what you preach." "Well," said he, "the difference between your preaching and mine is, that you make out that salvation is got by Christ's death, and I make out that it is attained by His life." "Now, what do you do with the passages bearing upon the death?" and I quoted the passages, "Without the shedding of blood there is no remission," and "He Himself bore our sins in His own body on the tree," and asked him what he did with them, for instance. "Never preach on them at all." I quoted a number of passages more, and he gave me the same answer. "Well, what do you preach?" I finally asked. "Moral essays," he replied. Said I, "Did you ever know anybody to be saved by that kind of thing — did you ever convert anybody by them?" "I never aimed at that kind of conversion; I mean to get men to Heaven by culture — by refinement." "Well," said I, "if I didn't preach these texts, and only preached culture, the whole thing would be a sham." "And it is a sham to me," was his reply. I tell you the moment a man breaks away from this doctrine of blood, religion becomes a sham, because the whole teaching of this book is of one story, and this is that Christ came into the world and died for our sins.

I want to call your attention to the nineteenth chapter of John and the thirty-fourth verse: "But one of the soldiers with a spear pierced his side, and forthwith came thereout blood and water." "Came thereout blood and water." Now, it was prophesied years before that there should open a fountain which should wash away sin and uncleanness, and it seems that this fountain was opened here by the spear of the soldier, and out of the fountain came blood and water. It was the breaking of the crown of hell and the giving of the crown to Heaven. When the Roman soldier drove out the blood, out came the water, and it touched that spear, and it was not long before Christ had that Roman government. It is a throne and a footstool now, and by and by it will sway the earth from pole to pole. This earth has been redeemed by the blessed blood of Christ. Peter says in his first Epistle 1:18: "Forasmuch as ye know that ye were not redeemed with corruptible things, as silver and gold, from your vain conversation received by tradition from your fathers; but with the precious blood of Christ, as of a lamb without blemish and without spot." You are not redeemed by such corruptible things as gold or silver, but by the precious blood of the Lamb — "the precious blood of Christ — as of a lamb without blemish." If silver and gold could have redeemed us, it would have been the easiest thing to have made a pile of gold ten thousand times larger than the bulk of the earth. Why, the poorest thing is gold in Heaven. But gold couldn't do it. The law had been broken, and the penalty of death had come upon us, and it required life to redeem us. Now, it says we shall be redeemed. My friends, redemption is to me one of the most precious treasures in the Word of God — to think that Christ has bought me by His blood. I am no longer my own, I am His. He has ransomed me.

A friend of mine once told me that he was going out from Dublin one day, and met a boy who had one of those English sparrows in his hand. It was frightened, and just seemed to sit as if it pined for liberty, but the boy held it so tight that it could not get away. The boy's strength was too much for the bird. My friend said: "Open your hand and let the bird go. You will never tame him; he is wild." But the boy replied, "Faith, an' I'll not; I've been a whole hour trying to catch him, an' now I've got him I'm going to keep him." So the man took out his purse and asked the boy if he would sell it. A bargain was made, and the sparrow was transferred to the man's hand. He opened his hand, and at first the bird did not seem to realize it had liberty, but by and by it flew away, and as it went it chirped, as much to say, "You have redeemed me." And so Christ has come down and offered to redeem us and give us liberty when we were bound with sin. Satan was stronger than we were. He has had six thousand years' experience. He did not come to buy us from Satan, but from the penalty of our sin.

Another thought about the blood. It makes us all one. The blood brings us into one family, into the household of faith. I remember during the war Dr. Kirk, one of the most eloquent men I ever heard, was speaking in Boston. At that time, you recollect, there was a good deal said about the Irish and the black man, and what an amount of talk about the war of races. He said while preaching one night: "I saw a poor Irishman and a black man and an Englishman, and the blood of Christ came down and fell upon them and made them one." My friends, it brings nationalities together; it brings those scattered with the seeds of discord together and makes them one. Let us turn to Acts 17:26, and we read: "And hath made of one blood all nations of men for to dwell on all the face of the earth, and hath determined the times before appointed and the bounds of their habitation." That's what the blood of Christ does. It just makes us one. I can tell a man that has been redeemed by the blood; they speak all the same language. I don't require to be in his company ten minutes before I can tell whether or not he has been redeemed. They have only one language, and you can tell when they speak whether they are outside the blood or sheltered by it. The blood has two voices — one is for salvation and the other for condemnation. The blood tonight cries out for my salvation or for my condemnation. If we are sheltered behind the blood, it cries for our salvation, for we see in Galatians: "It cries for our peace." There is no peace till a man has been sheltered by that blood.

Again, I would like to call your attention to the twenty-sixth chapter of Matthew, twenty-eighth verse, where we find Christ speaking of His blood: "For this is My blood of the New Testament, which is shed for the remission of sins." This blood was "shed for the remission of sins." Then in Hebrews ninth and twenty-second, where it says, "Without the shedding of blood is no remission of sins." Men don't realize that this is God's plan of salvation. Said a man to me last night after the meeting: "Why, God has got a plan to save us." Certainly He has. You must be saved by God's plan. It was love that prompted

God to send His Son to save us and shed His blood. That was the plan. And without the blood what hope have you? There is not a sin from your childhood — from your cradle — up till now that can be forgiven, unless by the blood. Let us take God at His word: "Without the shedding of blood there is no remission of sins." Without the blood no remission whatever. I don't see how a man can fail to comprehend this. That's what Christ died for; that's what Christ died on Calvary for. If a man makes light of that blood what hope has he? How are you going to get into the kingdom of God? You can not join in the song of the saints if you don't go into Heaven that way. You can not sing the song of redemption. If you did, I suppose you would be off in some corner with a harp of your own, and singing, "I saved myself; I saved myself." You can't get in that way. You must accept the plan of redemption and come in through it. "He that climbeth up some other way the same is a thief and a robber."

Then, in the tenth chapter of Hebrews, we find Paul, if he wrote this, just taking up the very thought: "He that despised Moses' law died without mercy under two or three witnesses." You know when a man made light of the law under the Mosaic dispensation, whenever two witnesses came into court and swore that he hadn't kept the law, they just took him out and stoned him to death. Take up the next verse: "Of how much surer punishment suppose ye, shall he be thought worthy who hath trodden under foot the Son of God, and hath counted the blood of the covenant wherewith He was sanctified an unholy thing, and hath done despite unto the spirit of grace." My friends, what hope is there if a man tramples the blood of Christ under his foot if he says, "I will have nothing to do with that blood?" I ask, in all candor, what mercy is there? What hope has he if he "hath trodden under foot the Son of God, and hath counted the blood of the covenant wherewith He was sanctified an unholy thing?" This is the only way to get to Heaven — no other way. Turn again to the eleventh verse of the same chapter, and we see: "But this Man after He had offered one sacrifice for sin"

— mark that, He had settled the question of sin — "forever sat down on the right hand of God." The high-priests could never sit down; their work was never done. But our High-Priest had put sin away by one sacrifice and then ascended to God. And in this same chapter of Hebrews we see again: "Having therefore, brethren, boldness to enter into the holiest by the blood of Jesus, by a new and living way, which He hath consecrated for us through the veil, that is to say, His flesh, and having a High-Priest over the house of God, let us draw near with a true heart, in full assurance of faith, having our hearts sprinkled from an evil conscience, and our bodies washed with pure water. Let us hold fast the profession of our faith without wavering, for He is faithful that promised." I want to call your attention to the twentieth verse more particularly — "by a new and living way." Now Christ has opened a new and living way. We can not get to Heaven by our own deeds now. He has opened "a new and living way." We don't need a high-priest to go once a year and pray to God. Thank God, we are all kings and high-priests. We can go right straight to the Father in the name of the Lord Jesus Christ. When Christ died that veil was rent from the top to the bottom — not from the bottom to the top — and every poor son of Adam can walk right in and worship — right into the presence of God, if he only comes by the way of the blood. Yes, thank God, He has opened a new and living way whereby we can come to Him. Let us thank Him for a new and living way. We don't need any bishop, we don't need any pope, we don't need any priest or prophet now; but every one can be made king and priest and we can come through this living way to His presence and ask Him to take away our sins. There's not a man in this assemblage but can come to Him tonight.

There's a good deal about the blood in Hebrews that I would like to bring up; time passes, and I have just to fly through the subject. Now I don't know any doctrine I have preached that has been talked about more than the doctrine of blood. Why, the moment Satan gets a man to leave out this doctrine of blood, he has gained all he wants. It is the most pernicious idea to leave it out. A man may be a brilliant preacher, he may have a brilliant intellect, and may have large crowds of people; but if he leaves this out, no one will be blest under his ministry, no one will be born in God's kingdom. If a man leaves out this blood he may as well go and whistle in the streets, and try to convert people that way, for all the good he will do in saving souls. It is said that old Dr. Alexander, of Princeton College, when a young student used to start out to preach always gave them a piece of advice. The old man would stand with his gray locks and his venerable face and say, "Young man, make much of the blood in your ministry." Now, I have traveled considerably during the past few years, and never met a minister who made much of the blood and much of the atonement, but God had blessed his ministry, and souls were born into the light by it. But a man who leaves it out — the moment he goes, his church falls to pieces like a rope of sand, and his preaching has been barren of good results. And so if you find a man preaching who has covered up this doctrine of blood, don't sit under his ministry; I don't care what denomination he belongs to, get out of it. Fly from it as those who flew from Sodom. Never mind how you get out of it — leave it. It is a whited sepulchre. There is no life if they don't preach the blood. It is the only way we've got to conquer Satan — the only way we can enter Heaven, and we can not get there unless we have washed our robes in the blood of the Lamb. If we expect to conquer, we must first be washed by that blood. A man who has not realized what the blood has done for him, has not the token of salvation. It is told of Julian, the apostate, that while he was fighting, he received an arrow in his side. He pulled it out, and taking a handful of blood, threw it into the air, and cried, "Galilean, Galilean, thou hast conquered!" Yes, the Galilean is going to conquer, and you must bear in mind if you don't accept the blood — don't submit to it and let it cleanse you — the rock will fall on you, because the decree of Heaven is that every knee shall bow to the will of Heaven. The blood is a call of mercy now. He wants you to come — He beseeches you to accept and be saved.

I heard of an old minister who had preached the Gospel for fifty years faithfully. "Ah!" many here will say, "I wish I was as safe to go to Heaven as him." When he was reaching his end he asked that his Bible be brought to him. His eyes were growing dim in death, and he said to one of those about him, "I wish you would turn to the first epistle of John 1:7," and when it was found, the old man put his dying finger on the passage where it says: "But if we walk in the light as He is in the light we have fellowship one with another, and the blood of Jesus Christ His Son cleanseth us from all sin," and he said, "I die in the hope of that." It was the blood in his ministry that cleansed him. And so it is the only way by which our sins can be washed away. Why, there was a question once asked in Heaven when a great crowd were gathering there, "Who are those?" and the answer was, "They are those who have come up through great tribulation, and have been washed by the blood of the Lamb."

Now, the question is, what are you going to do with that blood? I would like to ask you, what are you going to do about it? You must do either of two things — take it or reject it. Trample it under foot or cleanse your sins by it. I heard of a lady who told a servant to cook a lamb. She told him how to do it up and all about it, but she didn't tell him what to do with the blood. So he went to her and asked, "What are you going to do with the blood of the lamb?" She had been under conviction for some time, and such a question went like an arrow to her soul. She went to her room and felt uneasy, and the question kept continually coming to her, "What are you going to do with the blood of the lamb?" and before morning she was on her knees asking for the mercy of the blood of the Lamb.

Now the most solemn truth in the Gospel is that the only thing He left down here is His blood. His body and bones He took away, but He left His blood on Calvary. There is either of two things we must do. One is to send back the message to Heaven that we don't want the blood of Christ to cleanse us of our sin, or else accept it. Why, when we come to our dying hour the blood will be worth more than all the kingdoms of the world to us. Can you afford to turn your back upon it and make light of it? Dr. King, when the war was going on, went down to the field with the Christian Commission. He used to go around among the soldiers, and during one of his visits he heard a man cry, "Blood! blood! blood!" He thought that, as the man had just been taken off the battle-field, the scene of carnage and blood was still upon his mind. The doctor went to him and tried to talk to the man about Christ, and tried to divert his mind from the scenes of the field. "Ah, doctor," said the man feebly, "I was not thinking of the battle-field, but of the blood of Christ;" and he whispered the word "blood" once more and was gone.

Dear friends, do you want all your sins washed away from you? It was shed for the remission of sins, and without the shedding of blood there would be no remission. There is blood on the mercy-seat. "I am not looking to your sins now," God says, "but come and press in, press in and receive remission." Thank God, the blood is still on the mercy-seat. It is there, and He beseeches you to accept it. What more can He do for your salvation? Now, my friends, don't go out of this Tabernacle laughing and scoffing at the precious offering made to you, but just bow your head and lift up your voice, "Oh, God of Heaven, may the blood of Thy Son cleanse me from all sin." The blood is sufficient.

Some years ago I was journeying to the Pacific coast, and nearly every stage-driver I met was talking about a prominent stage-driver who had just died. You know that in driving over those rocky roads they depend a good deal upon the brake. This poor man, when he was dying, was heard to say: "I am on the down grade and can not keep the brake." Just about that time one of the most faithful men of God, Alfred Cookman, passed away. His wife and friends gathered around his death-bed, and when his last moments arrived, it seemed as if Heaven had opened before him, as with a shout he cried, "I am sweeping through the gates washed by the blood of the Lamb." What a comfort this must have been to his friends; what a comfort it must have been to him, the blood of the atonement in his last hours.

My friends, if you want a glorious end like the end of that sainted man, you must come to the blood of Christ. Let us bow our heads in prayer; let us have a few moments of silent prayer, and let us ask the Lord to let us see this great truth.

Mr. Sankey sang the following hymn, as a song-translation of the story told by Mr. Moody, at the conclusion of his sermon:

> I am now a child of God,
> For I'm washed in Jesus' blood;
> I am watching, and I'm longing while I wait.
> Soon on wings of love I'll fly
> To my home beyond the sky,
> To my welcome, as I'm sweeping thro' the gate.
>
> Refrain — In the blood of yonder Lamb,
> Washed from every stain I am;
> Robed in whiteness, clad in brightness,
> I am sweeping thro' the gates.
>
> Oh! the blessed Lord of light,
> I loved Him with my might;
> Now His arms enfold and comfort while I wait.
> I am leaning on His breast,
> Oh! the sweetness of His rest.
> And I'm thinking of my sweeping thro' the gate.
>
> Burst are all my prison bars,
> And I soar beyond the stars;
> To my Father's house, the bright and blest estate.
> Lo! the morn eternal breaks
> And the song immortal wakes,
> Robed in whiteness, I am sweeping thro' the gate.

BIBLIOGRAPHY

A Barry: *The Atonement of Christ,* London, 1871, pp. 59-74

Charles J. Brown: *The Word of Life,* New York, 1874, pp. 86-98

Charles Jerdan: *For the Lord's Table,* 2nd ed., Edinburgh, 1903, pp. 113-118; 152-157; 263-267.

Alexander Maclaren: *Expositions of Holy Scripture — Matthew XVIII — XXVIII,* pp. 243-252

David Smith: *The Pilgrim's Hospice,* New York, 1906, pp. 63-70. Also, in his *The Feast of the Covenant,* London, n.d., pp. 41-57

Charles H. Spurgeon: *Metropolitan Tabernacle Pulpit,* Vol. 33, 1887, No. 1971, pp. 373-384

Mr. Moody's sermons on the blood appeared in a great number of volumes, among which are the following: *Addresses by D. L. Moody delivered in England, in 1874-1875,* London, 1875, pp. 100-120; *The Blood, Two Addresses,* London, 1875. *Fifty Evenings at the Great Revival Meetings Conducted by Moody and Sankey,* Philadelphia, 1876, pp. 207-227; William R. Moody and A. P. Fitt: *The Life of D. L. Moody,* London, n.d. pp. 100-120; W. H. Daniels: *D. L. Moody and His Work,* Hartford, 1876, pp. 424-433; *New Sermons, Addresses and Prayers,* New York, 1877, pp. 156-164.

DWIGHT L. MOODY
(1837-1899)

Probably all will agree that Dwight L. Moody contributed
more to the advancement of the kingdom of God on this earth in
the nineteenth century than any other single individual. It is
generally recognized that he spoke to more different people in
the last quarter of the nineteenth century than any other man
during that significant era. That, in itself, is, at least in part, a
measure of the influence he exerted. The writings of no other
nineteenth century Christian have had such enormous sales, and
been so widely distributed throughout the world as those of
D. L. Moody, during his lifetime and in the nearly half century
that has followed with the exception of the sermons of Charles
H. Spurgeon. As long ago as 1902, Dr. John R. Mott said, "I
can safely say that I have not visited a country in Europe, Asia,
or Africa, where the words of Mr. Moody are not bearing fruit.
Next to the words of the Bible, and possibly those of Bunyan, his
words have been translated into more tongues than those of any
other man. Oh, the infinite possibilities of the surrendered, sub-
jugated, consecrated tongue!"

Biographical details need to be presented here only in barest
outline. D. L. Moody was born February 5, 1837, in Northfield, Massachusetts, the son of Edwin and Betsy Holton Moody.
With very little education in the local schools, at the age of
seventeen the young man went to Boston looking for work, and
was at once employed in a shoe store owned by a relative of his.
After a little more than two years in Boston, Moody felt compelled to leave New England and venture into the Middle West,
arriving in Chicago September 18, 1856, not yet quite twenty
years of age. In spite of the fact he was still in his teens, without any previous connections with business men in the city, and
without any externally visible talents, the young Dwight soon
became one of the outstanding Christian citizens of that growing metropolis. In 1858, he organized the North Market Hall
Sabbath School, and became so interested in Sunday School
work and the Y.M.C.A. that in 1861, he felt led to give up his

44

profitable business as a traveling salesman. At the end of 1864 he founded the Illinois Street Independent Church, out of which ultimately was formed what came to be known as the Chicago Avenue Church, now the Moody Memorial Church. Two years later, in 1866, he was made President of the Young Men's Christian Association of Chicago, and in the following year he made his first of seven visits to Great Britain, during two of which, 1873-1875, and 1881-1884, he conducted the greatest evangelistic campaigns that had been seen in Great Britain since the days of Wesley and Whitefield, the results of which still abide.

Mr. Moody seemed to have, like many men who exercise national influence, unlimited energy. In 1879, he was enabled to launch the Northfield Seminary for Girls, and in 1881, the nearby Mount Hermon School for Boys. The first of the great Northfield Bible Conferences was held in August 1880, and for the next twenty years, most of the greatest Biblical expositors in the Western world were to be heard at these summer gatherings. For three years, 1886, 1887, and 1888, Mr. Moody also conducted at Northfield a conference for college students, to which annually over 250 students from some eighty colleges would gather. The lists of delegates seems to be almost a catalogue of the men who were to be the Christian leaders of America at the beginning of this century, such as Robert Speer, John R. Mott, etc.

The evangelist just could not confine his activities to any one area, and in addition to his great campaigns on both sides of the Atlantic, and the famous conferences at Northfield, as well as the church in Chicago, Mr. Moody felt led to launch in 1889 what was then called the Bible Institute of the Chicago Evangelization Society. In 1896 it took the name of the Bible Institute of Chicago, and a few months before Mr. Moody died, was known as the Moody Bible Institute, the greatest institution of its kind in the Western world. Mr. Moody was taken ill during his evangelistic campaign in Kansas City, and as a result was compelled to travel back to Northfield, where he passed away, December 22, 1899.

My own opinion, after an extensive amount of research into the subject, is that more has been written in periodicals and books about Mr. Moody than about any other religious leader of the nineteenth century, even more than Charles H. Spurgeon. (Most of this literature appearing in books, as well as much appearing in periodicals, I have carefully listed in my *Annotated Bibliography of D. L. Moody,* published in 1948, and now long out of print). I know of at least eight doctoral degrees which have been written on the life and work of D. L. Moody during the last thirty years, and, no doubt, more will yet be written. Some areas of Mr. Moody's life have never yet been carefully explored, as for example, his visits to California, especially those of 1871, 1888, and 1899.

I believe D. L. Moody, with his world-wide influence, radiating from a transparent life, energized by the Holy Spirit, saturated with the love of God, ever exalting the Lord Jesus, seeking out broken and lost men, marshalling the forces of the Church, and interesting leaders of our country and abroad in the things of Christ, ever honoring the Word of God, glorying in the cross of Christ, setting forth the great tasks men should be undertaking for the Saviour in a world of such great needs — I believe the influence of this one man, in less than half a century, did more to arrest and turn back the waves of unbelief that were battering at the foundations of the Christian Church, did more to deliver men from the chilling, paralyzing effects of rationalistic criticism, did more for the relief of the distressed, and the exaltation of righteousness, did more for the genuine miraculous regeneration of men and women, and for the permanent, Christ-centered inspiration of college men on both sides of the Atlantic, than can be ascribed to any other Christian man of his generation.

THE SUFFERINGS OF CHRIST
by
George Milligan

"Ought not Christ to have suffered these things, and to enter into His glory?" — Luke 24:26

On the afternoon of the first Easter-day two men — we know that the name of one of them was Cleopas — had left Jerusalem to return to their homes in the little village of Emmaus. They had been disciples of Jesus, and had doubtless gone up to keep the Passover at Jerusalem, under the belief, shared by so many others, that their Master would seize that opportunity of announcing and vindicating His claim to be the Messiah of Israel. And, instead, they had witnessed a mock trial, a cruel scourging, a shameful death. All their hopes seemed to be for ever dashed to the ground. There was nothing left for them but to return to their old homes and former occupations.

As they went along the road, dispirited and sad, but still eagerly discussing the events of the past few days, and unable to agree regarding them, a stranger joined them. And at once, without further introduction, He broke in upon their eager questioning and doubting with the words, "What manner of communications are these that ye have one to another as ye walk, and are sad?" They did not resent the interference: they only wondered that one coming like themselves from Jerusalem could have any doubt as to the thoughts which were engrossing their minds concerning Jesus of Nazareth, "which was a prophet mighty in deed and word before God and all the people" — notwithstanding their disappointment they still clung with fond reverence to the memory of what Jesus had been and done — "and how the chief priests and our rulers delivered Him to be

47

condemned to death, and have crucified Him." "But we," they continued, in words amongst the most pathetic in the gospels, "trusted that it had been He which should have redeemed Israel." They were mourning not only the loss of a personal Friend and Master: they mourned still more the loss of Israel's Messiah. And, as they thus recalled the failure of their hopes, they further recalled how that very morning they had heard strange tidings of an empty tomb, of a vision of angels, and of a risen Christ. And yet to them such tidings had been matter only of wonder; and they concluded their recital of the women's tale with the despairing words — "But Him they saw not."

Then it was that the stranger, still to them unknown, but so soon to be welcomed as in very truth the Master they had lost, met their sorrow and doubt with the gentle remonstrance — "O fools, and slow of heart to believe all that the prophets have spoken: ought not Christ," or rather the Christ, the Messiah, "to have suffered these things, and to enter into His glory?" The stumbling-block in the disciples' path, the cause of all their unbelief was the suffering of Jesus. That the Messiah should die — die shamefully on a cross — they could not believe. Was not that in itself a proof that His enemies had conquered, and not He? But now, Jesus Himself showed them that it was just because of the cross that He was the Messiah, that it was necessary for Him so to suffer in order that He might enter into His glory.

Such then were the circumstances under which the words of our text were first spoken. And significant as they still are at all times, have they not a very special meaning for us today, in view of the solemn service in which we are so soon to be engaged? We are about to commemorate in His own appointed rite the death of our Lord, and to claim for ourselves the benefits of His sufferings. And that being so, there can surely be for us few more practical questions than, Why were the sufferings of Christ necessary? Why must we still turn to a crucified King if He is to be a true Saviour for us?

There seem to me to be at least four reasons. Let us notice them briefly.

I.

We have the reason to which Christ Himself pointed in
the passage before us. His sufferings were necessary
that the Scriptures might be fulfilled.

It was trusting to their own interpretation of the Scriptures
that the two disciples had turned away from a crucified Jesus.
They had thought that they pointed only to a glorious and triumphant king, but now Jesus, "beginning at Moses and all the
prophets, . . . expounded unto them in all the Scriptures the
things concerning Himself."

How we should like to have been present at that exposition!
We can imagine Jesus going back to the first prophecy of all
regarding Himself as the bruiser of the serpent's head, and show-
ing how that could only be accomplished, and the victory over
evil won through suffering and toil; or pointing to Himself as
the true paschal lamb, the sin-bearing sacrifice, the brazen serpent lifted on high that the people might be healed; or recalling
some of the many figures under which prophecy had pointed to
the Messiah, as the lowly King, the pierced Victim, the smitten
Shepherd; or, summing up all, finally, in the great words in
which the evangelical prophet described so clearly the Messiah's humiliation, that we can hardly understand how the Jews
could have ignored it: "He is despised and rejected of men, a
man of sorrows, and acquainted with grief. . . . Surely He hath
borne our griefs, and carried our sorrows: yet we did esteem
Him stricken, smitten of God, and afflicted. . . . He is brought
as a lamb to the slaughter, and as a sheep before her shearers is
dumb, so He openeth not His mouth" (Isaiah 53:3,5,7). The
whole Old Testament, Jesus would show, was Messianic; and
the whole Old Testament, exhibited to those who read it aright,
a suffering, as well as a triumphant Messiah — a Messiah passing through suffering and death to glory and life. Everywhere,
with the golden thread of victory, there was interwoven the
scarlet thread of sacrifice.

II.

But we must look deeper than the letter of Scripture, if
we would understand aright the cause of the sufferings

of Christ. We must look at the purpose, the work He came to accomplish.

What was that work? Not, as the Jews fondly imagined, to make of them a great nation, and raise them to the chief place among the nations of the world; but to save the Jews, and with them to save the world. It was in very truth to establish a kingdom, but no outward kingdom of power and glory, but an inward kingdom of "righteousness, and peace, and joy in the Holy Ghost" (Romans 14:17).

If men had remained in the state in which God had first created them, if there had been no Fall, the work of Jesus would have been easy. But instead He came, to whom? To men sinful and disobedient, who had passed under the power of evil, and were subject to death. How could He save them, except by Himself passing through death, that He might "destroy him that had the power of death, that is, the devil; and deliver them who through fear of death were all their lifetime subject to bondage" (Hebrews 2:14,15).

You know how often the sin and misery in the world tend to turn away men's hearts from God. And, indeed, if we look at them only in themselves, can we wonder that they do so? But look at them in the light of the cross of Christ, and is not all changed? The cross shows us what God thinks of sin. It shows us what a power evil must be, that it could only be overcome by the death of God's own Son, and it shows us once more how great is the redeeming love of God, who "commendeth His love toward us, in that, while we were yet sinners, Christ died for us" (Romans 5:8).

We are, let us frankly acknowledge it, face to face with a great mystery, when we think of the death of Christ, the Holy suffering for the unholy, the Just for the unjust. But we can never hope to understand the meaning of these sufferings at all, unless we see ever above and behind them the love of God.

> "Inscribed upon the cross we see
> In shining letters, 'God is Love,' "

Or, as we are taught in those simple, but far-reaching words,

words in which the whole gospel is summed up, — "For God so loved the world, that He gave His only begotten Son, that whosoever believeth in Him should not perish, but have everlasting life" (John 3:16).

"In the heavenly crown," it has been beautifully said, "Christ could say nothing else to a magdalen, or a publican, or a paralytic, than 'Depart from Me.' But in His crown of thorns, it is in His power to say to those guilty souls, 'Go in peace; your sins are forgiven you.'"

Ought not, then, the Christ, as the Saviour, the Redeemed of the world, as our Saviour, to have suffered these things, and to enter His glory?

III.

The Christ ought to have suffered these things that He might be "a merciful and faithful High Priest in things pertaining to God. . . . For in that He Himself hath suffered being tempted, He is able to succour them that are tempted" (Hebrews 2:17,18).

The Christ by His sufferings made Himself one with the whole human race, able to enter into every sorrow, and to strengthen in every temptation or trial.

In the presence of great want or great sorrow, I say nothing now of great sin, we must often have felt how vain and presumptuous our attempts at sympathy were. Who were we that we should bid this poor, struggling one not lose heart, it seemed so easy for us in our comfort and plenty to speak, or call upon this broken-hearted mourner not to despair, beside whose loss our own sorrows seemed so small? But one thing we could do. We could point to One, Himself the Son of man as well as the Son of God, who, while He lived upon our earth was homeless, friendless, forsaken — "a man of sorrows and acquainted with grief." Is not this one reason at any rate which gives the cross its attractive power? No one, however great his sorrow or his need, can feel himself beyond the range of the love and sympathy of the Saviour, who hung there.

There is a fine legend in early church history, which tells us

how on one occasion when St. Martin, the soldier-saint, was praying in his cell, suddenly the cell was filled with a glorious light,
and there appeared before him a figure clothed in purple, and
crowned with gold. At first no word was spoken, and then the
visitant said, "Recognize, Martin, him whom thou beholdest, I
am Christ. I am about to visit the earth; and it is my pleasure
to manifest myself to thee beforehand." And when Martin made
no reply he continued, "Why dost thou hesitate to believe when
thou seest? I am Christ." Thereupon, as by a sudden inspiration,
the saint made answer, "The Lord Jesus did not foretell that He
would come arrayed in purple and crowned with gold. I will not
believe that Christ has come, unless I see Him in the dress and
shape in which He suffered, unless I see Him bear before my
eyes the marks of the cross." Thereupon, so the story concludes,
the apparition vanished, and Martin knew that he had been
tempted by the evil one.

It is only an old story, but is it not a story with a deep meaning
for us still? A Saviour without the cross would be no Saviour for
us toiling and struggling men and women. It is only He who
Himself has been lifted up on high out of the earth, who will
draw all men to Himself.

IV.

Once more the Christ ought to have suffered these things,
    "leaving us an example, that we should follow His
    steps."

It must ever be in suffering, in fear and trembling, that sinful
men "work out" the salvation which God is working in them,
therefore "it became Him for whom are all things, and by whom
are all things, in bringing many sons unto glory, to make the
captain of their salvation perfect through sufferings" (Hebrews
2:10). As our great Leader and Commander, Christ has gone
before in the way in which we are called upon to tread. He leads
His people through no darker turn than He Himself has passed
through before. It is for us, therefore, to take up our cross and
follow Him. As the good Duke said when they would have

crowned him king of Jerusalem, "No, by no means, I will not wear a crown of gold, where Jesus was crowned with thorns." And have we not His assurance that "if we suffer, we shall also reign with Him?" (2 Timothy 2:12).

Let it be ours then, as we surround this Holy Table, and partake of that broken bread and poured-out wine which symbolize for us the sufferings of our Lord, to claim the benefits of these sufferings for ourselves, and, dying in Christ's death, live anew in His risen life. For

> " . . . all the fulness of (man's) life,
> And all the greatness of his thought,
> And all the peace of his long strife,
> Root in that everlasting *Ought*."

BIBLIOGRAPHY
G. H. Knight: *The Master's Questions to His Disciples*, New York, 1904, pp. 332-338
George Milligan, in *Eden and Gethsemane*, Manchester, 1903, pp. 137-147
Wm. Robertson Nicoll: *Sunday Evenings*, London, n.d., pp. 323-330

GEORGE MILLIGAN
(1860-1934)

The distinguished Scotch theologian and exegete, George Milligan, was born at Kilconquhar, April 2, 1860. His theological studies were carried on at Aberdeen, Edinburgh, Goettingen, and Bon. For eleven years, he was the minister at St. Matthews, Morningside, and for the next sixteen years, at Caputh, Scotland. His great gifts for Biblical interpretation were early recognized and in 1910, he was appointed the Regius Professor of Divinity and Biblical Criticism in Glasgow University, a chair which he continued to adorn for twenty-two years. Other ecclesiastical honors were conferred upon him from time to time, the most important of which was the Moderatorship of the General Assembly of the Church of Scotland in 1923. He will always be remembered as the co-author with James Hope Moulton of *The Vocabulary of the Greek New Testament,* followed by his interesting volume, *Here and There Among the Papyri.* He also wrote volumes on the Epistle to the Hebrews, and on the two letters of St. Paul to the Thessalonians. Dr. Milligan died November 25, 1934.

CHRIST REIGNING FROM THE CROSS
by
Brooke Foss Westcott

"I, if I be lifted up from the earth, will draw all men unto myself." — John 12:32

The student of the Gospels cannot fail to be deeply impressed by the contrast that St. John's record of the passion which we have heard today offers to that of the other Evangelists. It is from the beginning to the end a revelation of majesty. No voice of suffering, no horror of thick darkness, find a place in it. Every indignity is so accepted by the Lord as to become part of a gracious and willing sacrifice. The words with which He goes forth to die are a declaration of a victory which has been already achieved: *I have overcome the world.* The words which precede His voluntary death are the ratification of a work perfectly accomplished: *It is finished.* The Betrayal is fruitless till He places Himself in the hands of His enemies. He is Himself the Judge of His judges. 'The man' and 'the King' are offered to the people that the thoughts of their hearts may be made known. No remonstrance of high-priests can move the Roman governor to alter the title in which he had written the prophetic sentence of Christ's dignity. Hanging upon the Cross the Lord discharged with calm and tender authority the last offices of personal affection, the last requirements of the Scripture which He came to fulfill. He gave up His Spirit; and still He lived through death. And so we read that *he that hath seen hath borne witness* of that crowning sign of the blood and water, that we *also may believe.*

There is as we know another aspect to the scene. Here as elsewhere glory and shame answer to the judgment of GOD and the judgment of man. We must take account of both. But we

55

must not for one moment rest in the images of outward dissolution. We must look through the suffering to the triumph: through the material to the spiritual: through the manhood which died to the manhood which rose again in the unbroken unity of the Person of the Son of GOD. We must keep together in closest union the Resurrection and the Passion, Easter Day and Good Friday, Life and Death. The Crucifix with the Dead Christ obscures our faith. Our thoughts rest not upon a dead but upon a living Christ. The closed eye and the bowed head are not the true marks of Him Who reigns from the Cross, Who teaches us to see through every sign of weakness the fulfilment of His own words, *I, if I be lifted up from the earth, will draw all men unto Myself*.

I, if I be lifted up from the earth, will draw all men unto Myself. The words follow, as you will remember, on the last and fullest declaration of the fruitfulness of sacrifice, the fruitfulness of death. The law which is true in nature, true in the intercourse of men, finds its fullest expression in the work of Christ. For us as we strive in our earthly conflict, *as chastened and not killed, as sorrowful yet always rejoicing, as dying and behold, we live,* the Cross is the symbol of Christ's throne from which He reigns, till the last enemy shall be subdued, with a sovereignty new, and universal, and present, and divine: a sovereignty exercised through us, and effective for the world.

1. The sovereignty of Christ from the Cross is a new sovereignty. It has destroyed for ever the formula of material tyranny that might is right. It has put to shame the self-assertion of false heroism. It has surrounded with imperishable dignity the completeness of sacrifice. It has made clear to the pure heart that the prerogative of authority is wider service. We all felt a few days ago that the founder of the German Empire had read his lesson well, when he confessed that he trembled to take the Imperial crown from the Altar in order to place it on his own head till his eyes fell upon the Crown of thorns. So from age to age the truth moves forward, and asserts its power in unexpected ways. The Divine King rules for ever by dying.

2. The sovereignty of Christ from the Cross is a new sovereignty and it is also a universal sovereignty. It appeals in its principle to every man as based on love and not on fear. It claims with the attractiveness of blessing the service of every man. It speaks to every type of character. It leaves none desolate or uncared for or unoccupied. It brings to all the brotherhood of a divine origin, the equality of a common destiny, the freedom of self-surrender. For the isolating thought of right it substitutes the thought of duty which is the spirit of a larger life. For the prospect of material happiness it substitutes the vision of a fellowship of saints, when every joy grows greater as it is shared by more.

3. The sovereignty of Christ from the Cross is again a present sovereignty. It is not for some distant future only, when there shall be no more sorrow and no more sin. It is for the transformation of the world which He has conquered. It corresponds with the circumstances of our troubled state. It is extended by the forces by which it was established. It is exercised still from the Cross, and through the Cross. It is directed to bring our common impulses under the conscious rule of a will harmonious with the will of GOD. We pray for the Coming of GOD'S Kingdom, and yet our King Himself is with us all the days.

4. Yet more the sovereignty of Christ from the Cross is a divine sovereignty. It answers to the very nature of GOD. GOD is love, and in love He reveals Himself as King. Christ upon the Cross establishes His own words in a way beyond the imagination of man: *He that hath seen Me hath seen the Father.* The sovereignty of Christ is in other words the victory of love, a victory won once for all by the Son of man and appropriated slowly by men as the years go on. But meanwhile there rises before us all, more prevailing than we know, the image of the suffering Son of GOD, the ideal to which we turn, and by which we are insensibly fashioned. Knowledge requires love for its perfect work, even as love requires knowledge. Mere dogma is powerless in itself to stir the heart; but when it is seen in a Person the soul feels its influence. Devotion flows from the joyful sense of dependence on a living Lord. *We love Him because He first loved us.*

5. This sovereignty of Christ from the Cross new, universal, present, Divine, is exercised through His people. They share in Him the Divine life for which they were made. They follow in Him the Divine method through which He was made perfect. Their sufferings contribute through His grace to the furthering of His purpose. And have we not all felt in the range of our own efforts that we live, so far as we truly live, by incorporating the Divine? That our meat is to do the will of Him Who sent us to do some fragment of His work? that we receive exactly as we give? that we require to learn obedience through suffering that we may in turn commend it? So we come to understand the social destination of every gift with which we have been endowed. Each in our place we represent Him Who reigns from the Cross, strong by the virtue of His Presence, prevailing by the power of His Life.

6. Yet once again the sovereignty of Christ from the Cross is an effective sovereignty. Our hearts, I fancy, often misgive us, even as the hearts of the first disciples misgave them, and we also ask in sadness: *Where is the promise of His coming?* The same question has been put in every age, and it is well that we should put it now. If there were no generous discontent there could be no substantial progress. We must feel the evil, and trace it to its spring, before we can apply the remedy. I would not extenuate the multiplying wretchedness of our great cities. I would not disguise my horror at the spectacle of an armed continent. I tremble when I hear an African Christian arraign our commerce as the destruction of his people. I bow in shame when I am told that the Missionary is looked upon by thoughtful men among negro races as the decoy of the trader. But none the less that grief, that horror, that thrill of indignation, that depth of abasement, is as the royal voice of Christ Who makes His purpose known to us and demands our loyal action. It is enough that we should recognise His living call, and hold ourselves in readiness to move where He opens the way.

But His ways are not as our ways. His seasons are not measured by the circuits of the sun. His vision is not bounded by the limits of our discernment. We look back, and we see that the discipline of centuries ended to our eyes in the tragedy of the Passion and in the apostasy of the chosen race. And yet that tragedy was a revelation of love which, as far as we can see, could not have been made otherwise: that apostasy became the prelude to the glorious freedom of a Catholic Church. The discipline of centuries was not in vain: the stern schooling of Israel, the manifold development of the nations. In the fulness of time Christ came *of the seed of Abraham after the flesh,* gathering into Himself every fruit matured by the long toil of lawgiver and prophet and psalmist: and a world was made ready for Him, conscious through bitter trials of the wants of humanity and of the powerlessness of natural forces to satisfy them.

Even so it may be that GOD is working still. It may be that He is preparing through His Church — the spiritual Israel — some new revelation of His Son, for which the nations, weary and wasted, are even now waiting. It may be that the Risen Lord is coming among us otherwise than we have expected, in some fresh form of self-sacrifice in which we can see no beauty. It may be that like the Jews of old we shall be blind in the day of our visitation, and reject to our own ruin the Saviour whose Advent we have prepared. It may be: and the thought may well move us to humblest self-questioning. Yet it may be tht GOD in His great mercy will enable us to take to heart the failure of our spiritual fathers, and to stand prepared to recognise Him at His coming.

One sign we may be sure will not be wanting. However Christ may come, He will claim the offering of love moved by love, of suffering hallowed by suffering: He will bear in this sense the marks of the Cross. The truth finds expression in a beautiful vision of St. Martin which will bear repeating. That soldier-saint in a time of deep distress and perplexity, when it seemed that the end of the world must be at hand, suddenly, as he prayed, saw his cell filled with a glorious light. In the centre stood a figure of serene and joyous aspect, clothed in royal array, with a jewelled crown upon his head, and gold-embroidered shoes upon his feet.

Martin was half-blinded by the sight; and for a time no word was spoken. Then his visitant said: 'Recognise, Martin, him whom thou beholdest. I am Christ. I am about to visit the earth; and it is my pleasure to manifest myself to thee beforehand.' When Martin made no reply he continued, 'Why dost thou hesitate to believe when thou seest? I am Christ.' Thereupon Martin, as by a sudden inspiration, answered, 'The Lord Jesus did not foretell that He would come arrayed in purple and crowned with gold. I will not believe that Christ has come, unless I see Him in the dress and shape in which He suffered: unless I see Him bear before my eyes the marks of the Cross.' Forthwith the apparition vanished, and Martin knew that he had been tempted by the Evil one.

This story, told by St. Martin himself, is a true parable for all time. The Christ Who comes to us, the Christ for Whom we look, the Christ Who reigns over men, fashioning them to His own likeness, reigns from the Cross. *I, if I be lifted up from the earth, will draw all men unto Myself.* In that exaltation through suffering to glory, through death to life, lies the unchanging secret of His power, of our confidence.

Brethren, in the past week we have ventured to meditate upon great mysteries: to meditate upon a truth, one and manifold, which gathers into a harmonious unity the facts of life: upon an aim, which inspires with a generous nobility the smallest service and the greatest: upon a power of love, divine and human, which transforms the sorrows of our chequered experience into occasions of a closer communion with GOD in Christ, a closer likeness to Christ in GOD.

We have seen that the natural fellowship of man with man, which lies inevitably in our circumstances and in our being, becomes the condition of a spiritual fellowship through which there is opened to us the sight of one transcendent life, to which we all contribute and which it is GOD'S will that we should all enjoy.

We have seen that the law of sacrifice, which rules the efficacy and the joy of human action, is ratified in the order of redemption, so that the ministries of love, by which we are able to bring to others solace and peace, are found to be faint reflections of the counsel of eternal wisdom, whereby our Father brings back to Himself His wandering children and conforms them to His likeness through the sufferings of His own Son.

We have seen that the gift of the Son of GOD'S love Who made all that is ours His own, our weaknesses and temptations and sins, and Who has been made perfect in the fulness of humanity, has brought back to us the right and the fact of sonship, so that He now fulfils through us the offices of His earthly sovereignty, imparting to our afflictions the virtue of His Cross, and crowning them even now with the joy of His peace.

We have seen, in a word, however imperfectly it must have been, that the Victory of the Cross is the satisfaction of the necessities, the instincts, the aspirations, the activities of the soul of man.

In the endeavour to convey these thoughts I have made, I know, a heavy demand upon the attention of those who have listened to me. The preacher can speak only from the fulness of his heart and as he sees the truth. But such thoughts are not so much difficult as strange. They are not mere speculations of the closet. They are not for students and scholars only but for every believer who looks directly to Christ. They reach to the inmost depths of our common life. And if we have been allowed to regard them during this Holy Season, in quiet contemplation for a while, it is that GOD by His Spirit may teach us to bring them afterwards into the cares and distresses of our daily work. There is in the soul that which leaps up in quick response to the greatest hope. The soul was made to strive with unwearied desire towards an unattainable ideal. Only let the principle of the Christian life, which we too readily dwarf to the proportions of conventional littleness, be recognised in its breadth and power, and the life will clothe itself in the form through which it will conquer.

We need, at the present time, an energy of spiritual force, and our chief encouragement is that the need is acknowledged on every side. It is evil, and we know that it is evil, when religion tends to externalism and philosophy loses the inspiration of the unseen: when poetry becomes the amusement of an idle hour: when statesmanship is content to accept material tests as the criterion of national welfare; and to write history becomes a process of criticism and not a message of prophecy. It is evil; and no natural irony, no shrinking sense of our own unworthiness, no distrust born of past failures, should hold back the boldness of our confession of this evil.

We need an energy of spiritual force to purify the accumulated, and often unconscious, selfishness of our lives: to concentrate in one sympathetic whole the fragmentary labours of all who have been touched by the Divine love. We need, that is, to look yet again, as with eyes that cling to a vision half-understood, to the Cross of Christ, not as it has been moulded by art into a form of earthly grace, but in its stern, dread reality, that we may feel the shame and take it to ourselves, that we may feel the power and use it for the world which Christ died to save.

We need, I repeat, an energy of spiritual force. The world is full of eager and restless endeavours to better the conditions of life, to bring amusement and knowledge within the reach of all. It is well, but it is not enough. You cannot bring back life to the dead by painting and clothing the corpse. As long as we remain within the region of material and intellectual powers, our highest hopes will be doomed to disappointment. Selfishness in the accumulation and the use of wealth — of wealth of body and mind — will assert its supremacy. We must invoke and receive the new life of GOD: we must see ourselves and others in connexion with the unseen. We must confess and use the powers of the new age. We must appeal to the spiritual of which all else is a transitory symbol.

Life — life with all its joys and sorrows, with all its trials and opportunities — is as the man is. Earth itself answers to our view of heaven. If we are mean and narrow and unloving, we shall be beggars in the midst of luxury and desolate among a multitude of flatterers. If we behold GOD, if we behold Christ reigning from the Cross, suffering will be made the fuel of a purer joy.

I, if I be lifted up from the earth, will draw all men unto My-self. This is our faith; and we owe it to the world to proclaim it boldly. Men advance by association. And our fellowship is not with earth only but with heaven. Our fellowship is not with our kinsmen in religion only, but with all for whom Christ died. We shape no theory to define the ways of GOD which are past find-ing out; and we surrender no hope which His Spirit has put into our hearts. No ideal which we can form is able to reach, much less to surpass the end which answers to the Divine wisdom and the Divine love. 'The ideal,' it has been most truly said, 'is not the creation but the gradual discovery of the human intellect.' It *is,* and we only dimly divine it.

Do I find love so full in my nature, God's ultimate gift,
That I doubt His own love can compete with it? here, the
     parts shift?
Here the Creature surpass the Creator, the end, what Began?

I, if I be lifted up from the earth, will draw all men unto My-self. The noblest prae-Christian ideals failed, and we can discern the reasons of their failure. They were partial. They failed to take account of the contrasts in life. But the Christian ideal deals alike with the glory and the shame of humanity, with earth and heaven. On the Cross we see joy through suffering, life through death.

I, if I be lifted up from the earth, will draw all men unto My-self. Christ, the living Christ, reigns from the Cross with a do-minion which knows no bounds; and the Cross itself was taken in old times as the object to which St. Paul referred when he spoke of apprehending *the breadth and length and height and depth* in connexion with the love of Christ. 'Christ stretched forth His hands in His Passion' — in the words of an early father — 'and took the world in His embrace, to shew even then that a great host gathered from east and west would come beneath His wings and receive upon their brows that most noble and august sign.'

That sign, brethren, is on our brows, the sign of Christ Born, Crucified, Risen, Ascended. May God in His mercy grant that we may confess His Faith and live it.

64

BIBLIOGRAPHY

Samuel Cox: *Expositions,* 2nd ser., New York, 1886, pp. 285-298

A. C. Dixon: *The Glories of the Cross,* New York, n.d. pp. 25-30, reprinted Grand Rapids, 1962

Marcus Dods, in *Missionary Sermons, 1812-1924,* London, 1922, pp. 215-226

R. M. Edgar: *The Philosophy of the Cross,* London, 1874, pp. 19-34

P. T. Forsyth, in *Christian World Pulpit,* Vol. 63, pp. 305-312

John A. Hutton: *The Fear of Things,* London, 1911, pp. 106-115

Charles Jerdan: *For the Lord's Table,* 2nd ed., Edinburgh, 1903, pp. 380-383

J. H. Jowett: *The Transfigured Church,* New York, 1910, pp. 57-66

Alexander Maclaren: *Expositions of Holy Scripture: St. John IX-XIV,* pp. 140-150

N. J. Mc Leod: *Songs in the Night,* London, 1919, pp. 106-119

G. Campbell Morgan: *Westminster Pulpit,* Vol. IX, London, 1913, pp. 105-112

W. R. Nicoll: *Sunday Evenings,* London, n.d. pp. 263-270

Charles H. Spurgeon: *Metropolitan Tabernacle Pulpit,* Vol. III, 1855, No. 139, pp. 257-264; Vol. XIII, 1867, No. 777, pp. 589-600; Vol. XXIX, 1887, No. 1717, pp. 229-240

Alexander Stewart, in *Eden and Gethsemane,* Manchester, 1903, pp. 11-15

P. H. Swift: *The Magnetism of the Cross,* Cincinnati, 1904, pp. 9-30

R. A. Torrey: *The Gospel for Today,* New York, 1922, pp. 77-92

C. J. Vaughan: *The Wholesome Words of Christ,* 2nd ed., London, 1868, pp. 39-73

B. F. Westcott: *The Victory of the Cross,* London, 1888, pp. 95-110

For a biographical sketch of Bishop Westcott, see *Great Sermons on the Resurrection of Christ,* pp. 202-204.

THE CROSS A REVELATION OF DIVINE LOVE
by
R. McCheyne Edgar

"But God commendeth His love toward us, in that, while we were yet sinners, Christ died for us." — Romans 5:8

We have reached in this study of the Cross the position in which Christ is seen as an innocent substitute enduring the wrath due to human sin. By no other view can the death of Jesus be satisfactorily explained, as in no other light can it be reconciled with the interests of good government. If there were no Divine elements in the suffering endured, as some would have us to suppose, then it is hard to see how Jesus Christ was not the most faint-hearted of martyrs; while if He were not the representative and substitute for sinners, it is impossible to vindicate the permission of such a sacrifice. In other words, the doctrine that Jesus Christ was the solitary vicarious sacrifice for the sins of the whole world, exhausting in Himself man's deserved doom, is the only doctrine that gives any just account of the history. Here on the Cross, as nowhere else and at no other time, have you *Innocence* atoning for the guilty!

We have also seen that the entire tragedy was the result of a direct compact between the persons of the adorable Trinity, the Eternal Father commanding the willing and Eternal Son to lay down His life for the sheep, and He in the power of the Eternal Spirit offering Himself without spot to God. It was the assumption of the liabilities of man by the persons of the Godhead, and the wiping of them out by the blood of the obedient Son. It was God taking the side of man against Himself!

Nowhere, consequently, do we learn so vividly the wrath of God against sin as when we see it descending upon the Substitute.

The gathering waves of the Deluge, the flaming fire in Sodom, the sacking of Jerusalem, all famine, pestilence, and agony, do not proclaim so unmistakably as the Cross how real is the wrath, how terrible is the justice of the Most High in the matter of sin!

Yet, wonder of wonders, this same Cross of Christ, which is a revelation of Divine wrath, is also a revelation of Divine love. If the fire of wrath nowhere burns so fiercely as above the Cross, nowhere does the light of the Divine love break forth so brightly. Love was lavished upon our first parents in Eden in the provision and proscription of the garden; it has burst forth in no uncertain light in Providence; yet neither the bright dawn of love in the morning of creation, nor its progress in Providence ever since, can equal the summer noon which, to the open eye of a lost humanity, reveals its splendours around Christ's Cross. Upon Calvary love had its crowning manifestation; affection never welled forth as it did upon the day the dear Master died! "In this was manifested the love of God toward us, because that God sent His only-begotten Son into the world, that we might live through Him. Herein is love, not that we loved God, but that He loved us, and sent His Son to be the propitiation for our sins." (1 John 4:9,10).

But let us analyse this Divine love in the light of this text of ours, and in doing so we shall consider, I. The objects of this Divine love — men still sinners; II. The way in which the Divine love was revealed — by Christ dying for us; and, III. How the death of one Person can reveal the love of another — it is *God's* love which is revealed by *Christ's* death.

1. THE OBJECTS OF THIS DIVINE LOVE — MEN STILL SINNERS.

Now in order to understand the splendour of the Divine love which burst upon humanity in the Cross, we must remember that pity for the unfortunate, which seems at this hour almost *natural* to man, has been *made* so by the Cross. Up till the appearance of Christ, the law of the world was, "Thou shalt love thy neighbor and hate thine enemy." (Matthew 5:43). "I think it most disgraceful to a man," says C. Memmius in Sallust's *Jugurtha,* "to accept an injury without revenge." And we have already seen that the Divine wrath against human sin was most real and most righteous, especially when entertained in view of the crime of the Cross. How came it, then, that sinners became objects of Divine love instead of continuing objects of righteous wrath?

There have doubtless beeen instances in which one man has been willing to die for another: yet there must be in the person for whom the substitute dies something good and noble. A righteous man — that is, one strictly honest and honourable — would hardly find a substitute prepared to meet death in his room; man is not prepared to lose his life for the mere sake of *justice.* A good man, again, one who adds to integrity the attractiveness of goodness and geniality, might possibly secure a substitute in the hour of doom; yet even in this case there must be inserted a peradventure. A Christ again, with the attractiveness of sinless perfection and abounding love, may command martyrs in multitudes, for poor and pitiful is the soul that would not die for Him who died for us! Yet in all records of martyrdom and substitution there must be, you perceive, in the objects for whose sakes men sacrifice themselves, the attractive power of goodness and love. It seems beyond the bounds of mere human compassion to sacrifice life for the sake of those who have nothing attractive or winning about them.

But here in the Cross we have a new thing on the earth, self-sacrificing love expended upon *sinners.* Before there was in men anything attractive, anything lovely, anything fitted to engage a loving heart, the love of God came forth to them in the sacrifice of the Cross. It has been very properly said, "Supposing the object of love to be a being at once guilty, oppressed, and suffering, such as man must always appear to the view of God, and such as one man will sometimes appear in the eyes of a happier friend, a sacred thirst for sacrifice through love seems to waken naturally in the mind. How often when we suffer with the suffering we long to suffer *for* them, supposing this to be practicable; and to suffer with and for the guilty is but another form of this deep and generous yearning, native to so many hearts." But then this supposes what is the whole wonder and mystery in the question, how the guilty one becomes in the first instance the object of love. Doubtless if we have learned to love at Christ's Cross, we can understand how love becomes self-sacrificing for the sake of a loved one however guilty; but it is not so easy to come up to the love that makes the *guilty* its object.

That the guilty are the objects of human love and affection may be at once granted. We have Nancies lavishing their love even upon a Bill Sykes, the murderous housebreaker. But in such cases you have a sympathy with sin coupled with devotion to the sinner. It is entirely different when you try to realize how God Almighty, who is furious at sin, who abominates it, who knows its essence and meaning as virtual deicide, can nevertheless love the sinner *before* he had given up his sin. The whole difficulty of the atonement has its root here, and it is largely because men have occupied themselves with the details rather than with the first principle that they have ended in such confusion.

To love the unlovely, the hateful, the actively hostile, is something truly divine. Man never dreamed of overcoming evil with good till God put him upon the way by affording him the grand example. To furnish by the power of love a soul of good in things evil has been the master policy of God. But let us not mistake the truth here. Two very different courses may be taken in this mighty business. It is possible to find, or at least to *imagine* we have found, a soul of good in things evil; it is quite another thing to *put* the soul of good *into* the evil, and in time purge the evil away. Great masters, like Shakespeare and Dickens for example, have spent their powers in *finding* a soul of good in things evil; and often it is to be feared they have carried the good *imaginatively* into the evil, and thrown the halo of a false worth over what is base at best. But God undertakes to work out another problem, and it is to *put* good into what is evil, that the evil may pass away. He has nothing to start with: the evil is unmitigated, the creatures are lost, guilty, condemned, they are virtual murderers, their hands are full of blood; yet He girds up His loins to the task of transforming the evil into good. And this could only be by *love*.

Why did God love sinners, then? It was not because of anything in them, it was not because of "an inestimable preciousness that was hidden in humanity," for the inestimable preciousness was not hidden, but by *grace* bestowed; it could only have been because of what He knew He could make of man through the power of His Divine love! Just as a mighty engineer or agriculturist may contemplate the most unlikely raw material or desert ground, and rejoice lovingly in the possibilities that wait upon his skill if expended upon it, so God looked down on man, notwithstanding his fearful sin and guilt, and His holy eye kindled at the thought of what might yet be made out of His creature when He had lavished upon him His loving grace. "But God, who is rich in mercy, for His great love wherewith He loved us, even when we were dead in sins, hath quickened us together with Christ (by grace are ye saved), and hath raised us up together, and made us sit together in heavenly places in Christ Jesus: that in the ages to come He might show the exceeding riches of His grace in His kindness toward us through Christ Jesus." (Ephesians 2:4-7). The love of God to sinners, therefore, rested upon the assurance of His own *sovereign* power to subdue them and turn their sin to good. It was the Divine delight in the possibilities of His kingdom, when the stability of His kingdom seemed in peril. It was a Divine self-confidence, holy, just, and good, that saw in lost humanity an inviting field for the display of His powers!

II. THE WAY IN WHICH THE DIVINE LOVE WAS REVEALED.

The manifestation of love is one of the most curious and interesting in inquiries. It is easy understanding that a *profession* of love is something very far short of a manifestation. Proof is expected as well as profession, and the proof is in proportion to the gifts of love. Hence it is that we prize what embodies something of our friend's self; if he is a poet, our most precious acknowledgment will be to receive from him a poem; if he is a painter, a picture; if he is an author, a copy of his book. Now as we advance upon this line of thought, we can easily see that the heart's love may be tested by the amount of sacrifice which a person is prepared to undertake on behalf of the object of his love. Unless a heart is ready to risk *its all* for the object of its affection, love has not been made perfect.

Carrying this principle with us, we have to contemplate God as loving sinners so strongly that He gave up His only-begotten and well-beloved Son to the death for us all. Here in the person of Christ was an object of love, upon whom the Father had lavished His affection from all eternity. In the bosom of the Father He had experienced the Divine endearments before any creature had existed. The fellowship of the eternities crowded into their communion. Yet when the interests of us sinners come into competition, and justice demands a suitable sacrifice for human sin, God the Father gives up the Son to death for us all.

A circumstance in the patriarchal history seems designed to illustrate the very point before us. Abraham was commanded, you remember, to repair to Mount Moriah, and offer his son Isaac, the son of promise, so well-beloved, as a burnt-offering. It was a tremendous trial of the patriarch's faith, and, when considered in itself, it undoubtedly presents a moral difficulty. In fact it is only in the light of the Cross that this circumstance, like so many more, becomes at all clear. For God shows upon Mount Moriah how a faithful child of His is prepared to prefer the Divine will, when unmistakably expressed, to the nearest and dearest interest in life. Yet Abraham is spared the pain of taking away his son's life, — the voice from heaven arrests his hand before the deed is done. God the Father, however, reaches analogous circumstances in the fulness of time. In due season His Son, the well-beloved, is bound upon the altar. He is nailed upon the cross; and, as one has beautifully remarked, "This other Abraham has no one above Him to hold back His arm when prepared to strike," but for the sake of sinners, from the love He bore us, He took·away His Son's life with a stroke. Oh, what a devotion He exhibited to the interests of justice, and what a love He bore to man when He brought Himself to this!

To the Cross of Christ, therefore, do I point you as the incomparable commendation of love. No similar proof of God's devotion to the interests of sinners has ever been afforded. We may imagine that Divine love breaks forth more brightly in the sweet procession of nature, that it breathes in the summer breezes and smiles in cloudless skies and nights that speak of heaven, but nowhere have we such a revelation of love as when we witness the only-begotten and well-beloved Son given up by the Father to death for us!

And here let me remark in passing that nothing but a tremendous *necessity* could have brought about such an exhibition of love. "Ought not Christ to have suffered these things, and to enter into His glory?" This necessity must have been real, essential, dwelling deep in the very nature of things, else love would never have taken such shape as this. Doubtless there are many foolish, because needless, expenditures made in proof of human love, but in a matter which is Divine, and is concerned with life, there is no room for anything that is *needless*. This expenditure must have been necessary to secure the purposes of love, or it never would have been made. Had any material sacrifice been sufficicent, had a million suns with their incalculable fires been a sufficient holocaust, the Divine Word would doubtless have summoned them out of the nethermost night and illuminated the universe with His altar-fire. But with reverence must we say it, there was but one alternative presented, the sacrifice of sinners, or the sacrifice of the Son; and blessed be God, He preferred *our* salvation to His Son's exemption. He spares us, and spares not Him. (Romans 8:32). He lavishes His love on us, and lays our sins on Him! With ineffable compassion and delight, as if He had been ransacking the universe for a ransom, He at length exclaims in view of this Victim, Christ

Jesus, "Deliver from going down to the pit; I have found a ransom." (Job 33:24).

III.   HOW THE DEATH OF ONE PERSON CAN REVEAL THE LOVE OF ANOTHER.

We have, I hope, realized in the death of Christ the most precious of all proofs of the Divine love. It was about the greatest gift within the compass of the Divine generosity. I say *about* the greatest, because it does not at once appear that it *is* the greatest gift. Indeed it seems at first sight very like being generous at other people's expense, a cheap form of revealing love to give another person's life away. There are many who would be uncommonly generous with other people's wealth if they had it, who would respond to necessitous appeals out of other people's pockets, who would be reckless in a life and death matter with other people's lives. Indeed the world is full of these *shifted sacrifices,* this rolling of the burden upon the shoulders of others.

And, beloved, I speak it with reverence, the sacrifice of the Son has outwardly the aspect of a shifted sacrifice. If Christ be essentially different from the Father, if the sufferer be in substance other than the judge, — that is to say, if the doctrine of the Trinity be not true that the Father and the Son are essentially one, — then we can neither vindicate the property of the procedure, nor accept of it as a very high commendation of the Divine love. But this doctrine reconciles, harmonizes, sublimates all. By it Christ the sacrifice is seen to be the other self of the Father who delivers Him to death, and the atonement is neither more nor less than the virtual self-sacrifice of God! Admit that Christ and the Father are one in essence, then the ineffable sympathies of the Godhead demonstrate the depths of that Divine compassion which prefers to sacrifice the Son rather than sacrifice man; which prefers to strike *itself* rather than to strike lost man.

No wonder that atonement becomes a difficulty to those who reject the Trinity. It is easy to talk of legal fictions and forensic justification and such like when the essential unity of the parties to the great covenant of grace will not be recognized. But once we rise into this great mystery of the Trinity, and see in its sacred light that the atonement is really, through an assumed human nature, gathering up into the Godhead the doom that man deserves, that it is God taking sides with sinners against Himself, we see that we have left legal fictions far below us, and that we are in the midst of the realities of self-sacrifice. The atonement is the yielding up of a mortal nature by the Immortal Mind in the way of self-sacrifice, that a way of righteousness and mercy might be prepared for sinful man. It was the Divine discharge of human debt to keep straight the balances of the universe!

Let us, therefore, do the Father as well as the Son justice in our estimate of the tremendous transaction. The giving up of His other self in the person of His Son must have been a *self-denial* passing the bounds of all human thought, just as the submission of the Son to death and sorrow must have been an agony beyond compare. It is easy to read the words, "Therefore doth my Father love me, because I lay down my life that I might take it again. No man taketh it from me, but I lay it down of myself. I have power to lay it down, and I have power to take it again. This commandment have I received of my Father" (John 10:17, 18), and to utter a few platitudes about "the unbroken sense of the Father's favour;" but it is not so easy to enter into any due sense of the self-denial of the Father in giving the commandment to the Son to die, of the self-denial of the Son in responding thereto; in a word, of the *burden* which the Godhead assumed in the interests of the race.

The power of such Divine disinterestedness should melt the stoniest hearts. If God commendeth His love by such a death as this, oh surely our hearts will recognize it and respond to the Divine devotion! Shall we not be wooed and won by such a suitor as our self-sacrificing God? If He loved us beyond Himself, if He loved us so as to send His Son to die, while we were sinners, and deserved death instead of love, surely we will resolve in this solemn hour to love Him in return with all our heart, and soul, and mind, and strength! May Almighty Love who has commended Himself in such a fashion to us sinners, become a power in our hearts, leading us to love Him with all our might! Amen.

BIBLIOGRAPHY

R. M. Edgar: *The Philosophy of the Cross*, London, 1874, pp. 85-100
Herbert H. Farmer: *Things Not Seen*, London, 1927, pp. 144-153
J. D. Jones: *Richmond Hill Sermons*, London, 1932, pp. 90-105
Alexander Maclaren: *Expositions of Holy Scripture, Romans*, pp. 95-104
George H. Morrison, in *Christian World Pulpit*, Vol. 87, Feb. 24, 1915, pp. 118-120
Charles H. Spurgeon: *Metropolitan Tabernacle Pulpit*, Vol. II, 1854, No. 104, pp. 400-408; Vol. XXIII, 1877, No. 1345, pp. 169-180

BIOGRAPHICAL SKETCH

I greatly regret that I have not been able to find anything of importance for the biography of this well-known writer. His name is not to be found in any biographical dictionary or reference work known to me. All I know about Mr. Edgar, in addition to his being the author of two works other than the one listed above, *The Gospel of a Risen Saviour*, Edinburgh, 1902; and, *The Genius of Protestantism*, 1900; is that he wrote some of the Homilies in the *Pulpit Commentary* for Leviticus, Deuteronomy, the Gospel of Luke, Romans, Galatians, Ephesians, and Colossians.

"HE DIED FOR ALL"
by
John Henry Jowett

"And he died for all, that they that live should no longer live unto themselves, but unto him who for their sakes died and rose again." — 2 Corinthians 5:15

"Christ died for the ungodly." Yes, but what is meant by "to die"? The question suggests no fanciful inquiry, the pursuit of which will lead us into merely fruitless speculations. The question is of deep, practical, immediate, personal import. The word "death" is a cardinal word in the New Testament Scriptures. It enshrines a primary fact, out of which a great gospel is born. "I delivered unto you first of all . . . How that Christ died for our sins." "First of all." The fact takes first rank. It is all-determinative of our message. It must have priority and precedence over all other proclamations. All other proclamations must find their significance in this. This is the creative fact, primary and fundamental. "First of all. . . . Christ died for our sins." "Christ died for the ungodly." But what is meant by "to die"? We must have some large and worthy interpretation of the imperial fact if we would worthily appreciate the work of our Lord. Have we a sufficiently profound and pregnant interpretation of death? What is the prevalent interpretation? Our conception is too commonly narrow and impoverished. Our emphasis is false, and false emphasis always means distorted truth. The body is too obtrusive in determining our spiritual judgments. It constitutes the Alpha and the Omega of much of our thought. It defines and limits our outlook. Take the first hundred people you meet, and confront them with the inquiry —What is life? and half the hundred will immediately think of the body. Vary your inquiry, and launch the question — What is death? and the thought of the ninety and nine will immediately gather round about a body, a coffin, a graveyard. It is this dominance of the body, this intrustion of the body into all our conceptions, which impoverishes our comprehension of truth, and robs life of its heights and depths and far horizons.

Now, our Lord repeatedly proclaimed that the bodily aspects of things are not primary, but secondary, and that the way into the Kingdom of Truth is by a scrupulous observance of this divine order. No man rightly interprets his daily bread to whom its primary aspect is its relationship to the flesh. "Seek ye first" the spiritual aspects of common bread. Let it become to you a sacrament, and let its cardinal significance be its expression of the unseen and eternal. Let the body be subordinate and secondary, even in your interpretation of daily bread. That is the divine principle, the principle of succession in all ennobling and healthy thinking, and it seeks application in all the urgent affairs both of life and of death.

"Of death?" Yes; we misinterpret death if we allow the body to determine our thought. If we are to pursue the fruitful way of the divine order in our gropings round about this mystery of death, our first step must be to place this clamorous flesh in the rear. Death is not primarily, but only very secondarily, an affair of the flesh. This is our Master's teaching. Our investigations must find their starting-point here. The making of other starting-points has betrayed us into judgments which, I believe, have taken us far away from the Master's mind. You must have repeatedly noticed that what we ordinarily call death, our Master insisted upon calling sleep. When the bodily activities cease, we describe the cessation as death. Jesus described it as sleep, holding the word "death" in reserve. You will remember that when He came to the ruler's house, and one gave Him the intelligence that the little daughter was dead, the Master, even in the presence of the hired mourners, and surrounded by the trappings and wrappages of woe, made the surprising declaration, "The maid is not dead, but sleepeth." "And they laughed Him to scorn," so glaring was the apparent conflict between the declaration and the stern reality. "Not dead"; cessation of this kind does not constitute death; it is only sleep. The word "death" must be held in abeyance to express an experience of infinite and appalling significance.

You will remember, too, from that beautiful story which enshrines our Saviour's love for the family at Bethany, that when He heard of the black terror which had invaded their home, He used the same mild and gentle-toned expression, "Our friend Lazarus sleepeth"; and it was only because of the exigencies of the moment, and because of the practical bewilderment of the disciples, only because of their infantile grasp, and their inability to reach and grip the larger thought, that our Master, with a sigh that one can feel through the straining speech, condescended to their limitations, and using their own abused word confessed "Lazarus is dead."

Here, then, is a suggestive indication of the Master's mind. What too often constitutes our entire conception of death scarcely entered into Christ's conception at all. What we called death, Christ named sleep. The word death must be kept in the rear to suggest some other experience of awful and unspeakable import.

Now, let us advance a farther step. The Master repeatedly declares that He came to save us from that which He calls death. "If a man keep My word, he shall never see death." Insert the common interpretation of the word death in that phrase, and the sentence becomes a dark confusion. "If a man keep My word, he shall never see death." But the saintliest among us, they who have lived and walked upon the serene mountain heights, hand in hand with God, become worn in body, and grow weary, and cease, and we have to carry their remains over the same well-trodden way to the cemetery, along which we carry the remains of the lustful, the avaricious, and the proud. Yes, we have to dig graves even for saints. Do they then die? Nay, nay, they only sleep, for "if a man keep My word, he shall never see death." They sleep; yes, but they cannot die!

Listen again to the Master: "This is the bread which cometh

down out of Heaven, that a man may eat thereof and not die." But men and women do eat that bread. They make it their daily food, and yet they may be wayworn invalids, toilsomely dragging along in wearying infirmity, and long before they reach the limit of threescore years and ten they fall by the way, and we have to lay their wornout bodies beneath the soil. They fed on Heaven's bread; do they die? Nay, nay, they only sleep. "If a man eat of this bread, he shall never die." They sleep; yes, but they cannot die!

Let me give you one other of the Master's words. "He that heareth My word, and believeth on Him that sent Me . . . is passed from death unto life." "Is passed." The great transition is effected. He is alive for evermore. But men and women do hear His word, and they do fix their belief on the Father who sent Him, and yet they pass from physical strength through physical weariness to physical cessation. We hear their farewell. We draw our blinds. The mourners go about the streets, and we devise little memento-cards, on which we inscribe the words, "Died So-and-so!" "He that heareth My word and believeth is passed from death unto life." "Died So-and-so!" "If any man eat of this bread, he shall never die." "Died So-and-so!" "If a man keep My saying, he shall never see death." "Died So-and-so!" We are clearly using the word with quite another interpretation from that given to it by Christ. It cannot be repeated too often, or emphasized too strongly, that what we call death is to Christ our Lord not death at all. It is only sleep, and He came not to save us from sleep, but to deliver us from death. We shall all sleep, saints and sinners alike; but we shall not all die: for if any man keep the word of the Christ, he shall never see death; he is passed from death unto life; he abideth for ever.

But my text tells me that "Christ died." He did more than sleep; He died! What, then, was the Saviour's death? What do we commonly mean when we speak of the death of Christ? We fix our eyes upon Calvary. We see the Cross. We see the crucified body. We see the quivering flesh. We see the dripping blood. We see the face-lines of unutterable woe. We see the last gasp, and we almost feel the appalling stillness which follows the appalling pain. And we call that the death of Christ. That physical cessation we call the death. What if Christ should call that part of the stupendous crisis His sleep? When the little maid was lying in a precisely similar condition respecting the flesh, Christ named the condition a sleep. When all the physical activities of Lazarus had ceased, Christ named the cessation a sleep. May we reverently take the Master's own word "sleep," and use it to name the physical cessation on the Cross, and reserve the word death for something behind the physical cessation — something of untold and overwhelming horror? I think that even on Calvary the body may be too obtrusive in our thoughts. We see the rude, rough cross-beams; we see the hammers and the nails; we see the uplifted Saviour; and the vision is terrible and terrifying, and I pray that it may be burnt into our hearts in lines of fire. But on that awful Mount of Calvary we see the Saviour sleep; we do not, and we cannot, see Him die! But "Christ died." If the physical cessation were sleep, what was the Saviour's death? Since the crucifixion of the Master, hosts of His disciples have been similarly crucified, and have shared His bloody martyrdom. Like their Master, they slept; unlike their Master, they do not die. "Christ died." What was the Saviour's death?

I would not lead you along a way that I almost fear to tread. One can divine by instinct so much more than he can put into speech. We can feel so much more than we can express. And the way is very dim, with only here and there a guiding mark. Let us away into Gethsemane, at the midnight, that we may just touch the awful mystery. The Master is there, and He has taken with Him His three most intimate friends. They can accompany Him part of the way, and then He must leave them that He may continue the weird journey alone. Says the simple narrative, "He began to be sorrowful and very heavy." I think that marks the beginning of the dying. He has not yet begun to sleep; I think He has begun to die. "Sorrowful and very heavy." Just gaze into the hearts of these words. "Sorrowful" has a profounder content than the word appears to denote; it is significant of the grief of desolation; and as for the word translated "heavy," it suggests an awful sense of homelessness. Shall we insert these words in place of those that have become almost too familiar to us? "He began to be desolate and very homeless." Let us pause there. "Very homeless!" He who only a few hours before had spoken so comfortably about His Father's house with the many mansions, and who on the self-same day had joyfully proclaimed the unfailing presence and companionship of His Father — "I am not alone, my Father is with Me" — was now becoming burdened with the oppressive sense of homelessness. The Father's house was becoming dim, and communion with the Father was waxing faint, and this sinless Son of God was beginning to feel the chills of a homeless desolation. I think that was the beginning of the dying. He was beginning to taste death!

Go a little farther into the garden, and listen to the Master's agonised speech. "My soul is exceeding sorrowful, even unto death"; exceeding desolate, "even unto death." Desolation unto death! That is the wailing moan of the Saviour's soul. Is He shrinking from the Cross? Is He afraid of the nails? Does He recoil from the physical pain? I remember keenly that one of the distresses of my boyhood was a temptation, which I tried hard to resist, a temptation to suspect that Jesus was not so brave and fearless as some of His own followers, of whom I had read in my school-books. I had read how disciples of Jesus, when the flames of martyrdom were rising and curling about them, had almost toyed and played with the flames, as little children play with the fringes of the advancing tide. I had read of how young girls had been tarred from crown to toe, and then fired to illumine a sensualist's revels, and how they had sung in the flame. And did their Master shrink from that which they almost welcomed with a shout? "If it be possible, let this cup pass from Me." "My soul is exceeding desolate." Is he afraid of the Cross? Nay, nay, a thousand times nay; He fears not the sleep, but, oh, He does shrink from the death! Over His soul there is gathering and deepening a midnight darkness and desolation to which no other name can be given but the name of death. On now to Calvary, and let us hear the words in which the sense of desolation and homelessness deepens into an unspeakable and unthinkable intensity! "My God, My God, why hast Thou forsaken Me?" That was death. What would follow would be only sleep. That was death — appalling midnight in the soul, the horror of a great darkness, exceeding desolation, abandonment! That was death — the Father's house obscured, the Father's hand vanished, and the Son of God in the outer darkness, in the agonies of a consuming loneliness! That was death — the sinless Saviour out there in the night, in the abandonment which is "the wages of sin." What we call death, Christ called sleep. "Christ died."

Now, that homelessness of soul, that abandonment in the outer darkness, is "the wages of sin." But "Christ knew no sin." And so we are led to the music of the Gospel, which has brought cheer and assurance to a countless host, the Gospel that Christ Jesus walked that way of appalling darkness and alienation in place of His brethren. "Christ died for the ungodly." He died for our sins. A few soldiers with hammer and nails put Him to sleep on the Cross, but it was for the sins of a race that He died, that He voluntarily went into the outer darkness, into the awful eclipse of forsakenness and abandonment. "He tasted death for every man." He drank that cup for the race. "He died for all."

Now, the Scriptures affirm that apart from Christ I am still under the dominion of "the law of sin and death;" "sin and death," sin and abandonment, sin and homelessness, sin and forsakenness and terrible night. That is an indissoluble connection, stern and inevitable. It is a law, fixed and unchanging, "the law of sin and death." But the Scriptures further affirm that in Christ Jesus I come under the dominion of another law — the "law of the spirit of life" — and by this I am freed from the sovereignty of "the law of sin and death." Under "the law of the spirit of life," the lonely way of the outer darkness will never more be known. By Christ the way has once been trod, never to be re-trodden by those who are in Him. "There shall be no more death."

Let me now call up for review some of the Master's glowing

promises which I read to you at the beginning of my discourse, and let me read them in the light of the interpretation which I have been endeavouring to expound. "If a man keep My saying, he shall never see death." He shall sleep, but he shall never know the outer darkness of separation and abandonment. "This is the bread which cometh down out of Heaven, that a man may eat thereof and not die." He shall sleep, but he shall never die. He shall never pass into the cold, chilling eclipse of a homeless desolation. We have been "reconciled to God by the death of His Son," and in that Son death is abolished. There is "life for evermore."

Here, then, is the Glory of the Gospel. It is declared that I, a poor struggling, self-wasted sinner, may by faith be so identified with Christ, that Christ and I become as "one man." That is no ingenious phrase, the vehicle of a pious but fruitless fancy. It is the expression of a gospel, which a highly privileged ministry has the glory to proclaim, and which has proved itself to be the most august and blessed of realities to a great and uncounted host. An unspeakably fruitful identity with Christ, the mystic oneness of the believing race in the risen Lord! This is the possible heritage of all men, made possible to all men by the Saviour's atoning death. "He that is joined unto the Lord is one spirit;" he is "bound in the bundle of life with the Lord his God." He is a partner in the deathless or eternal life.

But now to me, and to all men, there is committed a great choice. I can choose to be one with Adam, or one with Christ; one with the old man, or one with the new; one under "the law of sin and death," or one under "the law of the spirit of life." I say the choice is ours, and we know it. If I make this the choice of my days — one with Thee, Thou deathless Christ, by faith and by faithfulness, one with Thee — I shall never die. But if my life be a deliberate affront to the deathless Son of God, if I turn my back upon His grace, if this be the choice of my days — one with thee, thou man of sin, by obedience and by spirit with thee — then I shall die, nay, even now I am dead, and the great day of unveiling shall reveal to me the appalling fact that

I am homeless, desolate, separated by a "great gulf" from "the inheritance of the saints in light." "These shall go into the outer darkness," into the night of awful loneliness, into the eclipse of death. They shall die.

Oh, pray that we may never know the death! When the hour of our departure comes, and the friends whom we leave behind shall speak of us as "dead," I pray that the word may be a misnomer, a pardonable fiction, not expressive of the reality of things. I pray that we may only sleep. May the good Lord put us into a gentle sleep, and in the great awakening may we find ourselves not homeless, but at home, glad to be at home, glad to meet the deathless One, and to see Him face to face!

BIBLIOGRAPHY

William Cunningham: *Sermons from 1828 to 1860, Edinburgh,* 1872, pp. 365-378

R. M. Edgar: *The Philosophy at the Cross,* London, 1874, pp. 174-188

Griffith John, in *Christian World Pulpit,* Vol. 54, Dec. 21, 1898, pp. 392-395

John Henry Jowett: *Apostolic Optimism,* London, 8th ed., n.d., pp. 171-185

Charles Kingsley: *Sermons on National Subjects, Works.* Vol. 22, London, 1885, pp. 230-241

Alexander Maclaren: *Expositions of Holy Scripture. Corinthians,* pp. 371-380

F. W. Robertson: *Sermons Preached at Brighton,* new ed., New York, n.d., pp. 495-504

James Saurin: *Sermons,* Vol. III, New York, 1804, pp. 169-194

JOHN HENRY JOWETT
(1863-1923)

Dr. J. D. Jones, a notable preacher himself, is probably correct in saying that Dr. John Henry Jowett was not only the greatest preacher among the Congregationalists of his generation, but was in many ways the greatest preacher of his age. John Henry Jowett was born August 25, 1863, in Halifax, England, son of a tailor and draper. Even when a boy he was an omnivorous reader, generally spending every evening in the excellent library of the Mechanics' Institute, concerning which his biographer gives us a most interesting anecdote.

"A little incident occurred one night in the Mechanics' Institute news room which was possibly pivotal in his life. As he was poring over a book an elderly gentleman, whom he had never seen before and never saw again, paused and looked over Jowett's shoulder to see, no doubt, what the boy was reading so assiduously. Then touching Jowett gently on the back he said, 'My boy, you must make your way to the University.' He passed out of the room and out of Jowett's life; but the words rang in the boy's ears and thrilled his soul. They breathed into him a new hope and vision. When he got home Jowett told his mother of the little episode. 'Oh,' she said, 'but I don't think we could ever afford to send you to the University.' Jowett possibly never dreamed that they could; but the train was laid by the stranger's stimulating words, and Jowett won his own way at last to the Universities of Edinburgh and Oxford."

It is not necessary here to enter into details regarding his life before his great ministry began, but one episode that exercised a great deal of influence upon him must be mentioned which occurred a few weeks after his father had "virtually completed all the arrangements for him to enter a Halifax firm of solicitors as an articled clerk. On the day before the articles were to be signed Jowett met his Sunday School teacher, by accident, in the street and told him what he was about to do. Mr. Dewhirst looked grieved. 'I had always hoped,' he said, 'that you would go into the ministry.' Jowett, with his profound affection for his Sunday

School teacher, was taken aback. He thought seriously over the suggestion and going home anxiously considered his whole future. He was strongly drawn to the ministry, but was he divinely called? Years afterwards recalling this crucial moment in his life, he said 'the grip' came to him as he stood by the harmonium in the parlour at home. From that moment he had no hesitation. His course was clear. 'It was the result,' he said, 'of no urgent argument, nor the issue of any calculation of profit and loss: it was a gracious constraint, an inclination born of love, a decision shaped by the worship of Jesus Christ.' "

Jowett was a student at Edinburgh University from 1883 to 1886, and upon graduation entered Airdale College for his theological training, followed by two terms at the newly-founded Mansfield College at Oxford. While in Edinburgh, he was powerfully influenced by the preaching of Alexander Whyte and the great messages of Henry Drummond. At the age of twenty-six, he was called to be the minister of the Congregational Church of Newcastle-on-Tyne, where at once he was recognized as a preacher of unusual gifts. The church became crowded from the very beginning, October 1889, and as has been said, from then until his last Sunday at Westminster Chapel, in London, "he never knew what it was to preach save to crowds." At the age of thirty-two, in October 1895, Jowett was called to the famous Carrs Lane Congregational Church, at Birmingham, following that mighty man of God, R. W. Dale, remaining here for sixteen years. In his first sermon at Carrs Lane, Jowett acknowledged — "I succeeded a great man who made it easy for his successor to labor. I succeeded a very great saint and a very great teacher and preacher who by the greatness of his personality, had created a liberal spirit at Carrs Lane. . . . If the stones of these buildings could be made to speak, I think that all their utterances would gather around about the redemption wrought for us in Christ."

Dr. Jowett was only thirty-seven years old when he was honored by being invited to preach the Union Sermon of the Congregational Union of Great Britain. In 1906, he was made Chairman of the Congregational Union, and later, 1910-1911, was the

President of the National Council of Evangelical Free Churches.

Dr. Jowett's first visit to America, in the summer of 1909, proved a turning-point in his career. His visit was primarily as a speaker at the Northfield Conference, but as the result of two sermons he preached at the Fifth Avenue Presbyterian Church, New York, he was invited to become its pastor, an invitation he declined. In 1910, the invitation was twice repeated. The congregation at Carrs Lane presented him with a resolution with 1400 signatures of members, pleading with him to remain in Birmingham. But in April 1911, at the age of forty-eight, he felt that this time it was God's will that he should go. In New York, from April 1911, for seven years, he carried on a phenomenal work. Jowett himself wrote to his friend, Dr. J. D. Jones, that the morning audience, which had dropped to 600 or 700, now had risen to over 1500, and that the afternoon services, which had dropped to 300, already were witnessing a similar crowded church, and at the mid-week service, which had become almost extinct, some five hundred people were ein regular attendance. I can bear witness myself to these great congregations. When still in my teens, I one morning went up to the Fifth Avenue Church to hear this man, about whom so many things were being said. The pews were held for the pew-owners until five minutes after eleven. A queue was lined up outside the church a half block long, waiting for the unoccupied seats to be made available. Dr. Jowett preached on 2 Kings 5:12, "Are not Abanah and Pharpar, the rivers of Damascus, better than all the waters of Israel? may I not wash in them, and be clean? so he turned and went away in a rage." I have never heard any man in any pulpit utter the word sin in such a way that it seemed to be a sword piercing one's own heart, as I heard that morning. The sermon never appeared in print — unfortunately.

Jowett lived for his pulpit. He was an indefatigable worker. In his famous Yale *Lectures on Preaching,* he said, "I used to hear the factory operatives passing my house on the way to the mills, where work began at six o'clock. The sound of their iron clogs ringing through the street fetched me out of bed and took me to my work."

Sir William Robertson Nicoll has correctly expressed one's reaction upon hearing Dr. Jowett preach: "Of the startling wealth and beauty of Dr. Jowett's diction, the incisiveness of his contrasts, the overwhelming power of his appeals it is impossible for me to write adequately. Excellent and inspiring as are his published sermons, one has to hear him in order to understand the greatness, and I had almost said, the uniqueness, of his influence. In Dr. Jowett everything preaches. The voice preaches, and it is a voice of great range and compass, always sweet and clear through every variety of intonation. The eyes preach, for though Dr. Jowett apparently writes every word of his sermons, he is extraordinarily independent of his manuscript. The body preaches, for Dr. Jowett has many gestures, and not one ungraceful. But, above all, the heart preaches. I have heard many great sermons, but never one at any time which so completely seized and held from start to finish a great audience. . . . Above all preachers I have heard Dr. Jowett has the power of appeal. That the appeal very deeply moved many who were listening was obvious, and no doubt it moved many who gave no sign. At times the tension of listening, the silence, and the eagerness of the crowd were almost oppressive. It was all very wonderful and very uplifting."

At the age of fifty-five, toward the end of the First World War, Jowett felt the leading of the Lord to return to England, in her hour of spiritual and moral need, and for the last five years of his active life, until December, 1922, he ministered with great blessing at the famous center of Congregationalism in London, Westminster Chapel, following Dr. G. Campbell Morgan. Dr. Jowett died after a lingering illness, December 19, 1923.

If Dr. Jowett as we have said, lived for the pulpit, his main theme in the pulpit was the divine revelation given to us in the Holy Scriptures. During his New York ministry, he wrote to a friend in England, "One thing is perfectly clear — there is a great hungering for the Word of God and a great desire to have its contents made known." To another friend, he wrote this just criticism. "I think probably the most novel thing in my ministry over here is the exposition of the Scriptures. Generally speaking the sermons in this country are topical and are not devoted to the immediate exposition of the Word of God. Such expositions have therefore the suggestion of novelty. I am glad to have so many students and ministers attending the services, as I have the opportunity of turning their minds to real delving work in the Bible. I am perfectly sure that what the churches of this country need is the nutriment of spiritual truth distributed at every service. I have met with many ministers who have confirmed my judgment."

"The longer I am in the ministry," said Dr. Jowett, when fifty years of age, "the more I am convinced that our work is to deal out the Bread of Life." About 1912, Jowett confessed in a letter, "I want the next ten years (he wrote on his fiftieth birthday) to be full of ripened service. I long to be able to expound the Word with greater power. But, O, the thing is so big, so wonderfully big that I seem as one who lifts a pebble from the shore, or one heather bell from these wide-spreading moors. The Book becomes increasingly wonderful to me. Every added experience in life gives me a new lens and deeper things are unveiled. But I suppose there is no bottom to the sea of grace, and that is the reason why we shall never lose our surprise through all eternity."

THE OFFENSE OF THE CROSS
by
Billy Graham

Galatians 5:11
"And I, brethren, if I yet preach circumcision, why do I yet suffer persecution? then is the offence of the cross ceased."
— Galatians 5:11.

At a moment when tensions in the cold war are reaching a new high, the whole world has been shocked by the tragic death of Dag Hammarskjold. The very existence of the United Nations is in jeopardy as the Soviet Union insists on a three-man secretariat which will make the UN unworkable. Diplomats brace themselves for further struggles and possible setbacks.

As one incident of crisis follows another, it seems to many as if demonic forces are at work to bring mankind to destruction. The Christian outlook has not been as black since the days of the first century. Never was the New Testament's message of hope more needed by a confused and alarmed people. Never has the cross of Jesus Christ towered so significantly in judgment over the events of time.

The late German theologian Karl Heim once said that the answer to the world's dilemma is the *kerygma,* or the proclamation of the Gospel; and that the heart of the *kerygma* is the cross. Yet the Apostle Paul referred to the cross as a "scandal" to the world. He asked the churches of Galatia why it was, if he preached "works," that he was being persecuted. If that were true, he said, "then is the offense (skandalon) of the cross ceased" (Galatians 5:11).

That expression, "offense of the cross," at first may sound

strange to the modern mind. We have crosses on our churches, embossed on our Bibles, and worn as pendants from our necks. The cross is an emblem of art to the poets. There may be nothing wrong with this sentimentality, but the Bible teaches that the cross as understood in New Testament days was an offense, a stumbling block, a scandal to men.

Christ is not always attractive to the human heart, no matter how he is presented. Isaiah says with prophetic vision as he looks down the corridors of time: "There is no beauty in him that men should desire him." Paul, living after Christ, found that the cross provoked the scorn and aroused the antagonism of men. When he held up Christ and him crucified, many were offended and turned away in contempt and rage. Today we hear the cry all over the Christian world, "Back to Christ." I want to ask, "What Christ are we to go back to?"

I attended a conference at Princeton Seminary some time ago. The president of one of our theological seminaries remarked, "I am convinced we are having a religious revival in America, but," he said, "it is not the Christian religion." Sometimes when we look at Christ, we get a wrong concept of him. Too often he is only the Jesus who walked in Galilee, only the picture of wisdom in Jerusalem, or an ideal created by a picturesque imagination. He is not the Christ of the cross. The cross in the days of Christ stood for a place of horrible execution. It was reserved by law for murderers, inciters of rebellion, and the lowest kind of criminals. The cross meant tragic suffering and slow death, for the victim was exposed to the elements and to the animals that prowled at night.

When Jesus said, "If you are going to follow me, you have to take up a cross," it was the same as saying, "Come and bring your electric chair with you. Take up the gas chamber and follow me." He did not have a beautiful gold cross in mind — the cross on a church steeple or on the front of your Bible. Jesus had in mind a place of execution.

Paul found that wherever he went he had no difficulty until he began to preach the cross. Wherever he went he found that the cross was an offense. People did not want to talk about it, and they did not want to hear about it. After two thousand years it has not changed. In America, in Europe, in Asia, in Africa, the cross of our Lord Jesus Christ is still a stumbling block to men who want to go to heaven but are not willing to pay the price of the cross.

There are four reasons why the cross is an offense:

WE SEE OURSELVES BY CONTRAST

First, the cross of Christ condemns the world. The thief on the cross beside Christ looked at Christ dying, confessed openly his sins, and said, "Lord, remember me, when thou comest into thy kingdom." The fact that Christ was dying and his blood was being shed had thrown the searchlight on his own wickedness. He saw the purity, holiness and righteousness of Christ, dying not for his own sins but for the sins of the whole world, and he recognized immediately that in comparison to Christ he was a sinner, and he cried out to God for salvation.

That is how I know I am a sinner. Not only because I have broken the Ten Commandments, sin being a transgression of the law, but because I have come short of the glory of God. The glory of God is Christ, and, if I have failed to live like Jesus, to be as holy, good, pure and righteous as Jesus was, I come short. I am a sinner. Who of you can stand up and say, "I am as good as Jesus?" None of you can. For all have sinned and come short of the glory of God, and the wages of sin is death.

Look at Herod Antipas, tetrarch of Galilee. He was living in adultery — committing the sin that broke the Seventh Commandment. But you can commit adultery several ways. Jesus said that if you look upon a woman to lust after her, you have committed it already. A word, the dirty joke, obscene language, filthy literature that plays upon the imagination — it is the same as if you committed it. Herod condemned Christ because his purity, love and graciousness shone upon Herod's sins. Herod did not like it, and the cross became an offense to Herod. Neither do you like the cross. Either it will make you turn away and harden your heart, or it will melt your heart and bring you to the foot of the cross, where Jesus will forgive you, cleanse and make you pure.

Caiaphas, the high priest, filled with pride and cold, crafty wisdom, faced Christ, and the shadow of the cross pointed as a dagger at Caiaphas. He saw his own selfishness, but he could not stand it, and the cross became an offense to him — and to all of you filled with your ego and pride.

SALVATION NOT BY OUR PRIDE

Pride was the sin of Lucifer, and it is the sin of the world today. We feel that we can please God by our works, and somehow get into heaven by valiant effort, even religious effort. But the Bible says, "By grace are ye saved through faith; and that not of yourselves: it is the gift of God: not of works, lest any man should boast." We don't like that. It offends us. This is the offense of the cross.

We have developed rockets and think we can do anything. We don't like to be told in our day that we have to become as little children to enter the Kingdom of Heaven. But I tell you salvation is of God. It is God who took the initiative, God who gives repentance, God who plants the seed of faith, God who regenerates.

The sin of Pontius Pilate was fear. He was a moral coward. How many people would give their lives to Christ, but they are afraid of what the crowd or the neighbors will say. They are afraid to face their family. They don't want to be called a "holy Joe." It is quite respectable to be baptized and confirmed and go to church at Christmas and Easter. That does not cost anything; that kind of churchgoing is simply a status-symbol of successful modern social living.

When it comes to real heart-commitment to Jesus Christ and personal daily fellowship with him many are like Pilate. They don't have it. They cannot say with Paul, "'I die daily to the things of this life."

HE CRINGED FROM THE CROSS

The cross shone in the direction of Judas, filled with covetousness, greed and ambition. He wilted and became a suicide, because the cross was a stumbling block. Judas could follow Christ when the people were cheering; Judas was right there in the parade on Palm Sunday when the band was playing and everything was going fine. But when the chips were down, and Jesus began to talk about a cross, Judas said, "Count me out." He was putting his money and his ambition above God.

Has money come between you and God? A few months ago a man accepted Jesus Christ and said, "From now on, although my business may go broke, I shall make only honest dollars." It may cost you that to give your life to Christ.

Look at the Apostle Paul. Wherever he went to preach, the cross was an offense. He preached before Felix, and the burning message of the cross condemned Felix so that he trembled, but he said, "When I have a more convenient season I'll call for you, Paul. Go away." There never came a more convenient season for Felix. That was his last hour and he did not know it. A man in the gallery one night during a Crusade trembled. He gripped the seat until his fingers throbbed with blood. He went home and dropped dead that night. Paul preached the cross to Festus, who cried out, "Paul you are mad; you are a raving maniac." The cross is an offense.

The Scripture says, "Men love darkness because their deeds are evil." The cross throws spiritual light into the dark recesses of our soul and shows us our sins. The cross becomes an offense because it condemns us as sinners.

GOD HIMSELF IS REPULSED BY SIN

Second, the cross is an offense because blood was shed there. People say this is a slaughter-house religion, a repulsive religion of blood. From Genesis to Malachi in the Old Testament, you will read of the blood of Christ. It is repulsive to some, but God put it there. Blood means life. "The life of the flesh is in the blood." When blood is shed, life goes. Jesus gave his life on the cross when he shed his life's blood.

It is the blood of *propitiation* — Romans 3:25; "Whom God

hath set forth to be a propitiation through faith in his blood, to declare his righteousness for the remission of sins that are past."

It is the blood of *redemption* — Revelation 5:9; "And they sung a new song, saying, Thou art worthy to take the book, and to open the seals thereof: for thou wast slain, and hast redeemed us to God by thy blood out of every kindred, and tongue, and people and nation."

It is the blood of *remission* or forgiveness — Hebrews 9:22; "And almost all things are by the law purged with blood; and without shedding of blood is no remission." If Christ had not shed his blood on the cross, we could never be forgiven of ur sins.

It is the blood of *reconciliation* — Ephesians 2:13; "But now in Christ Jesus ye who sometimes were far off are made nigh by the blood of Christ." We were separated from God by sins, but the blood of Christ brought us back to God again. That is why many of you are in deep distress. You make money, but you are not satisfied. You have glamor, you go to amusements, you drink alcohol, but you do not have satisfaction in yourself. Your soul was made in the image of God, but your sins and iniquities have separated between you and your God. There is only one way to find peace and forgiveness, and that is by the cross.

LUTHER'S ANSWER TO SATAN

It is the blood of *justification* — justified by his blood, we shall be saved from wrath through him, says the Bible. It is the blood of *peace*. Peace is found at the cross and only at the cross.

It is the blood of *entrance into his presence*: "Having therefore, brethren, boldness to enter into the holiest by the blood of Jesus" (Hebrews 10:19). Because Christ died and shed his blood on that cross, I have a right in the name of Christ to come into the very presence of God.

It is the blood of *Christ*: "If we walk in the light, as he is in the light, we have fellowship one with another, and the blood of Jesus Christ his Son cleanseth us from all sin" (1 John 1:7).

It is said the devil once confronted Martin Luther with a tabulation of his sins. Luther asked, "Is that all?" "No!" said the devil, "There are many more." Martin Luther said, "Put them down." The devil sneeringly wrote them down, and Martin Luther said, "Is that all you can think of?" The devil said, "Yes. Now what?" "Now," said Martin Luther, "write beneath them all, 'The blood of Jesus Christ cleanseth from all sin.' " There is a fountain filled with blood, drawn from Immanuel's veins; and sinners plunged beneath that flood lose all their guilty stains.

THE EXAMPLE OF THE CROSS

Third, the cross of Christ is an offense because it sets forth an imperative ideal of life. Jesus said, "If any man will come after me, let him deny himself, and take up his cross, and follow me."

We are busy in our churches today building astronomical figures — sending in reports: how many new members we took in, how many people affiliated with the church. Jesus worked on the opposite principle. Every time the crowd got too big, Jesus would say, "All right, deny yourself if you are going to follow me, take up the cross." That eliminated almost all of them. The crowd did not want self-denial; they wanted a kingdom, they wanted a crown, they wanted to rule, to live in a palace. They wanted all the blessings of the Christian life, but they were not going to go to the cross with Him.

How many chafe at the restraint of a life like Christ's! We refuse to give up what we know his cross condemns. In a great city, with its sensual indulgences of rich and poor, with its neglect of the miserable in the slum areas and the careless eye toward the wretched condition of thousands, with the selfish attitudes in the growing race problem, we see the evidence that the cross is an offense to us.

THIS WAY AND NO OTHER

Fourth, the cross of Christ is an offense because it claims to be the power and salvation of God. It demands from every man as his first duty that he get right with God. We do not like that. We like to think that there are other roads to heaven besides the one road. Jesus said that the gate to heaven is narrow. At the beginning of that gate is a cross, and no man will ever gain entrance to the Kingdom of Heaven unless he comes by way of the cross. The cross humbles us, the cross demands, the cross expects everything we have to be given to Christ. The cross condemns every other way of salvation. Man and his ego says, "I am going my own way." Many are sincere. They think they are going to make it, but if there were any other way to salavation, Christ would never have gone to the cross. He would never have died. He prayed in the Garden of Gethsemane, "If there is any other way, let this cup pass from me; nevertheless, not my will, but thine be done."

I tell you as a minister of the Gospel of Christ that there is no other way one can be saved but this. Have you been saved? Have you trusted in Christ? You can find a new life here and now and eternal life to come, for you become a partaker of God's life the moment you come to the cross. Jesus finished this work. You don't have to add to it. All you do is receive it.

BIBLIOGRAPHY

W. M. Clow: *The Cross in Christian Experience*, London, n.d., pp. 115-126
Billy Graham, in *Decision*, November, 1961
George H. Morrison: *The Wings of the Morning*, London, n.d., pp. 277-287
Dinsdale T. Young, *The Enthusiasm of God*, London, 1905, pp. 47-61

WILLIAM FRANKLIN GRAHAM, JR.
(1918-   )

There is no question about it that Dr. Billy Graham has contributed more to the proclamation of the saving gospel of Jesus Christ than any other one individual of the twentieth century. Biographical details may here be reduced to a minimum. Dr. Graham was born in Charlotte, North Carolina, November 7, 1918, in the year following the great Billy Sunday campaign in New York City. After choosing between a career in baseball and that of the Christian ministry, following some desultory studies in other institutions, recognizing his need of further preparation, he entered Wheaton College in 1940, graduating in 1943. For the first two years upon graduation, he was pastor of the small Baptist church of Western Springs, not many miles from Wheaton. In 1945, he resigned to identify himself with the then fast-growing Youth for Christ movement, becoming their official field representative, involving between 1946 and 1949 six different trips to Great Britain and Europe. More and more, however, this gifted young man felt called to devote himself exclusively to evangelism. It was in the fall of 1949, in the campaign in Los Angeles, that one may say, the great turning-point in Billy Graham's work of evangelism occurred. Only 200 churches cooperated in this campaign, and many a night the great tent had hundreds of unoccupied seats, though there was an average attendance, it is reported, of 4,000 each night. The campaign was scheduled originally for a period of three weeks, but Billy and his co-workers felt that there were reasons for continuing it for another week, and during that fourth week, Mr. Hearst sent notices to his papers that they were to give prominent notice to the Billy Graham campaign. The tent was soon crowded to capacity, and continued so throughout the remainder of that campaign, and I suppose one may safely say that from that time to the present accommodations secured for any great city campaign have continually been filled to capacity.

As with Mr. Moody, so with Dr. Graham, out of these

evangelistic campaigns, many more activities were born. In November, 1950, the first broadcast was given in what has been designated as the Hour of Decision, now heard over some 600 stations. This was followed by a great number of television programs of an hour each in length, projected across the entire nation at enormous cost. Then Billy Graham was asked to do a weekly newspaper column, and has continued to carry this extra activity for years. There then followed some famous films, which have been seen by millions, as well as records of his sermons and the songs of Beverly Shea. In addition to his evangelistic campaigns, Billy Graham from time to time has called together great numbers of leading business men for conferences regarding Christian activity. A few years ago was launched *Decision* magazine, which now has the phenomenal circulation of over two million copies each month, and will soon be appearing in other languages. In addition, Dr. Graham has found time for the writing of a number of widely-circulated volumes. As far back as 1947, before he was thirty years of age, he had written a vitalizing small volume, *Calling Youth to Christ;* but it was his volume, *Peace with God,* which appeared in 1953, that has reached the greatest number of readers, having been translated into twenty-four different languages. I can testify myself to the fact that I saw copies of this book in every Christian bookstore in the entire Mediterranean world. Let me just repeat this amazing number of channels which Billy Graham is using for proclaiming the saving Gospel of Jesus Christ: city evangelistic campaigns; radio; television; films; records; conferences; a weekly newspaper column; a monthly magazine; and books. The plans and programs for many of these activities center in the Billy Graham Evangelistic Association with headquarters in Minneapolis, where over two hundred people are employed.

I do not want to make this brief sketch a mere accumulation of statistics, but I cannot help but mention what I saw with my own eyes that final Sunday night of his great campaign in Los Angeles, August 25, 1963, what none of us had seen before, and never expect to see again: — 135,000 people gathered together to hear his closing message! Not only was every seat taken in the vast Coliseum, but the entire arena was so crowded with thousands of others in chairs and sitting on the grass, that at the end of the service Billy Graham found it impossible to ask those receiving Christ to come forward, for there was no room for them to move, so that each was dealt with by workers in separate areas.

It is not my purpose here to appraise the work of any of the men whose sermons we are using, but one cannot help but ask what is it that gives to these Billy Graham evangelistic meetings the enormous drawing power which they have manifested for these seventeen years? Well, I would say that, first of all, the whole world knows that Billy Graham has deep convictions regarding the absolute uniqueness of Jesus Christ as Saviour and Son of God, and regarding the Bible as the infallible word of God. In the second place, his work manifests continually the presence and power of the Holy Spirit. In the third place, to Billy Graham the Lord has given visions of great things to do, and he has thrown himself wholeheartedly into these vast and multiplied tasks, all centered on one major objective, the winning of souls to Christ. Then, all recognize that Billy Graham lives the life which he preaches: not a shadow of suspicion regarding any aspect of his life has ever been hinted at. Furthermore it is so evident that he has an enormous capacity for work. He is completely loyal to those to whom he assigns authority, no matter what the criticisms might be that reach him regarding these individuals. He is not only the greatest evangelist of modern times, but he has redeemed mass evangelism, which had been rejected by so many since the days of Billy Sunday. Finally, he is gracious in every contact and activity. He has been bitterly denounced, both by modernistic left-wing Christians, and by some outstanding Fundamentalists, but this does not keep him from continuing faithful to his divine call, nor prevent the undisputed effectiveness of his ministry.

GLORYING IN THE CROSS
by
Charles Jerdan

"God forbid that I should glory, save in the cross of our Lord Jesus Christ, by whom the world is crucified unto me, and I unto the world." — Galatians 6:14

To glory or boast is natural to the mind of man. If we are acquainted with the matters in which an individual glories, we possess thus far an accurate index to his character. One man, for example, glories in his material wealth; another in his social influence; a third in his intellectual culture; a fourth in his faultless moral life. And each of these may with reason be judged accordingly.

But the Apostle Paul scorned to make any such subjects as these ground for glorying. He was a Christian, and the Christian is one who glories only in the Lord. Paul "counted all things" — his culture, his character, his religious observances — "but loss" and "dung, that he might win Christ." Paul gloried in the Cross. Not, of course, in the outward, material cross; not in any miniature imitation of it; not in the mere sign of the cross; but in the great truth which the Cross suggests. The central and vital doctrine of the Christian faith is the suffering, self-denying, atoning death of the Son of God; and in this doctrine the Apostle gloried. His great soul was entranced evermore by the Cross. The excellent glory was there; and no other subject or object had any glory in Paul's eyes at all. He was resolved to rejoice in the Cross on earth and in heaven — in time and throughout eternity.

It is our privilege and duty to be like-minded with the Apostle. And do we not gather at the Communion Table, because we have experienced the holy attraction and the blessed fascination of the Cross? In what follows, therefore, let us briefly consider and answer the question — *Why do I glory in the Cross?* I do so for three reasons.

I

BECAUSE THE CROSS IS THE RESTORER OF MY LOST RELATION TO GOD

What was the relation to God in which man first stood, and in which all of us ought to stand? We were made to glorify God: to reflect His image, to accomplish His purposes, to do His work, and to show forth His praise. We were also made to enjoy God — as members of His household, as sons in His family, as heirs of His glory. But does not conscience tell us that by nature we are at enmity with God? We have made Him angry with us, and instead of being His obedient children, we are rebels, criminals, felons. The Lord is justly offended with us; there is no peace between Him and us, and we dare not call Him our Friend.

But, blessed be God! although this is our natural state, it need not be our permanent state. No one of us requires to remain in it for an hour longer. In the Cross of Christ, with its blood and shame, we behold the means of our restoration to the Divine favour. God loved the sinner in spite of his sin; but His justice, until it was satisfied on the Cross, placed an interdict, so to speak, upon the exercise of His love. The difficulty was this: How could God be just, and also the Justifier of the ungodly? How was it possible that justice could be satisfied, and yet love spare and save the sinner?

There is, of course, much that is mysterious in the great fact of the satisfaction of Christ; and there is a deep philosophy in it which the human understanding is unable to grasp. But Holy Scripture assures us that the agony and death of the Cross were necessary, before the infinite love of God to sinners could have full practical outcome. On the Cross pardon has been purchased for the guilty. The work of Christ finished there is the ground of every one's acceptance. And every sinner is invited to look and live.

I look, then, to the Cross, and see the love of God shining there without obstruction. I read in the sacred Book that "God so loved the world, that He gave His Only-begotten Son, that whosoever believeth in Him should not perish, but have everlasting life." And I accept of Jesus Christ as my Surety and my Righteousness. So soon as I have done this I know that I occupy a new relation to Him — to His justice, His law, and His love. I can now look up to God and call Him Father. He is propitiated towards me — pacified for all that I have done. My sin is entirely put away. The Law cannot condemn me; the Devil dare not accuse me; my own conscience ceases to upbraid me. "Who shall lay anything to the charge of God's elect? It is God that justifieth. Who is he that condemneth? It is Christ that died." The Cross is the solace of my guilty fears, because it is the restorer of my lost relation to God.

II

BECAUSE THE CROSS IS THE SPRING OF MY SPIRITUAL LIFE.

The death of Christ has changed the Christian man's relation to God, not only outwardly, but inwardly. It affects him in mind, heart, and life, and makes him "a new creature." It saves him not merely from God's wrath, but also from his own wickedness. Christ, who hung upon the Cross, is made unto us both "righteousness" and "sanctification."

And indeed this, so far as we ourselves are concerned, is the very end for which the Cross was set up. Christ died for us in order to our regeneration, — our restoration to the image of God, — our resurrection to spiritual life. And it is evident that Paul is here contemplating the Redeemer's work in this vital aspect of it. He speaks in the next verse (ver. 15) of "a new creature" — that renewal of the heart which is everything in personal religion, and without which all mere rites and ceremonies are worthless. And he manifestly traces the power which produces the new birth and the new life to the Cross of Christ.

Do we ask how it is that the Cross is the spring of a good man's spiritual life? It is so in three ways.

First of all, from the Cross is derived the *power* which produces holiness. This power is Divine — the power of the Holy Spirit of God. Regeneration involves almighty power, and the Holy Ghost is the Agent in it. Before we can become holy we must be "born of water and of the Spirit." But the gift of the Spirit is intimately connected with the work of Christ. His influences were promised to the Saviour as the reward of His mediatorial obedience and sufferings. Christ hath redeemed us from the curse of the law, that we might receive the promise of the Spirit through faith." "God saved us by the washing of regeneration, and renewing of the Holy Ghost, which He shed on us abundantly through Jesus Christ our Saviour." Had there been no Cross there would have been no gift of the Comforter, no illumination, no regeneration, no sanctification: all mankind would have remained alike "dead in trespasses and sins."

But again, from the Cross are derived adequate *motive* and stimulus towards holiness. Although our spiritual life is produced by the indwelling of the Holy Spirit, He requires us actively to co-operate with Him in furthering it. We must diligently use all the means of grace, and make earnest personal endeavours after holiness of heart and life. And where can weak man find motive strong enough and constant enough to act upon his wayward will, and sweetly incline it to the paths of righteousness and purity? Such motive is to be found in the Cross of Christ. There I see written the exceeding sinfulness of sin, and the abounding love of the Sin-bearer. Sin has murdered my best Friend; therefore I cannot but hate it, and make it the work of my life to destroy it. The dying love of Christ constrains me to ask, "Lord, what wilt Thou have me to do?"

and the answer from the Cross — from the "Lamb as it had been slain" in the midst of the throne — is, "If ye love Me, keep My commandments." To gaze believingly on the Cross supplies us wth the one all-powerful stimulus which we have to follow purity of heart and life.

Once more, in the Cross is exhibited an *example* of perfect holiness. The death of the Redeemer not merely brings down Divine power and presents abundant motive, it also reveals a perfect Example. The Cross is the standard of our obedience; it has in it the pattern of true spiritual life. We were made to "live unto God," — to concentrate our affections upon Him, — to have Him for our Friend, Counsellor, and Companion. And does not the Cross furnish us with the noblest of the models for such a life? Christ "came not to do His own will, but the will of Him that sent Him." He "was obedient unto death, even the death of the cross." "Christ also suffered for us, leaving us an example, that we should follow His steps." Our pattern is a Living Person — not a written essay or a spoken sermon. We are to catch His gracious spirit, and imitate His beautiful life. "For their sakes," Jesus said, "I sanctify Myself, that they also might be sanctified through the truth." And the Cross was the climax and consummation of our Lord's holy obedience. It is the supreme example of self-sacrifice; and self-sacrifice is the great law of our spiritual life.

III

BECAUSE THE CROSS IS THE SIGNAL OF MY DEFIANCE TO THE WORLD.

That is, it has not only a legal and a spiritual, but also a moral efficacy. Separation from the world is the natural outcome of true spiritual life. To live to God necessarily involves the cessation of communion with the world. The spiritual life is an unworldly life; and thus the Cross, which is its spring, is also the emblem of our defiance of the world. This, besides, is precisely the thought in the foreground of the Apostle's mind when he speaks of glorying in the Cross: "By which," he says, "the world is crucified unto me, and I unto the world."

By "the world" here we are to understand the sphere of the outward and carnal — the sphere of sense and self — the sphere in which unspiritual men seek for happiness, and in which they glory. The term includes the domain of wealth and power, appetite and passion, — "the lust of the flesh, the lust of the eye, and the pride of life," — all that is external, unspiritual, transitory, as opposed to the inward, spiritual, eternal. The Apostle's words imply that the world exercises a potent and fascinating influence over most men. It goes with our fallen human nature to love the world. God has dowered us with strong affections, which must have on outlet and an object; and our corrupt hearts are swift to attach themselves to the things of time and sense and sin. But God forbids us to love the world; for the love of the world is incompatible with the love of God, and only in the love of God can we find true blessedness. Paul has already described the world as "this present evil world," because it has an element of evil in it — in its maxims, fashions, and habits — which shall one day be its ruin, and the ruin of all who love the world.

Where is the power to be found that will be efficient and sufficient to deliver us from the grasp of the world? It is vain to look for such a power anywhere else than in the Cross of Christ. But the great Apostle found this power there, and so may we. He was rescued from the infinite peril of worldliness by looking to Golgotha. His perception of the meaning of the atonement broke the spell of carnality. He found in Christ's death the power to resist the temptation of worldly ambition. It was the Cross that impelled Paul to make all the magnificent sacrifices which he made as a Christian disciple and missionary. He was dead to the world, and the world to him: he was done with the world — it had become nothing to him.

It was not that Paul had drained the cup of earthly joys, and had begun to feel that "all was vanity and a striving after wind." It was not that he had simply become disgusted with the hollowness of the world. His glorying in the Cross was occasioned by the power of Christ resting on him — the expulsive power of a new affection. No one but a Christian has any right to speak of being "crucified unto the world," and in the mouth of any one else such language would be misanthropy. But the man who has learned the meaning of the Cross really does despise the world, and abjure it as his portion. His faith in the Crucified keeps him from visiting scenes, puts him on his guard against the deceitfulness of riches, and cleanses his soul from the love of earthly things. Christ "gave Himself for our sins, that He might deliver us from this present evil world."

> "When I survey the wondrous Cross
>   On which the Prince of glory died,
> My richest gain I count but loss,
>   And pour contempt on all my pride.
>
> Forbid it, Lord, that I should boast,
>   Save in the death of Christ, my God;
> All the vain things that charm me most,
>   I sacrifice them to His blood."

May God help us all, both when we sit down at the Lord's Table, and after we have withdrawn from it, to glory in the Cross as the signal of our defiance to the world!

BIBLIOGRAPHY

A. Barry: *The Atonement of Christ*, London, 1871, pp. 95-111
J. H. Beibitz: *Gloria Crucis*, London, 1908, pp. 1-14
Horatius Bonar: *Fifty-two Sermons*, Grand Rapids, 1954, pp. 138-156. (The original edition was entitled *Family Sermons*).
F. W. Boreham: *A Bunch of Everlastings*, London, 1920, pp. 237-249
F. W. Boreham: *A Handful of Stars*, London, 1922, pp. 239-249
S. Parkes Cadman, in *World's Great Sermons*, Vol. X, pp. 205-216
Raymond J. Drummond: *Faith's Certainties*, 2nd ed., London, 1910, pp. 125-146

R. M. Edgar: *The Philosophy of the Cross,* London, 1874, pp. 221-237
A. J. Gossip: *The Galilean Accent* Edinburgh, 1926, pp. 139-150
H. L. Goudge: *Glorying in the Cross,* London, 1940, pp. 95-101
J. G. Greenhough: *The Cross in Modern Life,* 2nd ed., London, 1897, pp. 1-13
F. A. Huegel: *Calvary's Wondrous Cross,* Grand Rapids, 1949, pp. 40-49
Charles Jerdan: *For the Lord's Table,* 2nd ed., Edinburgh, 1903, pp. 322-331
W. J. Knox-Little: *The Perfect Life,* London, 1898, pp. 149-160
Memoirs and Remains of Robert Murray McCheyne, Edinburgh, 1892, pp. 415-421
James Saurin: *Sermons,* Vol. 6, New York, 1807, pp. 299-327
W. B. Selbie: *The Servant of God,* New York, 1910, pp. 179-198
Matthew Simpson: *Sermons,* New York, 1885, pp. 241-254
Charles H. Spurgeon: *Metropolitan Tabernacle Pulpit,* Vol. 31, 1885, No. 1859 pp. 493-503

BIOGRAPHICAL SKETCH

I have not been able to discover any biographical data concerning Charles Jerdan in any biographical dictionaries or bibliographical works known to me. Even the British Museum Catalogue gives no indication of dates. However, in his very interesting *Scottish Clerical Stories and Reminiscences* he gives the information that he was a student in the Theological Hall of the United Presbyterian Church, 1861-1865, and that he held pastorates in various churches in Scotland, as for example, Dennyloanhead, then at Tay Square, Dundee, during the early 1880's and from 1889 to at least 1920, he was the minister of St. Michael Street Church of Greenock. Should a second edition of this volume be called for, it may be that by that time I would have had the opportunity of a more thorough search for additional biographical data when in Great Britain.

THE CROSS AND THE SINNER
by
G. Campbell Morgan

"In whom we have our redemption through His blood, the forgiveness of our tresspasses, according to the riches of His grace." — Ephesians 1:7

The sense of God as personal involves conviction of His supremacy. It has been objected that personality ought not to be predicated of God, because personality implies limitation; but that is to misinterpret personality. It is of man that personality cannot be perfectly predicated, because man is limited. Perfect personality is unlimited. God alone is perfect in personality.

The sense of the supremacy of God creates the consciousness of sin. If our doctrine of God lose the note that affirms His personality, our doctrine of sin will lose the note that brings conviction. If God be known as personal and sovereign, man is conscious of sin. We may call it by any name we please — I care nothing for the name; we may speak of it as failure, as missing the mark, as coming short; the fact remains that directly man is conscious of God, and of His supremacy in the universe, he is also conscious of the fact that he has come short of the Divine requirement. That is conviction of sin. I am not now accounting for this widespread conviction, but I affirm that it is present.

I go one step further. The sense of God as personal perpetually causes a desire to be free from sin; or, in other words, a desire for forgiveness. These three things are independent. To destroy in either order is to destroy wholly. Deny the doctrine of the personality of God, and you immediately weaken the consciouness of sin, and consequently man becomes careless about forgiveness. Let a man become careless concerning forgiveness of sin, it is not because his conception of sin is not that of disobedience, and such weakening invariably issues from some conception of God that dethrones Him from the place of actual supremacy in the universe.

The message of the Christian evangel is to the sinner — that is, to the man who is conscious of God, and of his own failure; and who, in the deepest of his heart, would fain be free from failure. The message of the Cross is to that man. While the ultimate meaning of the Christian message goes out into that sinless life which lies beyond the present one, it begins with the forgiveness of sins. The first thing that Christ says to the soul who turns to Him is, "Thy sins are forgiven." That is not final; it is elementary. But it is fundamental.

In this text we discover: first, this first issue of redemption, "forgiveness"; in the second place, the method of redemption, "through His blood"; and finally, the source of redemption, "the riches of His grace." The Apostle moves back from the initial experience, and indicates the channel through which it comes, until finally, in one phrase full of beauty, he reminds us of the source from which the stream flows forth.

"The forgiveness of our trespasses"; that is the first issue of redemption. "Through His blood"; that is the method of redemption. "The riches of His grace"; that is the fountain head of redemption, the spring amid the eternal hills whence the great river flows. Or to state these things in the other order. The fountain head: "the riches of His grace." The channel through which the river flows: "through His blood." The gift the river brings: "the forgiveness of our trespasses."

I

First, then, "the forgiveness of our trespasses." This is so universally understood as a need — observe carefully that I do not say the method is universally understood — this is so universally understood *as a need,* that I do not propose to dwell upon it, save to emphasise the strength of the thought as it is here stated.

Sir Oliver Lodge has declared that the intelligent man today does not think about sin. I believe the intelligent man does think about sin, because he has to face the fact of sin. He may call it by other names. He may invent scientific terminology to describe the fact of which he is conscious; but the fact is there, and the intelligent man never shuts his eyes to facts — he faces them.

Because man is universally conscious of sin, he is also conscious of the need for forgiveness. He may not explain the *need* as I would. He may have lost his sense of relationship to the throne of the Eternal. He may speak of forces where I speak of God. But there is no man who knows his failure who does not, in the deepest of him, wish it had not been, wish it could be undone, regret the fact of it. The passion for perfection is one of the common inheritances of the human heart. No man is really, in his deepest life, content with imperfection. Every man admires perfection. Every man would if he could realise it in every department of life. There is no man who loves sin. He may love the things that sin suggests to him, but every man is against his own sin.

In this text the Apostle makes use of two words, which we must note — "trespasses," and "forgiveness." The etymology of the Greek word here translated "trespasses" suggests a falling out — a falling out of line. Trench says that the word means falling, where one ought to have stood upright, whether wilfully or not. It is the fact of falling. This word you will find, as you study the New Testament, is used sometimes of what we in these days call the smaller sins, or faults; but it is also used of the final and most awful sin of actual and absolute apostasy. It is an inclusive term. It is a word which includes all those deviations from the will of God which trouble the soul of man. Swiftly and silently think back over the line of your own life. Trespasses! There they lie, back through the years. If we could undo some of them! Peccadilloes, faults, deviations from the straight line of duty; tragedies, vulgarities are all there! The word sweeps over the whole of them. I am not discussing the mystery of original sin. The Apostle does not refer to it here, save as these are the fruit of the underlying principle, save as these are the apples of Sodom growing out of the root which in itself is poisoned.

The etymology of the Greek word translated "forgiveness" suggests freedom. The root idea is that of being "sent out," "sent forth." This particular word is variously translated in the New Testament, "deliverance," "liberty," "remission," "forgiveness." Let the text be read with some of these words substituted, "In Whom we have our redemption through His blood, the deliverance of our sins," "the liberty of our sins," "the remission of our sins." It is a word which recognises all the bondage into which our sins have brought us, of guilt, of pollution, of power; and declares that by this redemption we are set free therefrom. Not free merely from the penalty. I did not name the penalty — not that the penalty is not included — but I named the things, which being removed, the penalty is also removed. Penalty is a consequence. Forgiveness is liberty from the guilt of sin, liberty from the pollution of sin, liberty from the power of sin. Forgiveness means far more than saying; Never mind, I will pass it over, I will make no further reference to it. God never forgives that way. He never violates the cosmic order by lightly passing over the activity of disorder which wrecks and ruins human life and human history. New Testament forgiveness I can never extend to my own child. I cannot free my child from the guilt of wrong done. I cannot cleanse my child from the pollution which has gathered upon his mind as the result of wrong done. I cannot break the power of habit in my child through forgiveness. Consequently, whenever I try to illustrate Divine forgiveness by human I fail; for the symbol cannot perfectly convey the infinite meaning. Forgiveness is to be set loose from sins, their guilt gone, their pollution ceased, their power broken. That is what the world needs. This is what the Christian message declares, and what Jesus Christ offers to men first. It is the beginning, it is not the last thing; but, blessed be God, it is the first!

II

Now concerning the method: "In Whom we have our redemption through His blood." It is impossible to read the New Testament without noticing the constancy of this figure. All the writers and teachers make use of it in one way or another. "Purchased with His own blood," "Justified by His blood," "Having made peace through the blood of His Cross," "Redeemed, not with corruptible things, with silver or gold . . . but with precious blood . . . even the blood of Christ," "If we walk in the light, as He is in the light, we have fellowship one with another, and the blood of Jesus Christ, His Son, cleanseth us from all sin." These are but illustrations. Reverently we ask; What is the meaning of it?

There are those who have taken objection to it, and have attempted to express the truth in some other way. They ask for a new terminology. I never object to new terminology — indeed, I prefer new terminology for a new thing, to the old terminology robbed of its essential heart and life and meaning. I am told we need a new terminology, and that it will be safe for us to say, *"redemption through His life."*

Let us think of this. It is perhaps by consideration of the suggested phrase that we shall begin to see the meaning of the great and awful and appalling words, "redemption through His blood." Is it not true that blood is life? Perfectly true. Under the Mosaic economy the requirements in this respect were direct and stringent. Either in so many words, or in other words equivalent, the declaration is repeated, "The blood is the life." These things were written long before science had come to illuminate them. I need hardly stay to remind you that men have only known anything concerning the circulation of the blood for about two and a half centuries; yet that discovery,

in all its wonderful unfolding and explanation, does but add
infinite meaning to the old Mosaic word. Scientific men tell us
that in blood there are certain vital facts: resistance, so that
the blood, in healthy life, maintains its temperature as against
heat and cold; organisation, so that if you break in upon the
flesh, and close it again, the organism will be renewed by the
action of blood; fluidity, so that the blood contains in fluid
form that which tends to solidity; and finally, hear the mystery
of it! death, the final proof of life. "The blood is the life."

Remember that the flesh in man is the outward symbol of
the man himself. Remember that the essential in human life
is the spirit. Yet the blood most perfectly sets forth the essential.
"The blood is the life." It is a purely physical declaration, yet
an absolutely true one.

The Bible however, does not teach that a man is saved by
that principle, but by the *shedding* of blood. Salvation is not
through life lived, but through life poured out. It is not by
the life of Jesus that we are redeemed; but by His life given
up in the pain and suffering of a shameful death, of which
death there is no sufficient symbol or method of expression
other than that of the shedding of blood. Redemption is provided, not by the richness of His life possessed, but by the
suffering of His life poured out. As the blood in the physical
life is the symbol of the spiritual, so in the actual outpouring
of the blood of the Man of Nazareth there was symbolized that
infinite mystery of essential Love bending to suffering and pain
and death, gathering into itself that which is against itself in
inherent principle, and suffering, in order that through that
suffering there might be accomplished something which cannot
be accomplished without it. It is through the *shedding* of
blood that there is remission.

The moment we destroy this outward symbolism of words,
we inevitably begin to contradict the infinite mystery which
lies behind them, and which they do symbolise. The moment
we begin to say there is no virtue in the actual blood, the
physical blood of long ago, we are on the verge of denying the

lonely, separate suffering of God in Christ, through which, and through which alone, it is possible for forgiveness, which is at once freedom from the guilt and pollution and power of sin, to be pronounced upon men. I lay this emphasis here because, as I have said, the question is often asked; Why may we not get rid of the phrasing, Cleansed by blood, and say, "Cleansed by life? Because when we get rid of the phrasing we get rid of the truth. It is not by the life, but by the life laid down; not by the richness and beauty of the ideal, but by the mystery of its breaking and buffeting and suffering and death that it is possible for forgiveness to be pronounced.

Concentrating the thought for a moment upon the Man Jesus, knowing that He is but the window through which we look into the infinite and eternal mystery which lies behind, let us very carefully understand that not by the beauty of the human example can He forgive sins; not by all the rich glory of the wonderful life that holds us in its thrall and fascination can He pronounce absolution; but only as that life was bruised, a symbol of the very bruising of the Infinite, for "God was in Christ." There can be no divorce between God and Christ if we would understand the Cross.

III

We pass to the last of these thoughts, which takes us back to the original source — "the riches of His grace." Our freedom from sin is through "the riches of His grace." The death which makes possible our freedom from sin is through "the riches of His grace." What a revelation of God we have here! I pause for poverty of words and for lack of ability to lead you to these great heights. One can speak of the realm of conscious sin, for how have we known it! One can say something in the realm of suffering through which we have been pardoned, or may be pardoned, for we know the Cross! But when man tries to pass behind these matters and come into those far-reaching, infinite things, expressed in this word, "the riches of His grace," what can we say? We can only reach these heights by coming again through the Cross. In the Cross the nature of God is revealed in His attitude toward the sinner. It is that of grace; not something sickly and sentimental, but the great necessity of loving; Love in action — that is grace; or, if you will, Love itself, that which precedes action, the thought, the will, the purpose; and we see the heart and nature of God in this unveiling of His thought and purpose toward sinning man.

Grace in the heart of God was not created by the Passion. The Passion was created by the grace. The work of the Cross, this blood redemption; the redemption of which blood and blood-shedding are the only fit sign and symbol — this work of the Cross did not persuade God to graciousness. God's grace did compel this Passion of the Cross, and therein is a revelation of the nature of God.

Therein also is unveiled the will of God in the work He did for the sinner. When man has sinned and is guilty and polluted and paralysed, in order to his saving, Love will go to the uttermost extreme. We know all the beauty of the declarations concerning love on the human plane until we see them placed in the light of the heavenly revelation. "Love is strong as death," mightier than the grave. Love will break through every barrier. The will of God becomes revealed in the light of this great Cross.

But more. Not only the nature of God and the will of God are revealed, but also the power of God. All these things are in our word "grace." Grace is that which is born amid the eternal hills; but it is also the river which proceedeth from the throne of God and of the Lamb. Notice Paul's word, "the riches of His grace," the fulness of His grace. There is a measurement for His grace. Take another of Paul's phrases, "the riches of His glory." What gleams of it we have had in creation, in government, in prophetic song and vision, in the hope that is in our heart of the ultimate victories! "The riches of His glory" is the measurement of "the riches of His grace."

As is His glory, so is His grace; so that this selfsame Apostle, writing to Titus, brings the two things into juxtaposition. *"The grace of God hath appeared,* bringing salvation to all men, instructing us, to the intent that, denying ungodliness and worldly lusts, we should live soberly and righteously and godly in this present world, looking for the blessed hope and *appearing of the glory* of our great God and Saviour Jesus Christ." In that great passage the thought of Paul was fixed upon the two advents of Jesus: the appearing of grace when He came, the appearing of glory when He comes; the appearing of grace in the loneliness of His first advent, His ministry, His patience, and His dying; the appearing of glory in the splendour of His second advent, and the triumph of His administration. Can you measure this? When you can measure this you can measure that. When you can understand the meaning of the glory which at last shall triumph, in the hope of which we rejoice even in affliction and limitation, then you can understand the fulness of His grace.

A spurious, latter-day refinement, which objects to the mention of blood, is both sickly and sinful. A deeper sentiment would be conscious that the awful blood-shedding of the Son of God is the most terrible revelation of the meaning of sin, and is in itself proof of the dire necessity for such means of salvation. Do not let us forget this. I want to utter this with all the solemnity of conviction. I pity from my heart the man who tells me he objects to the phrasing concerning blood. I pity him, for he is suffering from a soft sentimental ignorance of his own heart, and ignorance of the actual deceitfulness and heinousness of sin.

They say that the Cross of Jesus is vulgar! I know it. Never was there anything so vulgar in human history as the Cross of Jesus! But where is the vulgarity? It is in the sin that mauled Him and put Him there. It is your vulgarity. It is my vulgarity. It is the vulgarity that lies and cheats, that is impure, that laughs at sin, or speaks of it as though it were something to be pitied. It is the vulgarity that has lost its sense of the high throne of God and the white purity of His heaven. It is the vulgarity of the age which drags God off His throne and makes Him merely a force in His creation, and denies righteousness and purity. That is the vulgarity that lifted the Cross! Sin is so vulgar that it can only be dealt with by that which violates the essential life of God. The Cross? Yea, verily; but the rough, brutal Roman gibbet was only the expression in time of something far more terrible. Those two pieces of timber and a dying Man! Awful, terrible; but infinitely worse was the pain of God, which was invisible save through that Cross. In His rich grace He took hold upon sin and expressed, in the suffering of His only Son, its vulgarity.

Thank God, He did more, for that very Cross of blood and shame is radiant with the glorious light of the infinite Grace; for, even at the cost of such suffering as makes poor half-cultured man shudder, Love, determined on man's salvation, accomplished it. Yes, disease is vulgar; but the mother and the nurse who touch it, to heal it, are not vulgar. Contact with it in order to heal it is not vulgar. I come to the Cross to bow my head in shame, and smite my breast with remorse. Vulgar Cross; but that in it which is vulgar is my sin. Shining through it is the light that comes from the throne; and flowing through it is the great river of His grace.

Now hear me in this final word. You tell me that the only atonement possible to me is by my own suffering upward to something higher. If you could persuade me that God could be satisfied with such salvation, I cannot be satisfied with it.

"Out, damned spot!" That is the true cry of human nature. The stain canot be removed without blood, and that which is infinitely more, and deeper, and profounder, and more terrible than blood, of which blood is but the symbol — the suffering of Deity.

Blessed be God, this is the evangel for me. Oh soul of mine, guilty, polluted, paralysed, we have "our redemption through His blood, the forgiveness of our trespasses." There my conscience finds rest. There I begin a new life, lifting my eyes toward the ultimate ages, God's last purpose for me made possible because He is able to forgive my sins.

BIBLIOGRAPHY

John Flavel: *The Method of Grace*, New York, 1820, pp. 297-307
Alexander Maclaren: *Expositions of Holy Scripture, Ephesians*, pp. 26-35
W. W. Martin: *The Sufficiency of the Cross*, London, n.d., pp. 11-33
G. Campbell Morgan: *The Bible and the Cross*, London, 1909, pp. 65-84
James Orr, in the *Report* of the *Westminster Bible Conference, Mundlesly*, for 1910, pp. 342-357
Charles H. Spurgeon: *Metropolitan Tabernacle Pulpit*, Vol. 6, 1858, No. 295, pp. 73-80, Vol. 26, 1880, No. 1555, pp. 481-492, Vol. 37, 1891, No. 2207, pp. 309-312, Vol. 49, 1903, No. 2863, pp. 613-619
A biographical sketch of Dr. G. Campbell Morgan may be found in the earlier volumes of this series, *Great Sermons on the Birth of Christ*, pp. 193-196, and *Great Sermons on the Resurrection of Christ*, pp. 107

THE FELLOWSHIP OF CHRIST'S SUFFERINGS
by
J. D. Jones

"That I may know Him, and the power of His resurrection, and the fellowship of His sufferings, becoming conformed unto His death." — Philippians 3:10

I must not stay to discuss the context at any length or else I shall not get to my text itself. Suffice it to say that Paul is here giving the reason why, all of a sudden, he had resigned his place in the Sanhedrin, surrendered the great career that was opening up before him, and turned his back upon the prospects of wealth and fame and power. It was an inexplicable step to his old associates who had known him in the days when he was the trusted emissary of the Jewish authorities. Like Festus, they were inclined to think Paul was mad. But here the Apostle himself gives the explanation — he had abandoned his career, he had surrendered his hopes of wealth and fame, in order to gain Christ. It had suddenly dawned on Paul that Christ was the pearl of great price, and he had sacrificed everything in order to possess Him. Like Samuel Rutherford, he could say that one smile of Christ's was to him of more value than kingdoms, and so, to gain Christ, he suffered the loss of all things and did count them but dung. To "gain Christ" became Paul's one ambition — the great wish of his soul. "To gain Christ" and to "know Him." I do not think the two phrases stand for two different processes. I do not think that "gaining Christ" is one thing and "knowing Christ" another. I think the second phrase is explanatory of the first. We gain Christ by knowing Him. We possess Christ only as we apprehend Him. So that it is fair to say that here in my text you get the great ambition of

Paul's life, compared to which he counted everything the world had to give as of no more value than the very dust and refuse of the streets.

The Knowledge of Experience

"That I may know Him." I invite your attention to the exact words the Apostle uses. What the Apostle desired was not knowledge about Christ; he wanted to know Him in a direct, immediate and personal way. He wanted not simply to "know" but to recognize and feel and appropriate, says Bishop Lightfoot. He wanted to know Christ not in the sense of intellectual apprehension, but in the sense of practical experience. There is all the difference in the world between knowing a person and knowing about Him. We know about numbers of people whom we do not really know at all. Every movement of the members of the Royal family, for instance, is chronicled for an inquisitive public. Every reader of the newspapers knows all about the King — about his movements, his visits, what he did yesterday, what he is going to do to-morrow. The external life of the King, his royal activities are all public property. But though we know all about him, we do not know him. But there is a little circle — his wife, his children, a little handful of associates — who not only know about him, but who know him in a direct and immediate way.

Every public man lives more or less in the limelight. Thousands and tens of thousands are acquainted with the appearances of our leading statemen, for instance, who have never set eyes on the men themselves. They know all about their opinions and policies and characters. But there is all the difference in the world between the knowledge of the man in the street and the knowledge of those who live within the circle of the family and the home. In the family circle they know him; the man in the street simply knows about him.

Now it was this immediate and personal knowledge Paul coveted above everything else. He did not want to know Christ after the flesh simply. He was not content with knowing the

facts about Jesus. He knew these well enough. It is quite possible he knew most of them before he became a Christian. But
there was no saving quality in external knowledge of that kind.
What Paul desiderated was not to know about Christ, but to
know Him; not to know Him as a Figure on the page of history, but to know Him as a Christ in his own soul. It was only
a Christ in his own heart who could ever become to him a hope
of glory.

And if I may pause in my exposition for a moment, it is to
say this: that it is still this knowledge of Christ that saves —
the knowledge of personal experience. Do not misunderstand
me — I am not minimizing the importance of the historic. I
am not suggesting that knowledge of the facts about Christ is
unimportant. It is through the study of the facts that we gain
the personal and experimental knowledge which is the one
thing needful. We read the Gospel story, and suddenly we become aware that we are dealing not with some One who lived
and died nineteen centuries ago, but with a living Person actually in touch now with our souls. Still it remains true that
historical knowledge is one thing and experimental knowledge
is quite another. And this latter is the knowledge which saves.
Multitudes in England know about Christ. I suppose it is true
to say that all our people have some rudimentary knowledge
of the external facts of His life. But without any breach of
charity it may be said that vast multitudes of them remain
unregenerate and unsaved in spite of it. The fact is, men and
women can only be saved by a contemporary. They can be
redeemed and restored not by a figure of the dim past, but only
by a Living Presence and Power. It is not enough to know
about Christ, we must know Him directly, immediately, experimentally. Christ in us is the hope of glory.

A Progressive Experience

Look once again at the exact phrasing of the Apostle's
speech — "that I may know Him." The phrase is an infinitive
phrase in the Greek, but the translation, "that I may know

Him," rightly renders its meaning. Paul speaks as if this knowledge he desiderates were still a future experience. But did not Paul at the very time he wrote this letter know Christ in a direct and experimental way? Yes, he did. He had known Christ in that way for years. That was what happened on the way to Damascus: his knowledge of the facts about Jesus changed to an experimental knowledge of Christ Himself. He came into actual touch with Jesus. He discovered Him to be alive. He experienced His power. That is how he himself describes that mighty happening — "it pleased God to reveal His Son in me." Not "to me," you notice, but "in me." It was a mighty experience of Christ's power in his own life and soul that came to him on the way to Damascus. This is what he says in this very paragraph about the same mighty event — he was "apprehended by Christ Jesus"; he felt himself in the grasp of the Living and Mighty Lord. It was a direct and overwhelming experience of Christ that came to him on the Damascus road. And the experience was by no means confined to that great and critical occasion. It was continuous. "I live," he declares in one place, "yet not I, but Christ liveth in me." And yet here he speaks as if this experimental knowledge of Christ were a boon still to be gained. "That I may know Him." The fact is, this experimental knowledge of Christ is always progressive. It comes fresh to man, as the manna did of old, morning by morning. No man discovers all at once all that there is in Christ. "In Him are all the treasures of wisdom hidden." The best of men, as a result, know only in part. We say sometimes about our human friends, "I know so and so through and through." But nobody knows Christ through and through. There are heights of knowledge, and great breadths of wisdom, and vast depths of love which the best of men have never explored. Christ is constantly surprising men by new discoveries of grace, and fresh relevations of Divine wisdom. He is an exhaustless mine of truth; He is an infinite ocean of wisdom and love. "Oh, the depth of the riches both of the wisdom and the knowledge of God!" cries Paul himself, "how unsearchable are

His judgments, and His ways past finding out." He had been enjoying for years ever richer and fuller experiences of the love and grace of Christ, and yet he felt as if here only on the edge and margin of things. "That I may know Him," he cries. John declared that if all the things which Jesus did were written down all the world would not contain the books that should be written. And the same sense of the limitlessness of Christ breathes through an aspiration like this. Throughout all the years of life and throughout all eternity, Paul, with all saints, would be following on to know the Lord, seeking to comprehend what is the length and breadth, what is the height and depth of that love which passeth knowledge.

The experimental knowledge of Christ is a progressive knowledge. And in my text I think certain stages in the progress of that knowledge are indicated. "That I may know Him," says the Apostle, "and the power of His resurrection and the fellowship of His sufferings, becoming conformed unto His death." As I understand the verse, these various phrases represent stages in a man's experience of Christ. First, he knows the power of Christ's Resurrection, then he becomes a partner in Christ's sufferings, and ultimately he becomes so entirely one with Christ that he dies with Him. The order, I know, strikes a reader first as odd and strange, especially because resurrection is made to precede suffering and death. Bishop Lightfoot, for instance, feels the strangeness of it so keenly that he practically transposes the order and paraphrases like this: "When I speak of knowing Him, I mean, that I may feel the power of His Resurrection; but to feel this it is necessary first that I should share His sufferings." Now I know it looks like presumption to differ from the great bishop, whose commentaries on Paul's Epistles are practically the final word in exegesis, and I know that such difference is always at one's peril, yet in this case I am going to be presumptuous enough to challenge the bishop's interpretation. I am quite convinced he is wrong. He is not only wrong in his interpretation of the Apostle's thought, he is untrue to the facts of life and experience. Far from it being necessary to share in Christ's sufferings before a man can feel the power of his Resurrection, I am persuaded that not until a man has felt the power of Christ's Resurrection will he share His sufferings. In Christ's case suffering and death preceded resurrection; in the Christian's case resurrection must precede suffering and death. Indeed, the bishop himself, when he comes to comment on the actual words, modifies the interpretation he gives in the paraphrase. "The participation in Christ's sufferings," he says, "partly follows upon and partly precedes the power of His Resurrection." I should myself say "always follows." The arrangement of the Apostolic phrases seems to me to set forth the invariable order of spiritual experience. The first thing we know about Christ is the power of His Resurrection. Then, as we make more and more room for Him, we begin to become partners in His sufferings, until at length we become so completely and entirely Christian that we are ready to share in His death.

The Power of His Resurrection

This is the first stage in our knowledge of Christ — we know the power of His Resurrection. That is the very beginning of the Christian life. We rise from the death of ignorance and sin through the power of the Risen Christ. That is exactly where Paul's Christian life began. That was exactly his first experience of Christ. He knew Him as the Risen Lord. Paul — before the Damascus experience — had shared presumably in the current and popular Jewish belief that Jesus was an impostor and a malefactor whose career had been ended on the Cross. To him it was sheer blasphemy that any one should assert that this criminal was the long-expected Messiah and God's Son. In his honest indignation against these blasphemers he haled them, both men and women, and cast them into prison and persecuted them unto foreign cities. And then, on that never-to-be-forgotten day, it was flashed in upon Paul's conscience that Jesus was no dead criminal at all, but a living and exalted Lord. "I am Jesus whom thou persecutest." That was Paul's first glimpse of Christ — as the living Lord. That is when his Christian life began — with the experience of the power of Christ's Resurrection. And it was in the region of Christ's Resurrection Paul's life moved for some time. During those years in Arabia, I believe that Paul was revising his beliefs in the light of Christ's Resurrection — building up a new edifice of faith, trying to read the meaning of the Cross in the light of the Empty Grave. The distinctive Pauline theology was beaten out in those solitary months. He emerged from Arabia exulting in the belief that the Cross was the final sacrifice, and rejoicing in the assurance of the forgiveness of sins. That is where Paul's Christian life began, in a direct experience of the Risen Christ, and in the assurance of emancipation and release and the hope of glory, all of which were the products of the power of Christ's Resurrection.

And that, I repeat, is how the Christian life always starts. We come into touch with the living Lord. Christ ceases to be a Name and becomes a Presence. We feel Him at work within us breaking all our bondages, scattering all our fears, giving us liberty, life, and immortal hope. The Christian life starts with something that Christ does for us. It starts in triumph and exultation. The living Christ quickens us even when we are dead in trespasses and sins. We begin with the experience of the power of Christ's Resurrection.

The Fellowship of Suffering

But while the experience of the power of Christ's Resurrection is the beginning of our knowledge of Christ and the start of our Christian life, it certainly is not the end. The Christian life is not simply something done for us and given to us by Christ, it is something also which we give to and do with Him. It begins to dawn upon the man who has felt the power of Christ's Resurrection, that there is a deeper and more sacred and more intimate experience into which he may enter — he may share in the fellowship of Christ's sufferings. He may know Christ by becoming a partner with Him in His toil and sacrifice, in His sorrow and redeeming passion. He may know Christ by bearing His Cross, drinking His cup, being baptized with His baptism. And this is a deeper and more sacred knowledge. There is nothing for knitting men's souls together like partnership in danger and fellowship in sorrow. In the hour of danger conventions perish and the soul reveals itself naked and bare, and in such an hour men who stand side by side know one another and are knit to each other by ties that nothing can sever. I read recently, in the paper, of the death of one of the survivors of the Balaclava Charge. That ghastly and terrible ride into the jaws of death — that sharing of a common danger — had bound the survivors together with hoops of steel. They were men of all ranks and conditions, but after that experience, in which they had faced death together, all sense of distinction vanished and they were comrades.

When one man shares his sorrow with another it is the final proof of intimacy. To the outside world we carry our heads high, we stiffen the lip, we wear an air of indifference; but there are a few, who know us, to whom we can tell out the sorrows of our hearts. This is the very sign of deep and familiar knowledge. And so exactly we know Christ when we enter into the fellowship of His sufferings, when we share His griefs and sorrows. We are only in the A B C class so long as we simply know the power of His Resurrection in the way of the forgiveness of sins and the hope of glory; we really begin to know Christ when we share His spirit and His sorrow becomes our sorrow, His grief our grief, and His agony our agony; when we weep with Him over Jerusalem, agonize with Him in Gethsemane, and die with Him on Calvary.

"The fellowship of — the having in common — His suffering!" In what way can the sufferings of our Lord be common to us and be shared by us? I can only in a sentence or two suggest ways in which we may enter into this sacred and intimate fellowship. Of course, into our Lord's atoning sacrifice we may not enter. The Cross was the one perfect oblation and sacrifice. But there are certain aspects of our Lord's sorrows which we *may* share. In fact, we only really become Christians as we do share in them.

(1) We may and must share in the sufferings that came upon our Lord for righteousness' sake. He was the despised and rejected of men. He came to the judgment hall and the Cross out of loyalty to His Father's will. Every Christian may and must share in this suffering. For still it remains true that they who will live godly must suffer persecution. We can climb the steep ascent of heaven only through peril, toil and pain. Paul shared in the sufferings of Christ in this respect. It was given to him to suffer for Christ's name. "Thrice was I beaten with rods, once was I stoned, thrice I suffered shipwreck, of the Jews five times received I forty stripes save one." And as he suffered these things Paul felt himself strangely near his Lord. He spoke of the weals and scars they left as "the marks of Jesus." And although stripes and imprisonments do not come our way, we, too, must suffer with Christ. For He is still the scorned and reviled of men. He still stands at the judgment seat and at the scourging post, and He is still crucified afresh. And whoso would be faithful to Him must be content to stand in the pillory of the world's contempt. There is no being a Christian on easy terms. We must suffer hardship. We know Christ in a deep and real way only as we today enter into the fellowship of His sufferings.

(2) There is the suffering Christ endured on account of sin. He bore the burden of it on His soul. He felt the shame of it. He was moved to the depths of His soul for the victims and slaves of it. A woman was brought into His presence one day — convicted of sin — and our Lord felt the disgrace of it so vividly that He hung His head for shame. It was sheer torture to His soul. "When He beheld the city, He wept over it" — over its indifference, irreligion, wickedness and impending doom. And we simply do not know Christ unless we enter into the fellowship of His suffering in this respect — unless we feel the sin and shame of the world as a burden on our own souls. "I could wish myself accursed for my brethren accord-

ing to the flesh," said St. Paul. The sin and rebellion of the Jews burdened and haunted him. "Who is weak," he cries in another place, "and I am not weak?" He suffered, as Christ suffered, at the thought of the wandering, ignorant, sinning millions of the world. But what about us? Do we share in the suffering of Christ in this respect? We are quick to sympathize with physical suffering and loss. Our hearts went out to the widows and orphans down in Senghenydd and to those poor emigrants who had such a nerve-shattering time on the *Volturno*. But what about the multitudes who are losing their souls? "When He beheld the city He wept over it." Has the thought of our cities and their sin and shame and their indifference to God ever moved you to tears? We do not know Christ — really know Him — until we become partners in His sufferings.

(3) And then again there is this yearning passion of the Lord for the souls of men. He saw them as sheep not having a shepherd, and He yearned to gather them in, with a passion that was full of pain. "Them also I must bring," He cried, and His picture of the shepherd out in the wilderness seeking in the cold and the dark, in weariness and painfulness, his one lost sheep, is but a picture of Himself in His seeking and suffering love. Paul shared in this suffering. "I am ready to become all things to all men," he wrote, "if by all means I may save some." He spent a life of toil and labour in His passion to save. He was ready to be spent out for men's souls.

> "Oh, to save these! to perish for their saving,
> Die for their life, be offered for them all!"

But what about us? Do we share our Lord's passion and pain? Does the thought of the millions "in heathen darkness lying" give us any concern? I am persuaded that the Church has stopped short in its knowledge of Christ. We know something about the power of His Resurrection, but we have *not* entered into the fellowship of His sufferings. There is no suggestion of the thorn crown or of the nail-prints about us. We are easy, untroubled, satisfied. The thought of the world's deep need and of human sin causes us no trouble or pain. But do we know Christ in any real way if with so much wickedness and sin at our doors, and such myriads of unevangelized abroad we can remain unconcerned? It is this deeper and more intimate knowledge we need. When we become sharers in Christ's sufferings — when we possess His sorrow for sin and His passion for souls, the time will not be far off when the whole earth shall be full of the knowledge of the Lord as the waters cover the sea.

BIBLIOGRAPHY

J. D. Jones: *The Gospel of the Sovereignty*, London, 1914, pp. 160-172
J. H. Jowett: *The School of Calvary*, London, 1911, Grand Rapids, 1956, pp. 63-79
G. Campbell Morgan: *The Bible and the Cross*, London, 1909, pp. 79-97
John Owen: *Works*, Edinburgh, 1862, Vol. IX, pp. 579-581
Charles H. Spurgeon: *Metropolitan Tabernacle Pulpit*, Vol. X, 1864, No. 552, pp. 61-72

J. D. JONES
(1865-1942)

John Daniel Jones was born, as he himself remarked, the day before Abraham Lincoln was shot, April 13, 1865, in Towyn in Wales. After attending Owens College in Manchester, he went on for further study at the Lancashire Independent College, and then received his B.D. degree at St. Andrew's University. Dr. Jones himself later said, "I do not think I exaggerate when I say that no single college possessed a more brilliant teaching staff than Owen's did at that time."

At the age of twenty-four, in April 1889, the young theological graduate was called to be the minister of the Congregational Church in Newland, Lincolnshire, a town of some 1200 people, where he remained for nine years, until May, 1898. From there he was called to the great Richmond Hill Church, of 1100 members, at the famous seaside resort of Bournemouth, where he remained for nearly forty years, until his resignation June 6, 1937. Here fame came quickly, and Bournemouth knew that it was privileged to have one of the great preachers of that generation. Honors followed one another quickly. He was twice made Chairman of the Congregational Union of England and Wales, in 1908 and 1924, and was elected Moderator of the International Congregational Council in 1930.

In his delightful autobiography, *Three Score Years and Ten,* Dr. Jones allows us to see into one of the most sacred moments of his life, when Dr. Joseph Parker, at the installation of Dr. Jones at Bournemouth, said to the much younger man, just before going into the pulpit, " 'You are just about to begin your ministry in this Church — will you take an old man's blessing?' Upon that he laid his hands on my head and commended me to God. I am certainly no believer in any supernatural grace bestowed by the laying on of episcopal hands — but I have always been grateful that Joseph Parker, before I actually began my ministry at Richmond Hill, laid his hands in blessing on my head. I faced my task with greater courage because of it and it made me feel what a privilege and what a responsibility it was to be a preacher of the Holy Gospel."

What giants there were in those days, and especially in the Congregational Church of Great Britain: R. W. Dale (1829-1895); Joseph Parker (1830-1902); Andrew M. Fairbairn (1838-1912); P. T. Forsyth (1848-1921); C. Silvester Horne (1865-1914); and John Henry Jowett (1863-1923). As J. D. Jones himself, said when writing at the age of seventy-five, "We cannot muster their like today. In comparison, we moderns seem somehow a lesser breed. I believe it is quite true that the average of our ministry has been raised . . . but we have not the outstanding personalities of forty or fifty years ago." At the same time concerning his own ministry he wrote: "I have no doubt an examination of my sermons over the fifty years would reveal changes of emphasis. But in the central thing I have not changed. I have preached Christ crucified as the wisdom of God and the saving power of God. And one of the joys of my age has been to notice that there has taken place during recent years a very definite return to Evangelicalism."

THE BLOOD OF THE CROSS
by
Andrew Murray

"(God) having made peace through the blood of His cross, by Him to reconcile all things unto Himself; by Him, whether things in earth or things in heaven." — Colossians 1:20.

The Apostle uses here an expression of deep significance: — "the blood of His cross." We know how greatly he valued the expression "the cross of Christ." It expressed, in a brief phrase, the entire power and blessing of the death of our Lord for our redemption; the subject of his preaching; the hope and glory of his life. By the expression here used he shows how, on one side the blood possesses its value from the cross on which it was shed; and on the other, that it is through the blood that the cross reveals its effect and power. Thus the cross and the blood throw reflected light on one another. In our inquiry into what the Scripture teaches concerning the power of the blood, we shall find it of great importance to consider what this expression has to teach us; what is meant by the blood, as "the blood of the cross." It will enable us to view from a new standpoint, the truths which we have already discovered in that phrase "the blood."

Let us fix our attention on the following points: —
  I. The Disposition of our Lord from Which the Cross Derived its Value.
  II. The Power it Has Thus Obtained.
  III. The Love Which Bestows Everything on Us.

I. The Disposition from Which the Cross Derived its Power.
  We are so accustomed, in speaking about the Cross of Christ,

to think only of the work that was done there for us, that we take too little notice of that from which that work derives its value — the inner disposition of our Lord of which the cross was only the outward expression. Scripture does not place in the foreground, as most important, the weighty and bitter sufferings of the Lord, which are often emphasised for the purpose of awakening religious feelings, but the inner disposition of the Lord, which led Him to the cross, and inspired Him while on it — this, Scripture does emphasise. Neither does Scripture direct attention only to the work which the Lord accomplished for us on the cross; it directs special attention to the work that the cross accomplished in Him, and which through Him must yet be accomplished in us also.

This appears not only from our Lord's words which He spoke from the cross, but from what He said when on three different occasions He had previously told His disciples that they must take up their cross and follow Him. More than once He spoke thus when foretelling His own crucifixion. The thought he wished specially to impress upon them in connection with the cross was that of fellowship with, of conformity to, Him. And that this did not consist in merely outward sufferings and persecutions, but in an inward disposition, appears from what He often added, "deny yourselves and take up the cross." This is what he desires them to do. Our Lord further teaches us, that neither for Him nor for His disciples does the bearing of the Cross begin when a natural cross is laid upon the shoulders. No! He carried the Cross all through His life; what became visible on Golgotha was a manifestation of the disposition which inspired His whole life.

What then did the bearing of the Cross mean for the Lord Jesus? And what end could it serve for Him? We know that the evil of sin appears in the change it brought about both in the disposition of man towards God, as well as in that of God towards man. With man it resulted in his fall from God, or enmity against God; with God it resulted in His turning away from man, or His wrath. In the first we see the terribleness of its tyranny over man; in the second, the terribleness of the guilt of sin, demanding the judgment of God on man.

The Lord Jesus, who came to deliver man from sin as a whole, had to deal with the power of sin as well as with its guilt; first the one, and then the other. For although we separate these two things, for the sake of making truth clear, sin is ever a unity. Therefore we need to understand not only that our Lord by His atonement on the cross removed the guilt of sin, but that this was made possible by the victory He had first won over the power of sin. It is the glory of the cross that it was the divine means by which both these objects were accomplished.

The Lord Jesus had to bring to naught the power of sin. He could do this only in His own person. Therefore He came in the closest possible likeness of sinful flesh; in the weakness of flesh; with the fullest capacity to be tempted as we are. From His baptism with the Holy Spirit, and the temptation of Satan which followed, up to the fearful soul agony in Gethsemane, and the offering of Himself on the cross, His life was a ceaseless strife against self-will and self-honour; against the temptations of the flesh, and of the world, to reach His goal — the setting up of His kingdom — by fleshly or worldly means. Every day He had to take up and carry His Cross, that is, to lose His own life, and will, by going out of Himself and doing, and speaking nothing, save what he had seen or heard from the Father. That which took place in the temptation in the wilderness, and in the agony of Gethsemane — at the beginning and end of His public ministry — is only a peculiarly clear manifestation of the disposition which characterised His whole life. He was tempted to the sin of self-assertion but He overcame the temptation to satisfy lawful desires — from the first temptation, to obtain bread to satisfy His hunger, till the last, that He might not have to drink the bitter cup of death — that He might be subject to the will of the Father.

So He offered up Himself and His life; He denied Himself, and took up His Cross; He learned obedience and became perfect; in His own person He gained a complete victory over the power of sin, till He was able to testify that the evil one, "The prince of this world cometh and hath nothing in Me."

His death on the cross was the last and most glorious achievement in His personal victory over the power of sin, from this the atoning death of the cross derived its value. For a reconciliation was necessary, if guilt was to be removed. No one can contend with sin without at the same time coming into conflict with the wrath of God. These two cannot be separated from one another. The Lord Jesus desired to deliver man from his sin. He could not do this save by suffering death as Mediator, and in that death suffering the curse of God's wrath against sin, and bearing it away. But His supreme power to remove guilt and the curse did not lie merely in the fact that He endured so much pain and suffering of death, but that He endured it all *in willing obedience to the Father,* for the maintenance and glorification of His righteousness. It was this disposition of self-sacrifice, of bearing of the Cross willingly, which bestowed on the Cross its power.

So the Scripture says: — "He became obedient unto death, even the death of the cross. Wherefore God also hath highly exalted Him, and given Him a name above every name" (Philippians 2:8,9).

And again: "Yet learned He obedience by the things which He suffered; and being made perfect, He became the author of eternal salvation unto all them that obey Him" (Hebrews 5:8,9). It is because Jesus broke down and conquered the power of sin first in His personal life that He can remove from us the guilt of sin, and thus deliver us from both its power and guilt. The cross is the divine sign, proclaiming to us that the way, the only way to the life of God, is through the yielding up in sacrifice of the self-life.

Now this spirit of obedience, this sacrifice of self, which bestowed on the cross its infinite value, bestowed that value also on the blood of the cross. Here again God reveals to us the secret of the power of that blood. That blood is the proof of obedience unto death of the Beloved Son; of that disposition which chose to offer it (the blood), to shed it, to lose His own life rather than commit the sin of pleasing Himself; of the sacrifice of everything, even life itself, to glorify the Father. The life which dwelt in that blood — the heart from which it flowed — glowing with love and devotion to God and His will, was one of entire obedience and consecration to Him.

And, now, what do you think? If that blood, living and powerful through the Holy Spirit, comes into contact with our hearts, and if we rightly understand what the blood of the cross means, is it possible that blood should not impart its holy nature to us? But as the blood could not have been shed apart from the sacrifice of "self" on the cross, so it cannot be received or enjoyed apart from a similar sacrifice of "self." That blood will bring to us a "self" sacrificing disposition, and in our work there will be a conformity to, and an imitation of, the crucified One, making self-sacrifice the highest and most blessed law of our lives. The blood is a living, spiritual, heavenly power. It will bring the soul that is entirely surrendered to it, to see and know by experience that there is no entrance into the full life of God, save by the self-sacrifice of the cross.

II. The Power Which the Cross has Obtained by this Disposition.

As we pay attention to this we shall have a deeper insight into the meaning of the Cross, and "the blood of the cross." The apostle Paul speaks of the word of the Cross as "the power of God."

We want to know what the Cross as the power of God can accomplish. We have seen the twofold relationship our Lord has towards sin. First, He must in Himself, as man, subdue its *power;* then He can destroy its effects before God, as *guilt.* The one was a process carried on through His whole life; the other took place in the hour of His passion. Now that He has completed His work, we may receive both blessings at the same time. Sin is a unity, so is redemption. We receive in an equal share, both deliverance from the power of sin, and acquittal from its guilt, at the same time. As far as consciousness is concerned, however, acquittal from guilt comes earlier than a clear sense of the forgiveness of sins. It cannot be otherwise. He (our Lord) had first to obtain the blotting out of guilt, through His victory over sin, and then He entered heaven. The blessing comes to us in the reverse order; redemption descends upon us as a gift from above, and therefore restoration of a right relationship to God comes first, deliverance from guilt; along with that, and flowing from it, comes deliverance from the power of sin.

This two-fold deliverance we owe to the power of the Cross. Paul speaks of the first, deliverance from guilt, in the words of our text. He says that God has become reconciled, "having made peace by the blood of the cross" with a view to reconciling all things to Himself.

Sin had brought about a change in God; not in His nature, but in His relationship toward us. He had to turn away from us in wrath. Peace has been made through the cross of Christ. By reconciliation for sin God has reconciled us with, and united us to Himself.

The power of the Cross in heaven has been manifested in the entire removal of everything that could bring about a separation from God, or awaken His wrath, so that in Christ we are granted the utmost freedom of entrance to, and the most intimate intercourse with God. Peace has been made, and proclaimed; peace reigns in heaven, we are perfectly reconciled to God, and have been received again into His friendship.

All this is through the power of the Cross. Oh, that we had eyes to see how completely the veil has been rent; how free and unhindered is our access to God; and how freely His blessing may flow towards us! There is now nothing, absolutely nothing, to hinder the fullness of the love and power of God from coming to us and working in us, save only our unbelief, our slowness of heart. Let us meditate upon the power which the blood has exercised in heaven, till our unbelief itself is conquered, and our right to these heavenly powers by faith, fills our lives with joy.

But the powerful effect of the Cross with God, in heaven, in the blotting out of guilt, and our renewed union with God, is, as we have seen — inseparable from that other effect — the breaking down of the authority of sin over man, by the sacrifice of "self." Therefore Scripture teaches us that the Cross not only works out a disposition or desire to make such a sacrifice, but it really bestows the power to do so, and completes the work. This appears with wonderful clearness in the Epistle to the Galatians. In one place the Cross is spoken of as the reconciliation for guilt. "Christ hath redeemed us from the curse of the law, being made a curse for us; for it is written, cursed is every one that hangeth on a tree" (Galatians 3:13). But there are three other places where the Cross is even more plainly spoken of as the victory over the power of sin; as the power to put to death the "I" of the self life; of the flesh; and of the world. "I am crucified with Christ: nevertheless I live; yet not I, but Christ liveth in me" (Galatians 2:20). "And they that are Christ's have crucified the flesh with the affections and lusts" (Galatians 5:24). "But God forbid that I should glory, save in the cross of our Lord Jesus Christ, by whom the world is crucified unto me, and I unto the world" (Galatians 6:14). In these passages our union with Christ, the crucified One, and the conformity to Him resulting from that union, are represented as the result of the power exercised on us by the Cross.

To understand this we must remember that when Jesus chose the cross, and took it up, and carried it, and finally died on it, He did this as the second Adam, as the Head and Surety of His people. What He did, had and retains power for them, and exercises that power in those who understand and believe this. The life which He bestows on them is a life in which the cross is the most outstanding characteristic. Our Lord carried His cross all through His entire life as Mediator. By dying on that cross as Mediator, He obtained the life of glory. As the believer is united to Him and receives His life, he receives a life that, through the cross, has overthrown the power of sin, and he can henceforth say, "I am crucified with Christ." "I know that my old man is crucified with Christ"; "I am dead to sin"; "I have crucified the flesh"; "I am crucified to the world" (Romans 6:6, 11).

All these expressions from God's Word refer to something that occurred in a time now past. The Spirit and life of Jesus bestow on believers their share in the victory over sin which was achieved on the cross. And now in the power of this participation and fellowship they live as Jesus lived; they live always as those crucified to themselves; as those who know that their "old man," and "flesh" are crucified so as to be put to death. In the power of this fellowship they live as Jesus lived. They have the power in all things and all times to choose the Cross in spite of the "old man," and the world; to choose the Cross and to let it do its work.

The law of life for Jesus was the surrender of His own will to that of the Father, by giving up that life to death, so as to enter the heavenly life of redemption — by the cross, to the throne. So surely as there is a kingdom of sin, under the authority of which we were brought by our connection with the first Adam, so surely has there been set up a new kingdom of grace, in Christ Jesus, under the powerful influence of which we are brought by faith. The marvellous power by which Jesus subdued sin on the cross, lives and works in us, and not only calls us to life as He lived, but enables us to do; to adopt the Cross as the motto and law of our lives.

Believer, that blood with which you have been sprinkled; under which you live daily, is the blood of the Cross. It obtains its power from the fact that it was the complete sacrifice of a life to God. The blood and the cross are inseparably united: The blood comes from the cross; it bears witness to the cross; it leads to the cross. The power of the Cross is in that blood; every touch of the blood should inspire you with a fresh ability to take the Cross as the law of your life. "Not my will but Thine be done" may, now, in that power, become a song of daily consecration. What the Cross teaches you, that it bestows upon you; what it imposes upon you, that it makes possible for you. Let the everlasting sprinkling of the blood of the cross be your choice, and through that blood, the disposition, as well as the power of the cross, will be seen in you.

III.   The Love which the Cross Reveals, and which bestows upon us all that the Cross has gained.

We must now fix our attention on this, if we are to learn the full glory of the blood of the cross.

We have spoken of the disposition of which the cross is the expression, and of the powerful influence that disposition exercises in us and through us if we allow the blood of the cross to have its full power over us. The fear, however, often arises in the mind of a Christian that it is too much of a burden always to preserve and manifest that disposition; and even the assurance that the Cross is "the power of God" which produces this disposition does not entirely remove that fear, since the exercise of that power depends to some extent on our surrender and faith, and these are far from being what they ought to be. Can we find in the cross a deliverance from this infirmity, the healing of this disease? Cannot "the blood of the cross" make us partakers always, without ceasing, not only of the blotting out of guilt, but also of victory over the power of sin?

It can. Draw near, to hear once more what the Cross proclaims to you. It is only when we understand aright, and receive into our hearts the love of which the Cross speaks, that we can experience its full power and blessing. Paul indeed bears witness to this: "I am crucified with Christ; nevertheless I live; yet not I, but Christ liveth in me: and the life which I now live in the flesh I live by the faith of the Son of God, Who loved me, and gave Himself for me" (Galatians 2:20).

Faith in the love of Him "who gave Himself for me" on the cross enables me to live as one who has been crucified with Him.

The cross is the revelation of love. He saw that there was no other way by which His love could redeem those whom He so loved, save by shedding His blood for them on the cross; it is because of this that He would not allow Himself to be turned aside by the terror of the cross, not even when it caused His soul to tremble and shudder. The cross tells us that He loved us so truly that His love surmounted every difficulty — the curse of sin, and the hostility of man — that His love has conquered, and has won us for Himself. The cross is the triumphant symbol of eternal love. By the cross love is seated on the throne, so that from the place of omnipotence it can now do for the beloved ones all that they desire.

What a new and glorious light is thus shed on the demand the Cross makes on me, and on what it offers to do for me; on the meaning, and glory, and life of the Cross, to which I have been called by the Word — I, whose flesh is so disposed to go astray that even the promise of the Spirit and the power of heaven seem insufficient to bestow on me the courage I need. But lo! here is something that is better still than the promise of power. The Cross points out to me the living Jesus in His eternal, all-conquering love. Out of love to us He gave Himself up to the cross, to redeem a people for Himself. In this love He accepts of everyone who comes to Him in the fellowship of His cross, to bestow upon them all the blessings that He had obtained on that cross. And now He receives us in the power of His eternal and ever efficacious love, which ceases not for one moment to work out in us what He obtained for us on the cross.

I see it! What we need is a right view of Jesus Himself, and of His all-conquering, eternal love. The blood is the earthly token of the heavenly glory of that love; the blood points to that love. What we need is to behold Jesus Himself in the light of the cross. All the love manifested by the cross is the measure of the love He bears to us today. The love which was not terrified by any power or opposition of sin will now conquer everything in us that would be a hindrance. The love which triumphed on the accursed tree is strong enough to obtain and maintain a complete victory over us. The love manifested by "a Lamb as it had been slain in the midst of the throne," bearing always the marks of the cross, lives solely to bestow on us the disposition, and power, and the blessing of the cross. To know Jesus in His love, and to live in that love, to have the heart filled with that love, is the greatest blessing that the cross can bring to us. It is the way to the enjoyment of all the blessings of the cross.

Glorious Cross! Glorious Cross, which brings to us, and makes known to us, the eternal love. The blood is the fruit and power of the cross; the blood is the gift and bestowal of that love. In what a full enjoyment of love those may now live who have been brought into such wonderful contact with the blood, who live every moment under its cleansing. How wondrously that blood unites us to Jesus and His love. He is the High Priest, out of whose heart that blood streamed, to whose heart that blood returns, who is Himself the end of the sprinkling of the blood, who Himself perfects the sprinkling of the blood in order that by it He may take possession of the heart that He on the cross had won. He is the High Priest who in the tenderness of love now lives to perfect everything in us, so that the disposition which the Cross has established as the law of our lives, and the victory which the Cross offiers us as the power of our lives, may be realised by us.

Beloved Christian, whose hope is in the blood of the cross, give yourself up to experience its full blessing. Each drop of that blood points to the surrender and death of self-will, of the "I" life, as the way to God, and life in Him. Each drop of that blood assures you of the power of a life, a heavenly life, obtained by Jesus on the cross, to maintain that disposition, that crucified life, in you. Each drop of that blood brings Jesus, and His eternal love, to you, to work out all the blessing of the Cross in you, and to keep you in that love.

May each thought of the cross and the blood bring you nearer to your Saviour, and into a deeper union with Him to whom they point you.

BIBLIOGRAPHY

A. C. Dixon: *The Glories of the Cross*, New York, n.d., pp. 89-96
Thomas Guthrie: *Inheritance of the Saints*, pp. 325-344
John Leland, in Fish: *Masterpieces of Pulpit Eloquence*, Vol. II, New York, 1856, pp. 454-461
G. Campbell Morgan: *The Bible and the Cross*, pp. 101-119. (Also in the *Westminster Pulpit*, Vol. II, 1907, pp. 145-152 and Vol. VI, 1911, pp. 89-96)
Andrew Murray: *The Blood of the Cross*, London, 1935, pp. 34-45

ANDREW MURRAY
(1828-1917)

I think it would be quite safe to say that the two most widely read writers of Christian devotional literature in the nineteenth and early part of the twentieth centuries were F. B. Meyer and Andrew Murray. Andrew Murray was the fourth person in succession in the Murray line to be named Andrew. Both his father and grandfather were educated in Edinburgh University, and were gifted ministers in Scotland, especially in the area around Aberdeen. His father, Andrew Murray, emigrated to the Province of the Cape of Good Hope, in South Africa in 1821, becoming pastor of the Dutch Reformed Church, at Graff Reinet, where he continued to minister for forty-five years. It was here, on May 9, 1828, that the subject of our brief sketch was born. At the age of ten, Andrew and his brother John were sent to Scotland for education, Andrew graduating seven years later at the age of seventeen from Aberdeen, which was immediately followed by his departure for Holland where he undertook studies to prepare him for ministering in the Dutch language in South Africa. His first pastorate, beginning in 1849, was at Bloemfontein. In 1860, he became pastor of the church at Worcester, where occurred a great revival during the first year of his ministry, with the result that fifty young men offered themselves as candidates for the Christian ministry. It was during his days at Worcester that he published, in Dutch, *What Manner of Child Shall This Be?*, which was the basis of his exceedingly rich volume, *The Children for Christ,* which appeared in 1886.

After a pastorate of seven years at Cape Town, he was called to Wellington, in 1871, where he spent the next forty-five years. The congregation at Wellington was largely composed of descendants of the Huguenots, who had fled to South Africa to escape the fearful persecutions they were enduring in France. From the Dutch Reformed Church at Wellington, because of the unusual ministry of Andrew Murray, there radiated throughout that area an influence in the lives of thousands,

143

leading to a deeper experience with Christ, to a recognition of the infinite possibilities of life in the power of the Holy Spirit, accompanied with a deep passion for missions, and for the education of the young people of that district. Perhaps this description of one of the communion services, written by Mr. Murray's daughter, would not be out of place.

"Can one ever forget the Communion seasons at this time? There, gathered round the Lord's Table, 500 or 600 Communicants, and a Holy influence permeated the Church. Can we forget the Holy Awe, the deep reverence, the joy and often the rapture written on father's face? The holy joy that filled heart and soul at these never-to-be-forgotten seasons of communion, when 'Heaven came down our souls to meet!' One communion season I remember well. Father seemed to have really been taken up to the third heaven and a holy awe and deep solemnity rested on us all before he spoke again, and his words were, 'I live, yet not I but Christ liveth in me, and that life which I now live in the flesh, I live in *faith,* the faith which is in the Son of God who loved me and gave Himself for me.' More especially he emphasised those words *'who loved me.'* Oh! the wonder of it! the pity of it that we so little understand, and so fail to bask in the sunshine of this great love! Let us love Him and trust Him more and more!"

Mr. Murray was asked to speak at the Keswick Convention, in 1895, and so impressed was he with the need of such a gathering for South Africa, that for the next twenty-eight years, he was recognized as the Father of the Keswick movement in South Africa. In the same year, he was the principal speaker at the Northfield Conference, directed by D. L. Moody, where he left an abiding impression upon the hearts of thousands who were in attendance. His messages displayed unusual spiritual power, the source of which was in his disciplined life of prayer and in his appropriating by faith the New Testament promises relating to the indwelling of the Holy Spirit.

In spite of his heavy pastoral duties, and after speaking at conferences in South Africa and in Europe, his indefatigable labors in establishing schools and a theological seminary in South Africa, and faithful attendance at ecclesiastical conferences, Andrew Murray, like F. B. Meyer, still found time for a most amazingly fertile literary ministry. His official biographer, Dr. J. DuPlessis, is the authority for the statement that Mr. Murray wrote not less than 240 books and booklets, in the Dutch and English languages, many of which were translated into French, German, Spanish, and Danish. The first volume to appear in English was his penetrating study, *Abide in Christ,* published in 1882, when Murray was fifty-five years of age, and at the very prime of life. This was soon followed, in 1885, by probably his best known and most widely read work, *With Christ in the School of Prayer.* I cannot help here but quoting the letter of no less a writer and thinker than Alexander Whyte, addressed to Mr. Murray after his reading this particular volume.

"I have been spending a New Year week out of Edinburgh and up in this beautiful spot, sanctified for me by generations of praying progenitors. I have read a good deal during last week; but nothing half so good as your *With Christ.* I have read in criticism and in theology; but your book goes to the joints and the marrow of things. You are a much honoured man: how much only the day will declare. The other books I have been reading are all able and good in their way; but they are spent on the surface of things. Happy man! you have been chosen and ordained of God to go to the heart of things. I have been sorely rebuked, but also much directed and encouraged by your *With Christ.* Thank you devoutly and warmly this Sabbath afternoon. I am to send your book to some of my friends on my return to Town tomorrow."

We have already referred to the volume, *The Children for Christ,* which I would urge every minister and father and mother to secure. It is an unsurpassed study of some fifty important passages in the Old and New Testaments relating to the subject of children and parents. Among other of his better known volumes are *Holy in Christ,* 1887; *The Spirit of Christ,*

1889; *The Holiest of All,* 1894, a Commentary of 550 pages on the Epistle to the Hebrews; *Have Mercy Upon Me,* 1895, thirty-one meditations on the 51st Psalm; *The Ministry of Intercession,* 1897; *The Full Blessing of Pentecost,* 1907; and *The Prayer Life,* 1913. Two of his more important volumes I have never been able to secure, namely, *The Key to the Missionary Problem,* published in 1901, and a book of Lectures on the Dangers of Modern Theology.

Dr. Alexander Maclaren said of Andrew Murray's book on Missions, "I hope that Dr. Murray's heart-searching book may be widely read and prayerfully pondered. It is the Key to the Missionary Problem indeed, but it is also the key to most of our problems, and points to the only cure of all our weaknesses."

This mighty man of God, so prevailing in prayer, so profoundly manifesting the mind of Christ, so wholly devoted to his Lord and the church, passed away in Wellington, January 18, 1917, at the age of eighty-nine. Would that we had more of his type in this time of such great need, and yet such general spiritual superficiality.

THE CROSS THE INSTRUMENT
OF CHRISTIAN ZEAL
by
R. McCheyne Edgar

"Who gave Himself for us, that He might redeem us from all iniquity, and purify unto Himself a peculiar people, zealous of good works." — Titus 2:14

We saw on last occasion how the Cross secures sanctification, at once purging our consciences of defilement and setting before us the disinterested hope of helping others towards their sanctification through the careful cultivation of our own. And now we are to study the outcome of the consecrated spirit in a zeal for good works,— an outcome which is secured also by the Cross.

The text states unmistakably the purpose of the crucifixion. It tells us that Christ gave Himself for us, undoubtedly, upon the Cross: first, that He might redeem, or ransom us from all iniquity; secondly, that He might secure a purified and peculiar people; and, thirdly, that they might be zealous of good works. It is to the third of these purposes that we are now to address ourselves, in the hope that in once more contemplating Christ crucified we may receive an undying stimulus to good works.

I. THE CROSS OF CHRIST BASES GOOD WORKS UPON THE GRACE OF GRATITUDE.

It is admittedly most important to have a good foundation for any structure, but especially for such a structure as that of good works. If the foundation be sandy, the edifice will certainly fall before the storms of temptation; if the foundation be upon a rock, the structure will endure even the shock of worlds.

Now there are only two possible foundations for good works, *prudence* and *gratitude*. It has indeed been imagined that there is a higher service than either possible to man; that "a more disinterested love may spring from the contemplation of what God is in Himself than from the recollection of what He has done for us." But this overlooks the fact that God is known by what He has done, and we cannot *anticipate* His goodness and love. It is an anachronism, consequently, to insinuate the possibility of serving Him because of His absolute perfections, when those perfections are revealed to us in ways that should secure our gratitude.

Of the two sources of duty, of the two foundations of good works, prudence and gratitude, a little consideration is sufficient to show that gratitude is the stronger and worthier. "If we are to compare, as a source of duty, the grateful with the merely prudential temper, rather may we trust the first, as not the worthier only, but the stronger too; and till we obtain emancipation from the latter, — forget the computations of hope and fear, and precipitate ourselves for better or for worse on some object of divine love and trust, — our nature will be puny and weak, our wills will turn in sickness from their duty, and our affections shrink in aversion from their heaven." Yes, brethren, there may be much done through prudence. Money may be extorted through fear of judgment to come; irksome penances may be performed in the hope that men may be accepted on account of them at last; licentiousness and all excess may be avoided for fear of their effects; much that seems fair and good may be gone through in a prudent spirit; and yet there is nothing more certain than that this is a selfish, a vacillating, an unreliable temper upon which to build a good life.

I might indeed pause to show that this selfishly prudent spirit can produce nothing worthy of the name of "good works," for selfishness eats the very heart out of goodness; but I shall content myself with dwelling upon the superior power of gratitude as a basis for good works. You can easily understand that the soul that has been led to realize his obligation to another, and do him service in grateful recognition, is in a higher condition than he who serves in the hope of recompense. Impelled by a sense of obligation, contemplating with wonder the goodness shown us by our fellow, we devote ourselves heartily and disinterestedly to his service.

Now it is upon this grace of gratitude that good works are built. The order in the Gospel is grace bringing salvation through the Cross, acceptance of that salvation by faith, and a life of zealous service through gratitude. "Grace, faith, good works," these three words epitomize the Gospel. Hence, as Monod once said, good works become *practicable* through grace. Upon grace must they be built.

Well, then, I ask you, is not this what Christ's Cross secures? In view of the Cross, where is the sinner that is not called to gratitude? To think that the Eternal Son of God through loyal love to us gave Himself up to death, even the death of the Cross, is surely the mightiest motive to gratitude that can be conceived. Do not all other obligations under which our fellow-men have laid us dwindle into the most utter insignificance before the obligation of the Cross? No friend, however affectionate and true, can lay us under anything like the obligation of Jesus. He has done more for us than all the world has done or could do. And I care not how insensible you have become to your duty, oh, if you only honestly contemplate the Saviour as He dies for you, you will discover in the contemplated Cross a motive power that will, by the Spirit's blessing, rouse you into burning, because grateful, zeal. With streaming eye, on account of sin and short-coming, you will at once say, "One love deserves another," such self-sacrificing love deserves a similar return, and I must labour for such a Saviour's sake!

And here let me add that gratitude should bear more fruit than fear. It is sometimes pleaded that Protestantism, through refraining from the motives of fear urged by the Church of

Rome, canot be expected to contribute so largely and sustain so efficiently her Church organizations. But surely this is a libel upon grace, and an unjust compliment to prudence and fear. If gratitude be genuine, it should be more than a match for prudence. The love of the Cross is a power of liberality and of zeal, such as no amount of anathema can possibly produce. What is wanting is not a new motive, but a better notion of the old; what is wanting is more gratitude in the heart, and then there shall be more power and zeal in the life.

II. THE CROSS OF CHRIST DETERMINES THE MEASURE OF OUR CHRISTIAN ZEAL.

If we have comprehended the basis of our good works, we are in a position to consider the *measure* of our zeal in them. It is a bad thing to run into unreasonable extremes, and exhibit a zeal not according to knowledge. Is there, then, any measure of Christian zeal, any standard that we are to keep before us, to regulate our conduct in the good cause?

At the risk of repeating a truth already insisted upon, I ask your attention, brethren, to the *Cross* as the measure of our zeal. Our Master was so zealous in the Father's service, that it was said of Him, The zeal of His Father's house had eaten Him up. (John 2:17). So zealous was He that He risked His life in finishing the work that had been given Him to do. So zealous was He, that He "endured the Cross, despising the shame." There was no timidity about Him, no cool calculation of consequences, but obedience to the mighty passion that consumed Him, a passion for His Father's honour, a passion for lost men's salvation! Martyrdom upon Calvary was the measure of Christ's zeal.

And let us learn at the Cross that *martyrdom* must also be the measure of our zeal. We must be prepared to push our Master's cause even though death meets us in the path of zeal. The courage of His Cross is fitted to provoke the zeal of very many, and to awaken the courage of a martyr within us. Our love is a low one indeed, cool and calculating, that refuses the sacrifice of life for the dear Lord's sake.

History tells us of enthusiasm for a person often leading men to brave death in the hero's cause. A Napoleon could lead forth huge armies to battle against great combinations, — to battle against winter's wildest storms, and to die by the battalion on battle-fields or amid the snow. And if he could command martyrs in the cause of his ambition, if he could write his haughty and selfish name upon the hearts of his countrymen, and lead them forth to die in his cause, shall not Christ, the great unselfish, self-sacrificing Saviour, the Captain who took the place of honour in the forlorn hope, the Leader who carried the flag which, "like that of Sigurd, while it has ensured triumph to those who followed it, has brought destruction to him who carried it;" shall not He, I say, secure a band abounding in zeal sufficient for all obedience even up to death? Yes, it is the zeal of self-sacrifice, the zeal of the martyrs that we need; this is what the Cross claims, and all who understand it in the spirit will yield!

III. THE CROSS OF CHRIST DETERMINES THE METHOD OF OUR CHRISTIAN ZEAL.

If the Cross bases zeal upon gratitude, and determines martyrdom as its measure, it also affords such practical suggestions about *method* as are indispensable in such a matter. "Its very silence, and its patience," like Rosalind's, "speak to the people." A most marvellous Cross, surely, that entwines around it the ivy of highest speculation and the passion-flower of morals, that affords food for the head, and heat for the heart, and wisdom to guide the hand in its good works!

Of course, brethren, the *life* of Christ is of high practical importance. It is full of meaning as well as of mystery, and out of it there blooms many a flowery suggestion for the benefit of Christian workers. Yet may we discern in His death the vast principles that bloomed in His life, and sufficient practical suggestions for our present need. Thus,

(a) The Cross gives *intelligence* to our zeal.

We can all understand how zeal may exist without intelligence. Men may have a zeal of God, but not according to knowledge. (Romans 10:2). Our zeal may lead us even to persecute the true Church. (Philippians 3:6). It may take the form of bitterness and strife, and result in confusion and every evil work. (James 3:14,16). In such dangers, then, who will guide us? How shall we in our zeal let our light so shine among men that they may see our good works, and glorify our Father who is in heaven?

Christ by the kindly light of His Cross shall guide us. Nothing is more noticeable about His death than His recognition of it as a *divine arrangement*. Man might fret and fume around Him, man might unjustly condemn Him, man might nail Him upon the cross, yet it was all part of God's plan, and as such He accepted it. "It must be that offences come, but woe to that man by whom they come." The opportunity of saving men by death comes to Him as the express arrangement of the Father, the emergency that demands Him is the provision of God, and He accepts it most willingly.

Nay, this was the rule of His whole life. "His plan," as one has well said, "is not what He chooses, but what the Father provides for Him, and makes so straight, so luminous (I do not say so easy!) for Him, that He has only to follow it step after step, without hesitation or obscurity. It is not He who comes to seek His good works, it is His good works which come to seek Him, succeeding each other in their place before Him, each in its hour and in its turn, without crossing or embarrassing each other, God never allowing time to be wanting for the work, nor the work for the time. Such is the way of good works which God has prepared for Jesus that He may walk in them; and because Jesus responds to this plan of the Father with a simple eye, a right heart, a docile will, the entire life of Jesus is only a series of good works uninterrupted, and of which each has been expressly chosen of God for the moment and the circumstances where it ought to find its place marked."

Well, brethren, I ask if there is anything to hinder us from regarding our life-work as arranged for us as minutely and as accurately as that of Christ? May we not have an intelligent assurance that each work, whether painful or joyful, whether minute or mighty, whether secret or public, that comes to our hand is a divine opportunity to be devotedly in the spirit of the Cross? "that comes to our hand," I say, for I do verily believe that the uncertainty and interruption of our work come largely from the fact that instead of taking the work laid by infinite wisdom to our hand, we waste time in choosing something that we imagine would be grander and better. Oh, if we looked upon life with something like the eyes of Christ, and accepted whatever work God sends in our way, and did with our very best, we should discover a calm power in our life-work of which we have no idea now!

And think for one moment what a blessed truth this is, that we are God's workmanship, "created in Christ Jesus unto good works, which God hath before ordained that we should walk in them." (Ephesians 2:10). It is not more certain that man was introduced at the first into a world divinely prepared for his reception than that each one of us is providentially ushered into a sphere of work which is fitted for us. If we would only in a spirit of submission take every work as it comes to us, with its joy or pain, as God's sweet arrangement, and that we have no choice but to set about the hearty doing of it, then I am certain we should find a power as well as comfort in life past all conception. Every hour we are coming to a kingdom, a sphere of opportunity and effort; and if we enter with the crown upon our heads and the sceptre in our hands, — the crown of gratitude, and the sceptre of righteousness, — believe me, we shall reign! But we usurp dominions and thrones when we despise the little realm and attempt the great.

(b) The Cross commends *prayer* as the spirit of our zeal.

The work of Christ upon the Cross was prayerful. It was no light matter to die bravely under such conditions as His, and so He spent a considerable portion of the time of the crucifixion in prayer. He prayed for Himself, but He prayed also for His murderers; He bore the world's destiny upon His prayerful spirit in that hour. Read the twenty-second Psalm, as well as the accounts of the crucifixion, and you shall have some faint idea of the prayerful spirit of Christ in His crucifixion.

And there is nothing more important in good works than prayer. Through communion with God we contract a divine illumination, we see our work as he sees it, we rise to his standpoint, things come out in their true relations, the concerns of time and sense give way before the paramount interests of the spirit, and we devote ourselves as we could not otherwise to the work given us to do.

Not more important is steam to a locomotive than prayer is to Christian work. Not more important is wind to the sails of a ship than prayer is to progress in Christian activity. Let the white canvas of your Christian zeal be filled with the breath of prayer, and swift as the ships shall you pass through the waves of work, however high, towards the desired haven of accomplishment. Pray for yourselves that you may be workmen not needing to be ashamed; pray for others that you may benefit them by your work and be benefited by theirs; pray for the work of all that it may be patiently completed, and you shall prove Samsons in your land! "Pray without ceasing. In everything give thanks: for this is the will of God in Christ Jesus concerning you." (1 Thessalonians 5:18).

(c) The Cross shows us how to be *considerate* in our zeal.

There is indeed a danger of being inconsiderate in our earnestness. We get so absorbed in our work, it is so important that we feel straitened how to accomplish it. And as people come into contact with us we contract a certain abruptness in manner that in its measure defeats our work. Now it is well to be absorbed in a good work, and to lay our whole powers to it; yet we must remember that consideration for others is itself a field of work, and it is at our peril if we neglect it.

If ever there was an hour or a work when absorption with it was justifiable, it was the crucifixion. And yet where will you find such tender consideration for those around Him? Though dealing as the Representative with God above, He also deals affectionately with man below, and instead of reviling those who reviled Him, He blesses them altogther. The dying robber at His side solicits remembrance when the dying King enters on His reign, and he receives the tender answer, "Today shalt thou be with me in Paradise." His mother, who is standing near the cross, is comforted by being commended to the care of John. And all around the cross, whether weeping daughters of Jerusalem, or noisy soldiers, or scoffing priests, must have admitted that the utmost consideration is entertained by this dying Jesus for the feelings and interests of those around Him. In fact, if He was *absorbed* by one thought more than another on that memorable day, whether He pleaded with God or spake to man, it was with the interests of sinners. It was the most unselfish devotion that led Him up to the cross and past it to the crown.

And, brethren, if you consider Him and how you may reciprocate His tenderness, you shall be kept from marring your good work. Mary, when she anointed Jesus in Simon's house, wrought a good work upon Jesus. (Matthew 26:10). Her love was so deep that it crowned her act with fitting grace and tenderness. She was absorbed in Him, and only considered how much she could make of Him. And this is what we too are to consider. In being careful to maintain good works (Titus 3:8), we shall be most considerate and fruitful when we continually ask ourselves what Christ's love deserves, what His person should receive were He here bodily, and what these representatives of His roundabout us shall consequently be offered. Then is it that even our gainsayers shall be led, beholding our good works, to glorify God in the day of visitation. Then shall we with well-doing put to silence the ignorance of foolish men (1 Peter 2:12,15).

(d) The Cross teaches us how to be *patient* in our zeal.

If zeal in sight of the Cross becomes intelligent, prayerful, and considerate, it also becomes *patient*. For burning zeal is not necessarily "wild-fire," but a patient, steady glow, like the fire at earth's centre, taking its own time to enflame the world.

Occasionally it may burst into a volcanic eruption, but as a rule it burns patiently, out of sight, but not of feeling, until its purposes are completed and the universal conflagration comes.

"The patience of Jesus Christ," the patience of His Cross, is not sufficiently regarded. No noisy demonstration is enacted there. All is calm, sincere, earnest. It is zeal in its most patient and, as history shows us, most triumphant hour. He is not anxious to vindicate and justify His course to friends or foes. The Cross He knows well will subdue the ages, and vindicate Him at the last. Sapping and mining is He, zealously labouring beneath the foundations of worldliness, of misery, and of sin; and though men did not suspect the tremendous issue, He could quietly say "It is finished" before He gave up the ghost, assured that the mine was laid which is destined to blow into nothingness the pride and pomp of opposing principalities and powers, and secure the victory. Patient zeal proves a power, and compels submission.

Let us, brethren, follow His bright example in this matter of patient zeal. Let us carry our cross, ready to die if need be, ready to do a quiet, yet warm and earnest work for our great Master. Not that we are to expect little, and be content with little, but that we are to expect much in God's own season. If we feel that the work of each hour is what God has allowed us, a shot from the great shuttle of God as He weaves the web of our individual life, and if we do not endeavour to break away from our work and leave out a single thread, we can assure ourselves that the pattern will complete itself in time, and will be the larger and the nobler the longer we have to wait.

Let me, in conclusion, brethren, urge upon you this Christian zeal as the last purpose of God. His purpose, it is plain, is not to save men merely, but to make men workers. As a husbandman, He does not plant His property with fruitless evergreens, but with fruit-bearing vines. Plant your evergreens in the churchyard; let there be green amid the graves the whole year round; but in the vineyard of God, with its eternal sap, it is fruit-bearing vines that are demanded, and no alternative is there between fruitfulness and the fire. In a day of evergreen profession and comparatively little fruit, of barren fig-trees and woody vines, it is needful to insist on good works as the grand end of the Gospel system. "The grape filled with its precious juice is the natural product of the vinestock; it is the lovely ornament thereof, it is the distinctive mark of it; but it is more than all that: it is the end of it. The husbandman has planted the vine, and cultivated it only to obtain the grape; so much so, that if he had known any other way of possessing it, he would have spared himself the infinite cares wherein he wastes his life."

God had died for men, not that they may be redeemed only, not that they may be purified as a peculiar people only, but that they may be zealous of good works. To the great hive in heaven only "working bees" shall be invited. You, therefore, that are at ease in Zion, doing as little as you can for Christ, content to be indolent, to you I call now. Such sluggishness is unbecoming at Christ's Cross. Awake, awake, and work. There is work at your hand waiting for you — do it with your best; for if you would form part of the incomparable company who have washed their robes and made them white in the blood of the Lamb, and whose privilege it is to serve God day and night in His temple, you must learn to labour for Him now; now, while the light lingers in the west, and the shades of the night have not deepened down; now, while life and health are yours, and the gate of the vineyard is open. "My son," says the Infinite Father, "go work today in my vineyard." May we all do so! Amen.

BIBLIOGRAPHY

W. Hay M. H. Aitken: *The School of Grace*, London, 1879, pp. 281-317
B. H. Carroll: *The Way of the Cross*, Nashville, 1941, pp. 31-42
R. McCheyne Edgar: *The Philosophy of the Cross*, London, 1874, pp. 274-290
Alexander Maclaren: *Expositions of Holy Scripture, II Timothy-Hebrews,* pp. 171-180
G. C. Morgan: *Westminster Pulpit,* London, 1910, Vol. 5, pp. 169-192
Charles H. Spurgeon: *Metropolitan Tabernacle Pulpit,* Vol. II, No. 70, pp. 129-136

THE PRECIOUS BLOOD OF CHRIST
by
Joseph Parker

"The precious blood of Christ." — 1 Peter 1:19

My heart's desire has ever been to make known to men that there is no salvation but by blood, and not by blood only, but by the particular blood named in the text — even the precious blood of Christ. I am afraid that in these latter days some of us have tried to find out some other word to use instead of this word blood. We shrink from it. A dainty piety has forced upon us a dainty vocabulary. As the intensity of our love has gone down, the intensity of our speech has gone down along with it. We speak of the life of Christ and the love of Christ, but we too seldom speak of the precious blood of Christ; that would seem to our frigid piety to be an exaggeration, and our frigid piety is encouraged by our deceitful fancy, that tells us that love is a larger term than blood, and should always be used instead of it. Beware of the temptations of a worldly fancy. If your piety becomes the creature or the plaything of your imagination, you will commit the keeping of your soul to the most capricious and the most irresponsible of all powers. We need some term that lies away, infinitely beyond the airy and cloudy region of fancy; a broad and emphatic word — a word that carries its own single and definite meaning so plainly that mistake is impossible, and that sacred and inviolable term is blood. The world over, that word has but one meaning. Even the word love may be tortured into ambiguity by men skilful in definition, but the word blood is too simple, too energetic, too solemn, to take upon it the faintest gloss of the most reluctant expositor. It is blood; it is precious blood; it is the blood of Christ; it is the blood that cleanseth from all sin; and to attemper its passion by the use of supposed equivalents, is to trifle with the supreme purpose of God in seeking the salvation of mankind. In a case like this, even reverent paraphrase is in danger of becoming almost profane. What other word can take the place of the word blood? Even love itself is a word with many aliases, or a word which admits of many changes and partial substitutes: it is regard, it is affection, it is sympathy, it is forbearance, it is friendship, it is trust — but how will you replace the word blood? It stands alone. It will not clothe itself in the disguises of various terms. Its unquenchable ardour burns through the snow which you scatter upon its summit. No winter can loiter upon those ardent slopes. If you mean to tax your fancy for the production of equal terms you must go elsewhere, for the term "blood" can accept no humiliation and pander to no disguise.

We are sometimes asked to admit that it cannot be what is called real, literal, or merely physical blood. Why should it not be real blood, the actual blood of the actual body? Let us take care lest our vulgar conceptions deprive us of gracious meanings and privileges. It may be our notion that is at fault, and not the word of God. The reference is unquestionably to the real blood of Jesus Christ, "who his own self bare our sins in his own body on the tree." Who shall say that his bodily blood was limited, and could therefore have but limited application? Verily herein we are straitened, not in Christ, but in ourselves; yes, even in the very imagination which is supposed to create for itself such wide liberty! If the people could find no limit in the handful of bread with which Christ satisfied the throng, as the poor woman could find no limit to the oil blessed by the prophet, who shall take upon him to say that it was a shallow and measurable stream that flowed from the heart of Christ? Did he not work miracles upon his own body? Did he not conceal it? Did he not cause it to pass untouched and unhurt through the angry host upon the hill? Did he not keep it from sinking in the sea? And can he not crown these wonders by giving us his blood to drink? "How can this man give us his blood to drink?" We never could tell how Christ did his mighty works, but, praised be his sweet and tender name, dear Jesus, Heart of God, he did them, and therein is our joy satisfied! To me the controversy is mean which contends that Christ does not give us his flesh to eat and his blood to drink, in the sacred ordinance of the Supper. He who maintains the contrary can make the vulgar stare by his tricks in the use of words, and can impale on harmless horns the argument which he opposes, but he has never plumbed the depths of Christ's power, he has never known what alone can appease the heart's violence of grief, nor has he entered into the holiest of all, wherein the corruptible letter clothes itself with the incorruptible spirit. When my heart is stung to death by its own remorse on account of sin, when hell is moved from beneath to receive me as fit only for its devouring flames, I am in no mood to be satisfied with types and symbols; a real want demands a real remedy, a real sinner calls for a real Saviour, and real sin can be met only by real blood; in that infinite distress you must not meet me with etymologies and verbal dexterities, you must let the tormented soul have free access to the precious blood of Christ. I know well that the literalist can vex me with truisms, and confound my poor learning by his brilliant ignorance; he can tauntingly ask me, How can this man give you his blood to drink? and I have no answer in words; he entangles me in the thicket of his alphabet and holds me as his prey, but deep down in the contrite heart, in the solemn sanctuaries never defiled by common speech, I know that Christ's word is better than man's when he says, "Except ye eat the flesh of the Son of man, and drink his blood, ye have no life in you." If you ask me whether a morsel of sacramental bread is the actual body of Christ, my senses combine in a unanimous protest against an absurdity so manifest; but in this holy exercise I do not walk by sight, but by faith; my senses have slain me aforetime, so that I canot allow them to usurp a function they have so disastrously abused; I will not allow them to speak in this sanctuary; they can but degrade its sacredness: they have been liars from the begining, and in all heavenly mysteries they are liars still; I will listen only to the voice of the dying, mighty, holy, infinite Saviour — "Whoso eateth my flesh and drinketh my blood, hath eternal life; for my flesh is meat indeed, and my blood is drink indeed; he that eateth my flesh and drinketh my blood, dwelleth in me and I in him."

By no priestly incantation is common bread transformed into the body of Christ. I know nothing of sacerdotal magic. My soul resents with horror too solemn to be merely contemptuous the suggestion that priestly wizardry is needful to my participation in the blood of Christ. But this is my faith, the faith that brings things of heaven near, the faith that consecrates the very dust of earth, that if, in the burning agony of my contrition, shame, and helpfulness, I put forth a trembling hand, and seize the common bread which makes the body live, and eat it for love of Christ, it will be to me the very flesh of the Son of God, a real appropriation, a holy sacrament; foolishness, to the cold, low world, but wisdom divine and comfort infinite to the hungering and dying heart. I shall then know, not by some intellectual feat, the deep meaning of Christ's words: "This is the bread which cometh down from heaven, that a man may eat thereof and not die. I am the living bread which cometh down from heaven; if a man eat of this bread he shall live for ever: and the bread that I will give is my flesh, which I will give for the life of the world."

We need what is truly called a realising faith as well as a spiritualising power. We are sometimes under the spell of two voices and hardly know to which to yield. The one voice says, Spiritualise everything; clothe the stones of the field with mystic meanings; fill the winds with voices from worlds unknown; and turn the stars into eyes of holy watchers not yet named of man. The other voice says, Beware of making the simple mysterious; avoid the attenuation which destroys solid meanings; take the very first signification that occurs to the earnest mind, and suspect all explanations that are far to seek. These contrary voices make themselves distinctly heard in the interpretation of this text; the one voice exhorts us to escape the narrowness of a literal meaning, and the other exhorts us not to lose the real and the true in some vain search for the speculative and the doubtful. A realising faith does not make things less, it makes them more vivid, it sets them before the eyes with true naturalness, and constrains their hidden meaning into bold and noble expression. I would, then, pray to have a realising faith when I think of the blood of Christ; the life-blood; the blood that cleanses from all sin; the blood of sprinkling; the blood of atonement; the blood of the everlasting covenant. I would see it as blood. The grossness is not in the blood, it is in myself. The blood is holy. Is there aught in the great universe so holy as the blood of Christ? But we cannot realise the blood until we have realised the sin. Where there is no conviction of sin — conviction amounting to the very anguish of the lost in hell — there can be no felt need of so extreme a remedy as is offered by the outpouring of the blood of Christ. A self-palliating iniquity may be cleansed by water. The light dust which bespots the outer garment may be removed by gentle means. When a man feels that he has not sinned deeply he is in no mood to receive what he considers the tragic appeals of the gospel; they exceed the case; they destroy themselves by exaggeration; they speak with selfdefeating violence. But let another kind of action be set up in the heart; let the man be brought to talk thus with himself — "I have sinned until my very soul is thrust down into hell; my sins have clouded out the mercy of God, so that I see it no longer; I have wounded the Almighty, I have cut myself off from the fountain of life, I have blown out every light that was meant to help me upward; I am undone, lost, damned," and then he needs no painted Cross, no typical sacrament, no ceremonial attitude, no priestly enchantment, he can be met by nothing but the sacrificial blood, the personal blood, the living blood, the precious blood of Christ.

How far it is possible to sustain in constant experience those keen and vivid realisations of the blood of Christ is known to us all. Considering the infirmities of the flesh, the deceitfulness of the world, the subtle and persistent temptations of the enemy, the continual vexations, anxieties, frets, and chafings of a life that is one daily struggle, it is not too much to say that we could not bear the incessant realisation of all that is suggested by the expression, "the blood of Christ." But if this is our weakness, and it surely is, what shall we say of the strengthening might that is stored up for us in Christ? We can do all things through Christ which strengtheneth us! For observe that, though the painful sacrifice of Christ makes an unendurable strain upon our feelings at one period of our spiritual history, it becomes to us the tenderest solace, the richest grace, the sweetest reflection, and the serenest rest, as we advance in our holy course. No longer are our sensibilities torn by it. No more do we see the wild but passing cruelty of man; the crucifixion becomes an atonement, and then on the Divine side we see the pity, the righteousness, the wisdom, and the love of God.

The practical effects of realising all that is meant by "the blood of Christ" are most useful. The text ceases to be a mere expression, and becomes a most solemn and all-determining fact. It becomes indeed the regulative power of our whole life. See, for example, how it reduces us to a state of most utter and abject helpfulness in the matter of self-salvation! If we could be saved by the shedding of blood only, how could we save ourselves? If Christ had saved us by some lower method, we might have been tempted to think that our redemption lay within our own power. But when it required the outpouring of every drop of blood that was in the fountain of his great heart, either he made a fatal mistake in his method, or we make a fatal mistake in supposing that we could have redeemed ourselves. Immediately following this reflection is the thought that, if so much was done for us, what is there that we can do in return? "How much owest thou my Lord?"

> "Love so amazing, so divine,
> Demands my soul, my life, my all."

We are not our own; we are bought with a price; therefore we are to glorify God in our bodies and in our spirits, which are God's. "I beseech you therefore, brethren, by the mercies of God that ye present your bodies a living sacrifice, holy, acceptable unto God, which is your reasonable service." My soul, canst thou reckon a debt so immense? Hast thou a pen that can be dipped in a sea of ink and a hand that can wield it until the day of death, that the sum may be set down in the face of heaven? My tongue refuses the intolerable burden of complete acknowledgment. My age would wither away before the growing tale was well begun. I owe all to Christ. There is nothing mine but my hateful sin. He found me; he loosed my bond; he paid my debt; he sounded the depths of all my woe; he ransomed me with blood! "I will offer to him the sacrifice of thanksgiving, and call upon the name of the Lord." How poor my best return! How mean my gifts! How weak my service! But as he met me in the helplessness of my sin, so will he meet me in the imperfection of my work. He will make it worthy with his own merit; he will complete it by his own might; he will sanctify it by his own holiness. The blood of Christ! It did not flow on one day, it flows evermore! My soul, is thine but a geographical Calvary? or is it a Golgotha of the spirit, the place where thy Church is founded and where thy heaven begins? Have we outlived the efficacy of the blood of Christ, and is the tale of his Cross a sound from which all the music has gone for ever? We need the sun to-day as we have ever needed it; th wind is still the breath of health to our dying bodies; still we find in the earth the bread without which we canot live; these are our friends of whom we never tire: can it be that the only thing of which we are weary is God's answer to our souls' deepest need? Shall we keep everything but the blood of Christ? Shall the Cross go, and the sun be left? Verily, as the sun withdrew at sight of that Cross and for the moment fled away, he would shine never more were that sacred tree hewn down by furious man. The blood of Christ is the fountain of immortality! The blood of Christ, — it makes the soul's summer warm and beauteous! The blood of Christ, it binds all heaven, with its many mansions and throngs without number, in holy and indissoluble security! My soul, seek no other stream in which to drown thy leprosy. My lips, seek no other song with which to charge your music. My hands, seek no other task with which to prove your energy. I would be swallowed up in Christ. I would be nailed to his Cross. I would be baptised with his baptism. I would quail under the agony of his pain, that I might triumph with him in the glory of his resurrection. O my Jesus! My Saviour! Thine heart did burst for me, and all its sacred blood flowed for the cleansing of my sin. I need it all. I need it every day. I need it more and more. Oh, search out the inmost recesses of my poor wild heart, and let thy blood remove every stain of evil.

BIBLIOGRAPHY

A. Barry: *The Atonement of Christ,* London, 1871, pp. 21-35
Clarence Edward Macartney: *The Greatest Texts of the Bible,* New York, 1947, pp. 118-127
Andrew Murray: *The Power of the Blood of Jesus,* London, 1935, pp. 18-29
Joseph Parker: *The People's Bible,* Vol. 20, pp. 341-348. (Also, the same, in Vol. 27, pp. 290-296).

A biographical sketch of Joseph Parker appears in *Great Sermons on the Birth of Christ,* pp. 72-77.

CHRIST'S ONE SACRIFICE FOR SIN
by
Charles H. Spurgeon

"Now once in the end of the world hath he appeared to put away sin by the sacrifice of himself." — Hebrews 9:26

I need not read the text again, for I shall not go far away from it; but again and again shall we come back to these precious words about our Lord's one great sacrifice for sin.

What Christ meant to do on the cross, he actually did. I always take that for granted. He did not die in vain; he did not leave any part of his work undone. Whatever was his intent, by the laying down of his life, he accomplished it; for, if not, dear friends, he would come here again. If any of his work were left undone, he would return to the earth that he might finish it, for he never did leave a work incomplete, and he never will. Christ effected the redemption of his people by one stroke; coming here, and living, and dying. He put away sin; he did not merely try to do it but he actually accomplished the stupendous work for which he left his glory-throne above.

He did not die to make men salvable; he died to save them. He did not die that their sin might be put away by some effort of their own; but he died to put it away. "Once in the end of the world hath he appeared to put away sin by the sacrifice of himself." There was one death, one sacrifice, one atonement, and all the work of man's redemption was for ever accomplished; so that we can sing, —

> "Love's redeeming work is done;
> Fought the fight, the battle won."

If the mission on which Christ came to this earth had not been fulfilled, I say again, he would have returned to complete the work that he had begun.

That would have meant that he should often have been offered since the foundation of the world, an idea which we cannot hold for a single moment. For Christ to die twice, would be contrary to all analogy. He is the second Adam. He, therefore, is like unto men. Read the words of Paul in the verse following our text, "It is appointed unto men *once* to die" (not twice), "but after this the judgment: so Christ was *once* offered to bear the sins of many; and unto them that look for him shall he appear the second time without sin unto salvation." For him, who is the true Adam, to die twice, would be contrary to the analogy of things.

It would be also most repugnant to all holy feeling. For Christ once to die a shameful death upon the cross on Calvary, has made an indelible mark upon our heart, as though it had been burned with a hot iron. I have sometimes half said to myself, "God forbid that his dear Son should ever have died!" The price seemed too great even for our redemption. Should he die, the Holy One and the Just, the glorious, and blessed Son of God? The answer to that question is, that he has died. Thank God, he can never die again! It were horrible to us to think that it should be possible that he should ever be called upon to bear our sins a second time.

It would be traitorous to his person, it would be dishonourable to his gospel, to suppose that his sacrifice is still incomplete, and that he might be called up to die again because his first death had not satisfied the claims of divine justice. The simple suggestion, even for the sake of argument, is almost blasphemous. Christ either paid the ransom-price for his people, or he did not. If he did, it is paid; if he did not, will he come again, think you? That can never be. Toplady knew that truth when he taught the saints to sing to their Lord, —

> "Complete atonement thou hast made,
> And to the utmost farthing paid

> Whate'er thy people owed:
> Nor can his wrath on me take place,
> If shelter'd in thy righteousness,
>   And sprinkled with thy blood."

The idea that Christ's one sacrifice for sin is not sufficient to accomplish his purpose, is also opposed to revelation. We are told that, "Christ, being raised from the dead, dieth no more, death hath no more dominion over him. For in that he died, he died unto sin once: but in that he liveth, he liveth unto God." The sinner for whom Christ died is free because of his Substitute's death; and the Substitute himself is free, for he has discharged every liability, and given to God the full satisfaction that divine justice required.

> "He bore on the tree the sentence for me,
>   And now both the Surety and sinner are free."

Take a good look at Calvary; get the cross distinctly photographed upon your eyeballs; behold the five wounds and the bloody sweat. The whole gospel was hung on the cross. It was all there; the battle and the victory, the price and the purchase, the doom and the deliverance, the cross and the crown. See again, in the death of Christ on the cross, a clear idea of what he meant to do, and of what he actually did when he laid down his life for us; and be you glad that once, and only once, this great deed had to be done. Nothing more is wanted, Christ has put away the sin of those for whom the covenant was made, according to the word that we read just now, "Their sins and iniquities will I remember no more." "Now, where remission of these is, there is no more offering for sin."

That will stand as a preface. Now I want, with great earnestness, — I fear with much weakness, but still with great earnestness, — to set before you, beloved friends, a summary of the way in which Christ has saved his people. It matters not how feebly the truth is put to you; if you do but lay hold of it, and firmly grasp it by faith, your souls are saved. I shall have to speak to you briefly upon five things; first, *the gigantic evil:* "sin." Secondly, *the glorious Remover of it:* "He." Thirdly, *the memorable event:* "Once in the end of the world hath he appeared." Fourthly, *the special sacrifice:* "the sacrifice of himself." Fifthly, and lastly, *the grand achievement:* "to put away sin by the sacrifice of himself."

I. First, notice, in considering what our text says that Christ has done, THE GIGANTIC EVIL. "Once in the end of the world hath he appeared to put away *sin.*"

"Sin." It is a very little word, but it contains an awful abyss of meaning. "Sin" is transgression against God, rebellion against the King of kings; violation of the law of right; commission of all manner of wrong. Sin is in every one of us; we have all committed it, we have all been defiled with it. Christ came "to put away sin." You see, the evil is put in one word, as if wrong-doing was made into one lump, all heaped together, and called, not *"sins"*, but *"sin."* Can you catch the idea? All the sinfulness, all the omissions, all the commissions, and all the tendencies to rebel that ever were in the world, are all piled together, hill upon hill, mountain upon mountain, and then called by this one name, "sin."

Now, sin is *that which makes man obnoxious to God.* Man, as a creature, God loves. Man, as a sinner, God cannot love. Sin is loathsome to God; he is so pure that he cannot bear impurity, so just that the thought of injustice is abhorrent to him. He cannot look upon iniquity without hating it; it is contrary to his divine nature. His anger burns like coals of juniper against sin. This it is that makes sin so dreadful to us, because, in consequence of it, we have become obnoxious to God.

And sin, dear friends, also *involves man in punishment.* Inasmuch as we have committed sin, we are exposed to the just and righteous wrath of God. Wherever there is sin, there must be penalty. Laws made without the sanction of reward and punishment are inoperative. God will never suffer his righteous law to be broken with impunity. His word still declares, "The soul that sinneth, it shall die." Where there is sin, there must be punishment; and although the doctrine is not preached as often as it ought to be, yet every man's conscience knows that there is a dreadful hell, there is a worm that dieth not, there is a fire that never can be quenched, and all these are reserved for unforgiven sinners. This makes sin so terrible an evil. Unless God vacates the throne of the universe, sin must be visited with punishment, and banished from his presence.

Yet again, dear friends, *sin effectually shuts the door of hope on men*. The guilty cannot dwell with God while they are guilty. They must be cleansed from sin before they can walk with him in white. Into heaven there entereth nothing that defileth; and if you and I are not pardoned, we must be separated from God forever. Nothing we can do, while sin remains upon us, can bring us reconciliation with God. Sin must be put away first. It lies across the road to heaven, and blocks up the door by which we come to God; and, unless it be removed, we are lost, lost, lost, and lost forever.

Do you all know, in your conscience and hearts, what sin means? I remember that, when I learned that dread lesson, I felt that I was the most unhappy youth in all Her Majesty's dominions. Sin went to bed with me, and scared me with visions. Sin rose with me, and made the most glorious landscape dark and gloomy. I had a terrible sound of judgment to come ever ringing in my ears. I knew that I was guilty; I did not need for God to condemn me, I condemned myself; I sat in judgment upon my own heart, and I condemned myself to hell. Sin! If you really feel it, no burning-irons in the hand of the most cruel inquisitor would ever pain you as sin does. Speak of diseases, and there are some that cause intense agony, but there is no disease that pains like sin on the conscience. Sin on the conscience! It is a prison, a rack, a cross whereon all joy hangs crucified, and bleeding to death.

That is the first thing in my text, the gigantic evil. In proportion as you feel the evil of sin, you will rejoice to hear that Christ came to put away sin by the sacrifice of himself. That is my next point.

II.   In the second place, having spoken of the gigantic evil that needed to be removed, let me now speak of THE GLORIOUS REMOVER OF IT. Who was it that undertook to remove this mountain of guilt? "Once in the end of the world hath HE appeared." Who is this that has appeared to put away sin?

I will not delay for a moment, but tell you at once that he that appeared was *very God of very God*. He against whom sin had been committed, he who will judge the quick and the dead; he it was who appeared to put away sin. Is there not great comfort in this fact? It is the Son of God who has undertaken this more than Herculean labour. He appeared, sinner, to save you; God appeared, to put away sin. Lost one, to find you, the great shepherd has appeared; your case is not hopeless, for he has appeared. Had anybody else than God undertaken the task of putting away sin, it could never have been accomplished; but it can be accomplished now, for HE who appeared is one with whom nothing is impossible. Listen to that, and be comforted.

Who is it that appeared? It is HE, *the commissioned of the Father*. Christ did not come as an amateur Saviour, trying an experiment on his own account; he came as the chosen Mediator, ordained of God for this tremendous task. The Saviour that I preach to you is no invention of my own brain. He is no great one who, of his own accord alone, stepped into the gap without orders from heaven. No; but he appeared whom the Father chose for the work, and sent, commissioned to perform it. His very name, Christ, tells of his anointing for this service.

> "Thus saith God of his Anointed;
>   He shall let my people go;
> 'Tis the work for him appointed,
>   'Tis the work that he shall do;
>   And my city
> He shall found, and build it too."

"He appeared," he who was *pledged in covenant* to do it;

for, of old, before the world was, he became the Surety of the covenant on behalf of his people. He undertook to redeem them. His Father gave him a people to be his own, and he declared that he would do the Father's will, and perfect those whom the Father had given him. "He appeared." Ah, dear friends, if the brightest angel had appeared to save us, we might have trembled lest he should be unequal to the task; but when he comes whom God has sent, whom God has qualified, and who is himself God, he came upon an errant which he is able to accomplish. Think of that, and be comforted.

III. But now, in the third place, we come to THE MEMORABLE EVENT mentioned in our text. We are told that, in order that he might save us, Christ appeared: "Once in the end of the world hath *he appeared.*" He could not sit in heaven, and do this great work. With all reverence to the blessed Son of God, we can truly say that he could not have saved us if he had kept his throne, and not left the courts of glory; but he appeared. I have not to tell you, at this time, that he will appear, although that also is true, for "unto them that look for him shall he appear the second time without sin unto salvation," but he has appeared.

He appeared, first, as *a babe at Bethlehem,* swaddled like any other child. This babe is "the Mighty God, the Everlasting Father, the Prince of peace;" and he has "appeared" on earth in human form. Made in fashion as a man, he has taken upon himself our nature, the Infinite is linked with the infant, the Eternal with the puling child. He, on whom all worlds are hanging, hangs upon a woman's breast. He must do that, or he cannot put away sin.

Thirty years rolled on; and he had toiled, in obscurity, as a carpenter at Nazareth. The Baptist comes, and proclaims the advent of the Redeemer, and he is there to the moment. Into the waters of Jordan he descends, and John with him; the servant baptizes his Lord; and, as he rises from the water-floods, the heavens are opened, the dove descends, it rests upon him, and God proclaims him to be his Son, in whom he is well

pleased. Thus Christ, *anointed at Jordan,* appeared to in-
augurate his public ministry, and, by his baptism, to begin working a robe of righteousness which is for ever to adorn us, poor
naked sinners. "In the end of the world he appeared;" his
manifestation commenced at Bethlehem, and was continued at
Jordan.

Three more years rolled by, years of toil and suffering; and
now the great debt was to be paid, the bill was presented; would
he be there to meet it? The charge was laid; would he be there
to answer to it? Where should he be but among those olives
in Gethsemane, surrendering himself? The night is chill, the
moon is shining; and he is there in prayer. But what prayer!
Never did the earth hear such groans and cries. He is there
wrestling; but what wrestling! He sweats, as it were, great drops
of blood falling to the ground. The sinner is called for, and the
sinner's Substitute has put in an appearance on his behalf in the
lonely garden of Gethsemane, so rightly named, the olive-press.
In a garden man's first sin was comitted; in a garden man's
Substitute was arrested.

But now comes the darkest hour of all. Christ appeared *on
Calvary, atoning for sin.* The sun is veiled as though unable
to look upon such a scene of sorrow. Hear the dread artillery of
heaven; the Father thunders forth his wrath against sin. Behold
the flames of fire, the forked lightnings of God's anger against
all iniquity. Who is to bear them? In whose breast shall they
be quenched? HE comes. On yonder tree he presents himself;
he hides not his face from shame and spitting; and, at last, upon
the cross, he hides not himself from divine desertion. Hear his
piteous cry, "My God, my God, why hast thou forsaken me?"
Then was fulfilled the prophecy given by the mouth of Zech-
ariah, "Awake, O sword, against my shepherd, and against the
man that is my fellow, saith the Lord of hosts." That sword is
sheathed in Christ's heart.

> "Jehovah bade his sword awake,
>   O Christ, it woke 'gainst thee;

> Thy blood the flaming blade must slake,
> Thy heart its sheath must be!
> All for my sake, my peace to make:
> Now sleeps that sword for me."

Yes, Christ appeared; he was visibly crucified among men; and observed by the gloating eyes of cruel men of hate, he appeared in that dread day of judgment and of vengeance. So it was, and only so, that he was able to put away sin.

We have come thus far, and the path has been strewn with wonders; but only he who knows the meaning of the word "sin" will see any wonder in it. If sin has made the earth tremble under your feet, if sin has scorched you like the blast of a furnace, if sin has burned into your very soul, and killed all your joy, you will hear with delight that God appeared here as man, for this purpose, to put away sin.

IV. Now, we must go a step farther, and consider THE SPECIAL SACRIFICE which Christ offered. He who appeared put away sin by a sacrifice, and that sacrifice was himself: "Once in the end of the world hath he appeared to put away sin by *the sacrifice of himself.*"

There was never any way of putting away sin except by sacrifice. The Bible never tells us of any other way; human thought or tradition has never discovered any other way. Find a people with a religion, and you are sure to find a people with a sacrifice. It is very strange; but, wherever our missionaries go, if they find God at all thought of, they find sacrifices being offered. It must be so; for man has this law written upon his very conscience.

Christ must bring a sacrifice; but observe what it was; *he offered himself.* "He appeared to put away sin by the sacrifice of himself," *his whole self.* Christ did not give to us merely a part of himself; he gave *himself.* Let me say those sweet words again, "He loved me, and gave himself for me." His blood? Yes. His hands, his feet, his side? Yes. His body, his soul? Yes; but you need not say all that; "He gave *himself.*" "Who his own self bare our sins in his own body on the tree." Whatever Christ was in himself, he gave that; he offered himself as a sacrifice for sin. What a wonderful sacrifice! Ten thousand bullocks, myriads of sheep, enough to cover all the pastures of the earth, what would their blood avail? But God, God incarnate, Immanuel, God with us, offers himself. What condescension, what love, what infinite pity, that he should sacrifice himself for his enemies, for those who had broken his holy law!

Christ offered himself alone. He put away sin by the sacrifice of *himself;* not by the sacrifice of his Church, not by the sacrifice of martyrs, not by the offering of wafers and consecrated wine; but by the sacrifice of himself alone. You must not add anything to Christ's sacrifice. Christ does not put away sin through your tears, and your grief, and your merit, and your almsgiving. No, he put away sin by the sacrifice of *himself;* nothing else. You must take nothing from Christ's sacrifice, and you must add nothing to it.

That sacrifice, too, if I read the Greek aright, was *a slain sacrifice,* a bloody sacrifice. Christ gave his life. It is written, "Without shedding of blood is no remission." He shed his blood. "The blood is the life thereof," is true of Christ's sacrifice; for without blood-shedding it would have been of no avail. He poured out his soul unto death. In instituting that dear memorial feast, which you are bidden to observe in remembrance of him, he said, "This is my blood of the new testament, which is shed for many for the remission of sins." The putting away of sin was accomplished by Christ dying in the room, and place, and stead of guilty men. Christ says, "I will take the punishment of sin." He takes it; he bears it on the cross. Sinful man, hear this! Take that fact to be true, and rest your whole soul on it, and you are saved. Christ died for believers. "God so loved the world, that he gave his only begotten Son, that whosoever believeth in him should not perish, but have everlasting life." If you believe in Christ, that is, if you trust him; if you trust him now, if you trust him altogether, if you trust him alone, and say, "There I am resting, believing

that Christ died for me," you are saved; for Christ has put
away your sin; you shall not die. How can a man die when his
sin is put away by Christ's all-sufficient sacrifice?

> "If sin be pardon'd, I'm secure;
> Death hath no sting beside;
> The law gives sin its damning power;
> But Christ, my Ransom, died."

Christ's appearing, then, was that he might, as a High Priest,
present a sacrifice; he presented himself to the death on the
cross; he died, and by that dying he has put away sin.

V. That brings me to my closing point, THE GRAND
ACHIEVEMENT. Christ appeared *"to put away sin."* What
can that mean?

It means, first, that Christ has put away sin *as to its exclusion
of men from God.* Man, by his sin, had made this world so
obnoxious to Jehovah that God could not deal with its in-
habitants apart from Christ's sacrifice. He is infinitely merciful,
but he is also infinitely just; and the world had become so putrid
a thing that he declared that he repented that he had made man
upon the earth. Now this whole world of ours must have gone
down into eternal ruin had not Christ come. John the Baptist
cried, "Behold the Lamb of God, which taketh away the sin of
the world," the whole bulk of it. It was there and then removed at one stroke, so that God could deal with man, could
send an embassage of peace to this poor guilty world, and could
come upon gospel terms of free grace and pardon to deal with
a guilty race. That was done. You may thank God for that.

But there is more wanted than that. When God comes to
deal with men, we find, next, that Christ has for every believer taken away sin *as to its punishment.* I mean what I say.
God cannot punish twice for the same offence; and to lay sin
upon Christ, and then to demand its penalty of those for whom
he stood as Substitute, would be to demand compensation twice
and punishment twice for one offence; but this can never be.

> "Payment God cannot twice demand,
> First at my bleeding Surety's hand,
> And then again at mine."

That were a gross injustice; and the Judge of all the earth must do right. Behold, then, this fact. If thou believest in Christ Jesus, he bore the punishment of thy sin. In that short space upon the tree, the infinity of his nature enabled him to render to God's justice a vindication which is better than if all for whom he died had gone to hell. Had all been lost, God's justice would not have been vindicated so well as when his own dear Son —

> "Bore, that we might never bear,
> His Father's righteous ire."

He has made the law more honourable by his death at its hands than it could have been if all the races of men had been condemned eternally. Oh, soul, if thou believest in Jesus, the chastisement of thy peace was upon him, and with his stripes thou art healed! "He was made a curse for us, as it is written, Cursed is every one that hangeth on a tree." And was he cursed for me, and shall I be cursed, too? That would not be consistent with divine equity. The true believer may plead the justice as well as the mercy of God in the matter of his absolution. If Christ died, then all who were in Christ died with him; and when he rose, they all rose with him; and when God accepted him by raising him from the dead, he accepted all who were in him. Glory be to his holy name!

Further, Christ put away sin, *as to its condemning power.* You have felt the condemning power of sin; I have supposed you have done so. If so, listen. "There is, therefore, now no condemnation to them that are in Christ Jesus." Thou art a sinner, but thy sin is not imputed to thee, but to him who stood as thy Sponsor, thy Paymaster, thy Surety. Thy sins were numbered on the Scapegoat's head of old, even on Christ, the divinely-ordained Substitute for all his people. As David wrote,

"Blessed is the man unto whom the Lord imputeth not iniquity, and in whose spirit there is no guile!" Thy sin doth not condemn thee; for Christ has been condemned in thy stead. "Neither do I condemn thee," saith the Lord; "Go in peace."

Yet once more, sin is put away now *as to its reigning power;* for, if sin be pardoned through the atoning blood, we come to love Christ; and loving Christ, away goes every sin. The man for whom Christ died, who knows it, who knows that Christ put away sin, must love Christ; and loving Christ, he must hate sin, for to love sin and to love Christ at the same time, would be impossible. If he bore my guilt, then I am not my own; for I am bought with a price, even with his most precious blood. He that suffered in my stead shall now my Master be. I lie at his dear feet, and bless his name.

> "Oh, how sweet to view the flowing
> Of his sin-atoning blood,
> With divine assurance knowing
> He has made my peace with God!"

When you get as far as that, then you love Christ, and serve him. I have told you before of the bricklayer who fell off a scaffold, and was taken up so injured that it was seen that he must soon die. A good clergyman, bending over him, said, "My dear man, you had better make your peace with God." The poor fellow opened his eyes, and said, "Make my peace with God, sir? Why, that was done for me more than eighteen hundred years ago by him who took my sin, and suffered in my stead." Thank God for that! I hope that many of you could say the same; you would not then talk about making your peace with God, or about doing something to reconcile you to God. The very thought of adding anything to Christ's finished work, is blasphemy. Believe that he has done all that is required, and rest in it, and be happy all your days.

With this remark I finish. Sin is put away *as to its very existence.* Where has sin gone to when a man believes in Christ? Micah says, "Thou wilt cast all their sins into the depths of the sea," where they will never be fished up again. The devil himself may fish to all eternity, but he will never fish them up again. God has cast the sins of believers into the depths of the sea. Where have they gone? "As far as the east is from the west, so far hath he removed our transgressions from us." How far is the east from the west? Will you go and measure it on the globe? Fly up to the heavens, and see how far you can go east, and how far you can go west. Is there any bound to space? So far has God removed our transgressions from us.

A more wonderful expression is this, "Thou hast cast all my sins behind thy back." Where is that? Where is God's back? Is there any place behind his back? He is everywhere present, and everywhere seen. It must be nowhere at all, then; and our sins are thrown into the nowhere. He that believes in Christ may know of a surety that his iniquities have gone into the nowhere. Listen once more. "In those days, and in that time, saith the Lord, the iniquity of Israel shall be sought for, and there shall be none; and the sins of Judah, and they shall not be found." Thus is sin annihilated for all who trust the Saviour. Listen to Daniel's description of the work of Messiah the Prince, "to finish the trangression, and to make an end of sins." If he has made an end of them, there is an end of them. O my heart, sing hallelujah! Let every beat of my pulse be a hallelujah unto him who has put away sin! Poor sinner, if you are black as the devil with sin, crimson to the very core with iniquity, yet wash in the fountain filled with the blood of the Lamb, and you shall be whiter than snow; for the Lord Jesus, by the sacrifice of himself, hath for ever put away the sin of all who trust him.

Dear hearers, have you laid hold of this great truth? Then I do not care to what sect you belong; and I do not care what your standing in life is; and I do not care what your opinion in politics may be. Has Christ put away your sin? If he has, be as happy as the days are long in summertime; and be as bright as the garden is gay in June. Sing like angels; you have more to sing about than angels have; for never did they taste redeeming grace and dying love. They were never lost, and therefore never found; never enslaved, and therefore never redeemed. God in human flesh has died for you. God loved you so that he would be nailed to a tree for you. You have sinned; but you are today as if you had never sinned. "He that is washed is clean every whit." "And ye are washed." Oh, I say again, let your heart beat hallelujah! Let your pulse seem to say "Bless, bless, bless, bless, bless the Lord!"

"Oh!" says one, in a mournful and sorrowful tone, "I am afraid it is not so with me." Well, then, do not go to sleep tonight till it is. If thou believest in the Lord Jesus Christ, it is so. "Well, I hope that it is so," says one. Away with your hoping! What is the good of that? There are many people that go hoping, hoping, hopping, hopping. Get out of that hoping and hopping; and walk steadily on this sure ground: Christ died for all who believe in him, effectually died, not died according to that theory which teaches that he died no more for Peter than he did for Judas, and died for those who are already in hell as much as he died for those who will be in heaven. The universal theory of the atonement has precious little comfort in it; albeit that Christ's death was universal in the removal of the hindrance to God's dealing on terms of mercy with the world, yet he laid down his life for his sheep. He loved his Church, and gave himself for it. He hath redeemed us from among men, out of men. He hath taken us to be his own by the purchase of his blood; we are redeemed, washed, saved. If this is your case, go home, and be glad; let nobody beat you in holy merriment. There is a passage at the end of the parable of the prodigal that I like very much, "and they began to be merry." The parable does not tell us when they left off being merry; but I suppose they are merry still. I know that, ever since my Father put the ring on my finger, and shoes on my feet, and gave me the kiss of love, and I knew that I was forgiven, I have been merry, and I mean to be merry still, till my merriment is lost in the merriment above, where they keep perpetual holiday, and sing to the praise of the Redeemer, "Thou wast slain, and hast redeemed us to God by thy blood out of every kindred, and tongue, and people, and nation." To him be honour, and glory, and blessing, for ever and ever! Amen.

BIBLIOGRAPHY

Horace Bushnell: *Christ and His Salvation,* New York, 1864, pp. 393-412
G. Campbell Morgan: *Westminster Pulpit,* Vol. I, 1906, No. 52; Vol. IV, 1909, pp. 305-312
Charles H. Spurgeon: *Metropolitan Tabernacle Pulpit,* Vol. VIII, 1862, No. 430, pp. 37-48; Vol. XIII, 1867, No. 759, pp. 373-384; Vol. XVI, 1870, No. 911, pp. 37-48, and No. 962, pp. 649-660; Vol. XXXVII, 1891, No. 2194, pp. 145-156; Vol. XXXVIII, 1892, No. 2283, pp. 553-562

A biographical sketch of Charles H. Spurgeon will be found in *Great Sermons on the Birth of Christ,* pp. 25-27; and also in *Great Sermons on the Resurrection of Christ,* pp. 54-57.

CHRIST OUR SIN-BEARER;
OR, THE NATURE AND SCOPE OF THE ATONEMENT
by
James M. Gray

"Who his own self bare our sins in his own body on the tree, that we, being dead to sins, should live unto righteousness: by whose stripes ye were healed. For ye were as sheep going astray; but are now returned unto the Shepherd and Bishop of your souls." — 1 Peter 2:24,25.

I. *The Nature of the Atonement*

"Who his own self bare our sins in his own body on the tree." Suppose we had just heard these words for the first time; and suppose we had no prejudice or preconceived opinions as to the truth they taught, what idea would we obtain from them? Could the English tongue put the thought of substitutionary or vicarious suffering before us in plainer terms?

To quote the language of one of our theologians: "When a sovereign graciously allows one person who is under no obligation to do so, to discharge a service or suffer a punishment for another on whom such obligation rests, that is substitution. And when that service is discharged or that penalty suffered by the substitute, the service of the suffering becomes vicarious." The second of these two ideas is stated, and the first is clearly implied in these words of Peter: *"Who his own self bare our sins in his own body on the tree."*

This then, is the *nature* of the atonement of Christ; it is substitutionary and vicarious. And the thought is all the more confirmed by the light thrown upon it in the Old Testament. Take the whole sacrificial system of the Mosaic dispensation, for example, which every Bible student knows to have been symbolical of the person and work of Christ. Is it not based on the idea of the substitution of one life in the place of another? The offerer of the sacrifice laid his hand on the head of the victim and confessed his sins over it, thus identifying himself with it in the first instance and transferring his sins to it in the second. Here is substitution, and here is vicarious atonement.

Take the teachings of the prophets, the words of Isaiah particularly, so familiar to us all, and from which Peter quotes:

"He was wounded for our transgressions, he was bruised for our iniquities: the chastisement of our peace was upon him; and with his stripes we are healed. All we like sheep have gone astray; we have turned every one to his own way; and the Lord hath laid on him the iniquity of us all" (53:5,6).

Here again we have substitution and vicarious suffering. Or, take the Psalms, the 32nd, for example:

"Blessed is he whose transgression is forgiven, whose sin is covered. Blessed is the man unto whom the Lord imputeth not iniquity, and in whose spirit there is no guile."

Paul, in the fourth chapter of Romans, quotes these words to show that the psalmist apprehended the great truth of substitution and vicarious suffering, and that he was praising God for the non-imputation of his sin to him because it had already been imputed to another.

Of course, the New Testament is filled with declarations of this same truth. We hear Jesus saying in Matthew:

"The Son of man came not to be ministered unto, but to minister, and to give his life a ransom for many" (20:28).

And in John:

"I am the good shepherd: the good shepherd giveth his life for the sheep" (10:11).

It is the warp and woof of the teachings of Paul:

"Christ hath redeemed us from the curse of the law, being made a curse for us" (Galatians 3:13).

"Whom God hath set forth to be a propitiation through faith in his blood" (Romans 3:25).

"He hath made him to be sin for us, who knew no sin;

that we might be made the righteousness of God in him"
(2 Corinthians 5:21).

But to return to the text. When Peter says that Christ "bare
our sins in his own body on the tree," he means, of course,
that He bare the guilt of those sins which were laid upon Him.
But this is not to say that He suffered the very same sufferings
in kind and degree, or duration which would have been in-
flicted upon us in whose stead He suffered. Doubtless, the truth
is however, that He suffered precisely that suffering which Divine justice demanded of His Divine Person standing in our
place. A suffering which satisfied God's justice and which
rendered the exercise of His love consistent with His righteous
and holy character.

WHO STANDS FOR YOU?

In Dr. Bainbridge's *Around the World Tour of Christian
Missions,* written now twenty years ago, there is a curiously
interesting and suggestive incident.

When in his journey he had reached Tokyo, Japan, intending
to remain there some little time, he was waited upon one morning by an official, with this singular inquiry: *"Who stands for
you?"*

Supposing it to be a question of passports, he presented his,
but that was not what was wanted. He then offered some
letters of introduction he had, but they also were unsatisfactory,
and the question was repeated, *"Who stands for you?"*

It was finally explained that there was an ordinance in that
city to the effect that no foreigner could take up his residence
there for any length of time, unless he provided himself with a
"substitute." And as a matter of fact there were natives who
hired themselves out to foreigners for this purpose. If the
foreigner transgressed any law the substitute suffered the penalty for it. If the penalty were even death, the substitute
suffered death. Dr. Bainbridge secured a substitute, and was
thereafter permitted to remain in peace and security as long as
he chose.

The analogy does not hold good at all points, of course, and, like many another so called "illustration" of divine truth, if pressed too far it may hinder as much as it helps. But in this it is true, that all men are, by nature, alien from God through sin. That their standing before Him, or before His law, is only obtainable through the substitutionary work of His Son. That, (and this by contrast with the present illustration), the merits of His Son are obtainable by faith, and "without money, and without price." And finally, that once obtained, they secure to the believer eternal acceptance, perfect peace, complete satisfaction and glorious liberty.

May the reader of these words believe it and act upon it at once, if already it has not been done! Dr. Bainbridge could not satisfy the law of Tokyo in his own person, and without a substitute must be banished from its privileges. No sinner, such as we all are, can satisfy the law of God in his own person, and without Christ he must *"be punished with everlasting destruction from the presence of the Lord, and from the glory of His power"* (2 Thessalonians 1:9).

II. *The Design of the Atonement*

The design of the atonement is stated in the words: *"That we being dead to sins, should live unto righteousness,"* a two-fold design, as we see. The thought of God was not only punitive but remedial. He gave His Son not only to take away our guilt but to change our lives. Shall we then, say, that the design has both a negative and a positive aspect? Let us consider these words with the greatest carefulness.

1. That we should be *"dead to sins."* Rather a baffling and mysterious phrase this. What does it mean? It is almost identically used of Christ in the sixth chapter of Romans, and if we can grasp the meaning in His case we may in that of His believing people. In what sense is Christ said to have *"died to sin"?* Evidently, in the sense that sin, (not His own sin, for He was sinless, but our sin which He bore), caused Him to be crucified; and that, when once He paid its penalty by death,

it lost the power to bring Him into the place of penalty again.

There is a man in prison, let us say, awaiting the gallows or the electric chair to expiate the crime of murder. But when he has once expiated it, when he once dies in accordance with the law, the crime can never again bring him to judgment. He is dead to it forever, even though afterward were it possible, he should arise from the dead. So in the case of Christ, when He expiated human guilt He did so once and forever, and became dead to it thereafter.

But the believer on Jesus Christ, as we learn from this, and even more plainly from other scriptures, is so identified with Christ in God's purpose, is so entirely one with Him as his representative and substitute, that when Christ died to sin upon the cross the believer also died in Him. And if sin can not again bring his substitute into the place of penalty neither can it bring the one whose representative He was. Hence the significance of that Word in Romans 8:1: "There is therefore now no condemnation to them which are in Christ Jesus." This means no judgment, no penalty, no guilt to them that are in Him, i.e., bound up with Him in identity and substitution.

2. But Peter's phrase is in the plural: "dead to *sins*" — it is not "sin"; and this is even better yet, and more gracious and more satisfying to the soul.

For our present purpose, the difference between "sins" in the plural and "sin" in the singular may be stated thus: "Sin" refers to our sinful nature, the sin *in* which and *into* which we were born, while "sins" refers to the consequences or fruits of that nature in the actual transgressions of our lives.

How wonderful therefore, that the atonement of Christ not only covers our sin but our sins! That in Him we are not only dead to sin in our nature but dead to sins in our everyday life, the transgressions we have committed or even *may* commit! Neither sin nor *sins* can bring the believer on Jesus Christ into the place of penalty in the sense of eternal death. *Chastised* he will be for his sins and his transgressions, chastised it may be even to the extent of the taking away of his physical life (1 Corinthians 11:30), but judged in the sense of eternal death he can not be. The merits of the sacrifice of Christ have been imputed unto him not only for the putting away of sin but *sins*.

3. But the thought is not yet quite complete. Christ's work on the cross merited for us something more, even the gift of the Holy Spirit and all the operations of His grace within us. The moment we receive Christ by faith, we do also receive the Holy Spirit to dwell within us, regenerating us, creating within us a clean heart and renewing within us a right spirit, so that we become "dead to sins" not only in the judicial or imputed sense just referred to, but in the actual and experimental sense as well. That is not to say that sin becomes eradicated from our hearts and no longer dwells even latently within us (1 John 1:8); but that its power over us is broken. We do really come to hate the sins we used to love and to love the holiness we used to hate.

4. It is just here that the *positive* aspect of the design of the atonement presents itself. Christ died not merely that we should be dead to sins judicially and experimentally but that we might *"live unto righteousness."* As our substitute and representative He both died *and rose again.* And when He arose from the dead it was to live an entirely new kind of life as the God-man. New with reference to His relationship to God and to the question of sin. He had been obedient even unto death. He had glorified the Father. He had finished the work given Him to do. He had put away sin. The cross was behind Him and the throne of glory was before Him.

Now Paul tells us also in the sixth chapter of Romans already quoted that if we are united with Christ in the likeness of His death, we are also in the likeness of His resurrection. If we died with Him we also live with Him.

This is not merely that we *shall* live with Him by and by in a physical state of resurrection glory, but that we live with Him *now* in a spiritual state of resurrection glory. The death He died He died unto sin once, but the life He liveth, He liveth unto God. He liveth it unto God *now.* Even so we are to reckon ourselves not only to be dead indeed unto sin as we have already considered, but alive unto God in Christ Jesus (6:11), alive *now*.

In an imputed or judicial sense then, every believer in Christ Jesus is now walking before God in newness of life. Whether he is aware of it or not, whether it is the conscious possession of his soul or not, whether it is clearly manifested in his experience and daily history or not, he is now alive unto God, whereas before he was dead. He is now living a resurrection life in Christ his substitute, and with Whom he is identified as his representative. His is a new life compared with what it was before. Like that of Christ, new in relation to God and to the question of sin. It is a life unto righteousness in an imputed sense. Death, the penalty for sin is past, and glory is in the future.

5. Nor is it *only* in an imputed sense that this is true; but, as in the other half of this declaration, in an experimental sense as well. As we have just seen, the Holy Spirit within the regenerated man, not only enables him to hate sin but to love holiness and follow after it. No longer yields he his "members (as) servants to uncleanness and to iniquity unto iniquity," but as "servants to righteousness unto holiness." He crucifies the flesh with its affections and lust. He not only puts off all these: "Anger, wrath, malice, railing, shameful speaking out of his mouth"; but he puts on, as the elect of God, "a heart of compassion, kindness, humility, meekness, long-suffering, and above all these, love, which is the bond of perfection."

It is thus that *"by His stripes we are healed."* Perfectly healed. God having begun the good work in us perfects it until the day of Jesus Christ (Philippians 1:6). The man who receives Christ as his Saviour, and confesses Him as his Lord, need not fear as to whether he shall be "able to hold out." He need not wonder whether he will be tomorrow the same wilful sinner he was today. Let him commit himself unto God, let him take of the means of grace, let him feed on His Word, and wait. It is thus by *"His"* stripes, we are healed.

My sins laid open to the rod,
   The back by which from the law was free;
And the Eternal Son of God
   Received the stripes once due to me.

Nor beam was in His eye, nor mote;
   Nor laid to Him was any blame:
And yet His cheeks for me were smote —
   The cheeks that never blushed for shame.

I pierced those sacred hands and feet
   That never touched or walked in sin;
I broke the heart that only beat
   The souls of sinful men to win.

That sponge of vinegar and gall
   Was placed by me upon His tongue;
And when derision mocked his call
   I stood that mocking crowd among.

And yet His blood was shed for me,
   To be of sin the double cure;
And balm there flows from Calvary's tree
   That heals my guilt and makes me pure.

III. *The Need of the Atonement*

"For ye were as sheep going astray."

1. Ye were "going *astray*." The Greek word in this case (planaomai) like so many other words in that wonderful tongue, is full of figurative suggestion.

It gives us not only the picture of a wanderer, but an erratic wanderer. One who is moving about without any fixed destination. He is a wanderer lost in winding courses of labyrinthian ways. The idea of mental aberration is in the word, and with aberration, agitation. One may be mentally deranged without any conscious disturbance of his peace, and some of the most confirmed of the insane are apparently among the most happy of mortals, but it is not so in the case of a soul which, while normal in other respects, is astray from God. "The wicked are like the troubled sea; for it can not rest; . . . There is no peace, saith my God, to the wicked" (Isaiah 57:20,21,R.V.).

And finally, the thought of deception is in this word, i.e., the idea that the sinner has been seduced into his present straying and lost condition, precisely as we read in the story of the fall.

How perfectly true are all these figures to describe the sinner as we know him, as we have known ourselves! Seduced by Satan, he is now, like Cain, *"a fugitive and a wanderer in the earth."* His mind reprobate, his eyes blind, his soul restless and ill at ease, seeking good first in this direction and then that, and finding it not.

2. Ye were *"as sheep"* going astray. A sheep goes astray differently from any other animal, it is said. When once it wanders away its tendency is to pursue its wanderings, never returning again of its own accord. Should it ever come back, the shepherd must go out after it and bring it back.

The domestic animal, the cat, the dog, even the horse will return to its old home, if given liberty to do so. Yea, *"the ox knoweth his owner, and the ass his master's crib,"* but the sheep does not know and does not seem to consider. Hence the pathos of those parables of the 15th chapter of Luke and the 10th chapter of John.

What a type of the lost world have we here! There are those, wise in some other things, who are foolish enough to say that the world does not need a Saviour. Left to itself, it is affirmed, it will return to God of its own accord. Perhaps it has never wandered, but if it has, let it alone and it will come back again. Education will bring it back. Experience will bring it back. In fact, it is going back all the time, these prophets say. The world is growing better and better with every generation or every century, is their unthinking song.

And this in the face of history. Did not God leave the world to itself for 4,000 years to prove it whether it would return or not? Did He not send His prophets to it, rising up early and sending them, and with what result? Did not His merciful judgments fall upon it, and was not His goodness flowing towards it in streams of benefaction without ceasing, and did the world return and repent?

What is the witness of the centuries? What is the story they have to tell from the garden of Eden to the garden of Gethsemane? Did the world return to God at any time between the defeat of the first Adam and the victory of the Second? Had the world by searching found Him out in all these days?

HISTORY AND REASON CORROBORATING

Let the first century of the present era answer. When Jesus came what a paradox did the world present! It had reached its highest point of intellectual development, for it was the Augustan age. But it had reached its lowest point of moral degradation for it was the age of Nero, and of Herod, and the age that crucified the only holy man Who ever lived. It was going astray, the world. Like a sheep it was going astray.

And is it different now, or will it be different in time to come? *"What saith the Scriptures?"* Christ teaches that the tares will grow with the wheat till the end of the age (Matthew 13). Paul teaches that in the last days perilous times shall come (2 Timothy 3). Peter teaches that *"the earth and the works therein shall be burned up"* (2 Peter 3). All the New Testament prophets are a unit here.

But the world, in this sense, is only an aggregation of individual souls. If the world is going astray every individual soul out of Christ is going astray. If the world is like a sheep going astray every individual soul out of Christ is like a sheep going astray. If the world is getting farther and farther from God, every individual soul out of Christ is getting farther and farther from God.

God's Word needs no corroboration on this point from either history or reason, and yet the latter corroborates it as well as the former. For example, is it not an essential characteristic of moral evil that it grows by what it feeds upon? And is it not one of its fatalities that it renders impotent the very faculties by which alone it can be eradicated? Even Maurice, in his skeptical fulminations on future punishment, admitted that there were times when the possibilities of resistance in a human will to the loving will of God seemed to him, even in his own case, almost infinite. Had he not been wiser to have left out *"almost"?*

And Canon Kingsley, writing from the same point of view, affirms: "I believe it possible for me and for other men, to commit acts of sin against light and knowledge which would plunge me into endless abysses of probably increasing sin, and therefore of probably increasing and endless punishment."

"Can the Ethiopian change his skin, or the leopard his spots? then may ye also do good that are accustomed to do evil . . . saith the Lord" (Jeremiah 13:23,25).

What a motive to stir men to heed the warning; "Now is the accepted time"! and to obey the exhortation: "Today, if ye will hear his voice, harden not your heart"!

IV. *The Result of the Atonement.*
"But are now returned unto the Shepherd and Bishop of your souls."

Of course, Peter is speaking to Christians throughout the whole of this text, as indeed the whole of the epistle. He has in mind only such as have believed on Jesus Christ and have been regenerated by His Spirit, when he says, ye *"are now returned."*

But that word *"returned,"* how much it means! If one has returned to a place, the presumption is that he has been at that place before. And if one has returned to God it would seem that he had been with God before. But whenever, it may be asked, was man at home with God? Whenever was he in fellowship with *"the Shepherd and Bishop"* of his soul?

The only answer to this is the garden of Eden. Man was at home with God there. He had fellowship with the Shepherd and Bishop of his soul before he fell, and while he was still innocent. But he has had no fellowship since then.

The question therefore arises, whether the reconciliation effected by the atonement puts the believer back into as desirable a relationship with God as our first parents knew, prior to their sin?

The answer is, "Yes, and even a more desirable relationship." The relationship of Eden was based on a contingency. It was, "Do this, and live," or rather, "Fail to do this, and die." And man failed to do it, he failed to obey, and he died. But our new relationship through Christ is based on no contingency. It is believe, and live.

The noblest quality of man is his free-will, by virtue of which he attains a certain independence even from God Himself. But this his greatest glory is at the same time, his greatest peril. The prerogative is priceless, but as Tertullian once said, it can only be obtained at the hazard of an everlasting downfall. Free-will in the person of the first Adam met that fate.

The great Huxley is reported to have said, that if there were some being, or some power, to whom he could turn over his nature, by which of course he meant his will, to have it regulated like a clock, and kept regulated, he would hand it over immediately and absolutely.

This agnostic did not know that there was such a Being to Whom his nature, or his will, might be thus surrendered, to be set right and to be kept right.

That being is the Eternal Son of God, Who cries, and need such as Huxley's, is the occasion of His cry: "Come unto me, all ye that labor and are heavy-laden, and I will give you rest. Take my yoke upon you, and learn of me; for I am meek and lowly in heart: and ye shall find rest unto your souls" (Matthew 11:28,29).

The man who believes on Jesus Christ in the Gospel sense of that term commits and surrenders himself to Him absolutely, eternally, irreversibly. And Jesus Christ takes him and regulates him. He regenerates him, in other words, and then keeps him regenerated by the renewing of his mind, through the Holy Ghost. And the man finds rest, and he has peace.

JAMES M. GRAY
(1851-1935)

The future Dean and President of the Moody Bible Institute, James M. Gray, was born in New York City in 1851, though he moved to New England when he was still in his twenties. Of the early days of Dr. Gray very little is known, and he never talked about his years at college, or how he came to enter the denomination to which he belonged. The one church of which he was pastor, from 1879 to 1894, was the First Reformed Episcopal Church of Boston, Massachusetts. There he became a close co-worker of that noble man of God, A. J. Gordon, and taught a number of classes in the newly-organized Gordon Bible College. His great gifts for teaching the Bible were early recognized by Mr. Moody, who brought him to the Northfield Conferences in 1895, and then persuaded him to teach for a certain period each year in the then developing Bible Institute in Chicago. From 1894, Dr. Gray devoted all of his time, until his permanent association with the Moody Bible Institute, to Bible conferences. Finally, he was prevailed upon to move to Chicago, and identify himself with what was called, even before the great evangelist's death, the Moody Bible Institute. He served as the Dean of the Institute from 1904 to 1923, and as President from 1923 to 1934. In 1915, he assumed the editorship of the *Christian Workers' Magazine,* later known as the *Moody Monthly,* and continued to be the Editor-in-Chief for the next twenty years.

In spite of his heavy duties, both as an administrator and teacher, Dr. Gray authored over twenty different volumes, two of which had a very wide circulation. His *Synthetic Bible Studies,* first appearing in 1900, went through a number of editions, and was translated into some of the major European languages. In 1915, Revell published his *Christian Workers' Commentary,* which still is being considerably used. Dr. Gray served as one of Editors on the Tercentenary Bible Committee, which produced the so-called *1911 Bible,* projected by the Oxford University Press; and was one of the seven original editors of the famous *Scofield Reference Bible*. He also composed a few really worthwhile hymns, two of which are found in the current larger hymn books, "Nor Silver nor Gold," and, "Only a Sinner Saved by Grace."

Dr. Gray did not hesitate to enter the arena of theological disputes, when he felt so led. Probably the most influential single exposure of the errors of Dr. Fosdick was in his widely-quoted brochure, "The Deadline of Doctrine around the Church." He wrote extensively against Russellism, Evolution, Christian Science, a World Church, Modernism, etc.

In addition to his work at the Institute, and extensive writing, Dr. Gray was the leading speaker at many Bible conferences throughout his long ministry. In a note written to him by the late Dr. Gresham Machen, in 1929, when, remember, Dr. Gray was then seventy-eight years of age, he told his older and equally courageous defender of the faith of the great blessing he had received from an address by Dr. Gray given at Princeton Seminary one April evening of that year, "Your address on Tuesday evening at the Seminary seemed to me one of the most truly eloquent things that I have heard for a long time. Even the reading, with such impressive simplicity of that wonderful chapter of Nehemiah was of more value than whole volumes of ordinary sermons; and the address following was quite in keeping."

Dr. Gray, as has been said, rarely referred to any experiences or inner conflicts of his own and, therefore, the following words of his in a letter written to an unidentified correspondent, who asked some questions about the working habits of the President of the Moody Bible Institute, are significant. These words were written when Dr. Gray was eighty years of age. "You noted that my days were lived evenly, and as explaining that I may say, and perhaps I ought to say, that years ago I took Paul's admonition in 1 Corinthians 10:31 as a life motto, and the measure in which by divine grace I have lived up to it is, I believe, the secret of what you observed.

"There is also one other scripture which for a third of a

century has gone with it in perceptibly moulding my life. It is the word of our Lord in John 12:26. 'If any man serve me him will my Father honor.'

"These are two great rules of being for a young Christian believer, whose results are to be coveted above everything else in the world, and I commend them to you."

Dr. Gray died Sept. 21, 1935, at the age of eighty-four.

THE VICARIOUS SUFFERER;
OR, HOPE IN THE CROSS
by
Arthur T. Pierson

"Who his own self bare our sins in his own body on the tree, that we, being dead to sins, should live unto righteousness; by whose stripes ye were healed." — 1 Peter 2:24

"He bare our sins." Round about those four words the whole system of redemption might be constructed. They tell us in language that a little child can understand, the whole mystery of the sacrifice of Christ for the sins of men. "He bare our sins." How simple are these words, and yet how sublimely full of meaning.

One cannot read or hear them without thinking of a load. Sin is represented, from the beginning of the Word of God to its close, as a heavy burden; — a burden, first of all, of conscious guilt; a burden, second, of tyrannical power and despotic control; a burden, third, of penalty. And this threefold burden of the penalty, the power, and the guilt of sin, Jesus Christ has borne in His own body on the tree that you and I may no longer bear it. That is, in a few simple words, the doctrine of substitutionary sacrifice.

We can trace this burden bearing of the unforgiven sinner throughout the history of the race. Just as soon as Cain had committed the first murder of history, and the voice of his brother's blood cried from the ground to God for vengeance, God appeared to Cain in awful rebuke of his guilt, and the murderer said, "My punishment is greater than I can bear." It is a curious but a significant fact that the same word that is here translated "punishment" may be rendered "sin," and

197

is so translated in the margin in some cases. Cain's sense of sin carried with it a sense of overwhelming load — guilt, and power, and penalty, all at once; and so that first sin, committed after the fall in Eden, which has a definite record in Holy Scripture, wrings out from the transgressor that confession of deep despair, "My sin is greater than I can bear."

The sin of every evildoer is greater than he can bear. If your sin were left on your head, and heart, and conscience, it would sink you to the deepest hell. You would have to bear the load through all the years of your mortal experience, and then, when you toppled from the verge of life into the great chasm of the hereafter, you would go down, down, for ever, falling under the weight of that sin into the greater distance and alienation from God.

God foresaw that sin was going to be a heavier burden than any man could bear, and so He laid it on One Who is mighty to save, and Who, upon the broad shoulders of omnipotence, could sustain that burden. He put Himself beneath that awful load. He laid upon Himself not only the sins of those who shall finally be saved, but, however much unbelief may make the sacrifice of Christ unavailing in any case, there are two passages of Holy Scripture that leave no doubt that Christ assumed the load of sin and guilt, even in behalf of those who will not have Him to reign over them. In the first chapter of John and the twenty-ninth verse, when John the Baptist pointed at Jesus, he said, "Behold the Lamb of God, that beareth away the sin *of the world.*" Then, in the first epistle of John, in the second chapter, we read these words: "And he is the propitiation for our sins, and not for ours only, but also for *the whole world*" (literally rendered). So there must be some sense in which the sacrifice of Christ is *sufficient* for all, though it is *efficient* only to those who believe.

Let us seek, first of all, to get into our minds and hearts this great conception, that Jesus Christ came into the world, and put Himself not only under the load of one sinner, but under the load of the accumulated guilt of the whole world;

that He made a sacrifice that was so absolutely satisfactory to God that, if the whole world had believed, the whole world might have been saved. If that is not the gospel it is difficult to determine what is the meaning of such plain words as have been quoted.

In order that we may see further into the deep lesson of these four words, "He bare our sins," let us note in what sense these and similar words are used in the body of this Holy Book, by comparing Scripture with Scripture. Every book is interpreted according to the usage of language, or the way in which words are generally employed by its author; and, if you ask what these words mean which form the outlines of the body of all Christian theology, the only way to find out is to examine in what sense the Author of this book uses such words in other parts of this volume.

If we thus examine, from Genesis to Revelation, we shall find *four senses* in which the words "bearing sin," are used: First, *representation;* second, *identification;* third, *substitution;* and fourth, *satisfaction.* If we take those four conceptions, — representation — one standing as a representative before God; identification — one being made identical with those he represents; substitution — one substituted in the place or stead of others; and satisfaction — the furnishing of a satisfying atonement in behalf of others, — you have the scope of the meaning of these four words.

It may be well to take some illustrations from the blessed Word of God, to show the uses to which these words are thus put. In the twenty-eighth chapter of the Book of Exodus we shall find one of the early instances of this usage. In the thirty-eighth verse we read — with regard to the fore-front of the mitre on which were written or engraven the words "Holiness to the Lord," and which fore-front was bound round the edge of the mitre, and occupied a place immediately in front of and above the fore-head of the high-priest: — "And it" (that is, the fore-front with this inscription) "shall be upon Aaron's fore-head, that Aaron may *bear the iniquity* of the holy things, which the children of Israel shall hallow in all their holy gifts; and it shall be always upon his forehead, that they may be accepted before the Lord." It is very plain that here the words, "bear the iniquity of the holy things," are used in the sense of representation. Here was the great camp of Israel. They were coming up to offer various gifts and sacrifices before the Lord, and none of those sacrifices were perfect in His eyes, for they were all offered by sinners and contaminated by the touch of their guilt and uncleanness. When Aaron put on the fore-front of the mitre, and went up before the Lord, it was as though he was declaring that he was consecrated as perfectly holy unto the service of God. He stood for the people, as representing them. He represented the offerers with their gifts; he represented the consecrated gifts with all their imperfections; but he went to plead before the Lord that they might be accepted, notwithstanding the contamination of sin and selfishness. And we see in this very plainly, someone who was far beyond Aaron our great High Priest, and who can truly claim absolute holiness to the Lord, and in whom there is no sin to be atoned for on His own part before He can atone for the sins of the people. And when our blessed Master appears as our High Priest in the presence of God, His perfection makes up for the imperfection of our holiest sacrifices and offerings, and they are accepted before the Lord for the sake of His mediation. So we get here the first notion — that which lies at the bottom — of bearing iniquity. It is representation. It suggests the High Priest, as the type of our Lord, — one man standing for others in a representative capacity, and doing for them, and in their behalf, what shall be accepted before the Lord.

II.   The second thought connected with the idea of bearing sin is the idea of identification. You will find an illustration of this in the eighth chapter of the Gospel according to Matthew, and in the seventeenth verse, where we read: "Himself took our iniquities, and *bare our sicknesses.*" Here is the same verb, translated "bare" in the text — "bare our sins." St. Ambrose called the eighth chapter of Matthew, *"Scriptura miraculosa,"* or the miraculous Scripture. It follows immediately on the close of the sermon on the mount, which occupies the fifth, sixth, and seventh chapters; and the eighth chapter seems to be intended to place the sanction of divine authority and power on what Christ had spoken as God's prophet. We are told, in the close of the seventh chapter, that He taught as one "having authority, and not as the scribes." He did not refer men to the Holy Scriptures simply, but He declared, "I say unto you," as though He were, and as indeed He was, the Author of the very law, Himself. And therefore, in order that He might back up His authority for such teaching as man had never taught, by works of power such as no man had ever wrought, there are grouped together in the eighth chapter of Matthew representative cases of miraculous healing.

First, there is a leper who comes to Him and says, "Lord, if thou wilt, thou canst make me clean." And Christ put forth His hand, and touched him, and said, "I will; be thou clean." And immediately his leprosy was cleansed. Then the second miracle is wrought on the man who had the palsy, and whom Christ immediately cured, so that he rose and walked. The third miracle is performed on Simon Peter's wife's mother, who was sick of a fever. He took her hand, and fever left her: "and she arose, and ministered to her household." Then the fourth great miracle is the casting out of the demons from those that were possessed. To the Jew, all diseases had a *typical* character. He saw in various forms of disease the curse of God, and the typical representation of the guilt and power of sin. Leprosy was, to the Jew, a walking parable of death and judgment. Palsy was, to him, a representation in type of a moral inability — the loss of power to do the will of God. Fever represented the rage and fury of contending passions and lusts; and demoniacal possession represented a human soul under the complete dominion of the devil. How wonderfully Jesus, in these four great representative miracles, demonstrated His power to cure all the diseases of sin. Have you the leprosy of guilt? He can cleanse. Do you feel the impotence of inability? He can remove it. Have you the fever of malignant dispositions and terrible passions? He can quiet and quell that fever heat. Are you a slave of the devil? He can break your bonds.

In the midst of this chapter that contains these great miracles of healing there is a quotation from Isaiah: "Himself took our infirmities and bare our sicknessnesses." And if you compare the fifty-third of Isaiah you will see that sickness must here be the representative type of iniquity, the diseases of the body representing the diseases of the soul. How did Christ take those infirmities? How did He bear those sicknesses? By identifying Himself with the sinner and the sick. How beautifully pathetic is His whole conduct! When the leper came, and, kneeling before Him, besought Him, "Lord, if Thou wilt, Thou canst make me clean," we are told that Jesus put forth His hand and *touched* him, saying, "I will; be thou clean." There was no apparent need to touch him. He had only to say, "I will; be thou clean," and the same fiat that, in the darkness of the first creation, said "Let light be," so that light was, might have said also, "Let the leper be cleansed," and he would have been clean. But why did Christ put forth His hand and touch him? Remember that a leper, according to the law of Moses, when he went into the midst of clean people was to cry, "Unclean, unclean," and to have his head bowed down and a staff in his hand, as though to prepare the people for his approach, and to prevent anyone from possibly touching him. This leper whom Christ healed probably had not felt the touch of a clean human hand during all the days of his leprosy. Everybody shrank from him; everybody avoided him, and got out of his way when he cried and when they saw him coming. But Jesus drew near, and put out His divine hand, and touched him, and that touch must have been almost as grateful as the word of healing. Moreover, remember this: that touch *made Jesus Christ, Himself, ceremonially unclean.* The law of Moses, as given us in the fifth chapter of Leviticus, commanded that no one should touch an unclean person or thing, and that if he did so he should himself become unclean. The touch of a leper made a man for the time being, as it were, himself a leper. Our Lord wanted to show that leper that he was identified with his sickness and disease, and so He touched him and took, as it were, the level of ceremonial uncleanness alongside of him. I do not otherwise understand that touch of Christ. It is one of the sweetest and most beautiful incidents of which we read in the gospel.

There is a story about Hindoo mothers that a kind of disease sometimes takes hold upon their children, the remedy for which is so severe that it is not safe to administer it to the child directly; but, if the mother takes it herself, it passes into her circulation, and then as she nurses the child at her breast, the medicine which she has taken, modified by the action of her own system, and imparting healing qualities to the nutritious milk with which she nourishes her babe, saves the child's life. Our Lord took upon Him our infirmities and bare our sicknesses. Like that mother identified with her child, He chose to be identified with us. Do you shrink at the thought that he became ceremonially unclean when He touched the leper? The Bible tells us that He was *"made sin for us, though He knew no sin,"* — that God counted Him as a sinner and treated Him as a sinner when He offered up His sacrificial atonement. He took the sinner's place; He was identified with the sinner, and He stooped down to the level of the sinner's guilt, that He might lift the load from the sinner's heart and conscience.

III. So we come to the third thought, *substitution.* That thought is presented very plainly in the ceremonies of the Day of Atonement, in the sixteenth chapter of Leviticus. At the twenty-first verse, we read: "And Aaron shall lay both his hands upon the head of the live goat, and confess over him all the iniquities of the children of Israel, and all their transgressions, in their sins, putting them upon the head of the goat; and the goat shall *bear upon him all their iniquities* unto a land not inhabited." It is impossible to read those words without the impression that Moses intended to represent that scapegoat, *Azazel,* or goat of "removal," as a substitute for the sinners themselves. This double sacrifice of the great day of atonement can never lose interest to a true child of God. How vivid is the picture of atoning love there set before us! Two kids of the same age and undistinguishable from each other, one slain that by the shedding of blood remission of sin may be indicated, and the other brought alive into the presence of the Lord; Aaron, confessing his own sins and the sins of the people, and laying both hands on the head of the live goat, and, as the Jewish rabbis tell us, pressing hard on the head of the goat to indicate the weight of sin, — that goat, by the hand of a fit man, is led away from the presence of the camp out into an uninhabited place where he can no longer hear the bleating of others of the flock from which he has been withdrawn, or the noise of the camp in the service of worship, which might draw him back. There in the desert place he wanders about, never finding his way back to the camp, and so never bringing back to the thoughts of the people the sins that have been confessed upon his head. How plain it is what John meant when he pointed to Jesus Christ, and exclaimed, "Behold the Lamb of God, that taketh away, — *beareth* away the sin of the world."

What has become of your sin, believer? It was confessed, laid heavily, on the head of Jesus Christ as God's goat of Removal, and He went away, as it were into the uninhabited place, and thus bore your sins out of your sight, and out of God's sight, and they never shall be brought back by Him, either before your eyes or before God's eyes. *You* may bring them back by your unbelief; you may take a forgiven sin, a pardoned iniquity, and bring it up before yourself, and put it between you and God, but God will never do it, and Christ will never do it, and the Holy Ghost will never do it, for those sins are buried out of God's sight as in the depths of the sea — put behind His back as no longer to be seen, — borne into the wilderness never to be brought back into the camp.

Here is God's double substitution; Christ was the slain goat and the goat, Azazel, for He represented both the expiation for sin, and its removal from before the face of God.

IV. Now once more: *satisfaction.* Where shall we find the words of the text used plainly in the sense of satisfaction? In the 53rd chapter of Isaiah; and it is impossible for a candid student of the Word of God to escape the obvious force of these words. We read, "All we like sheep have gone astray, and have turned everyone of us to his own way, and the Lord hath laid on Him the iniquity of us all;" and, again, "Surely he hath borne our grief and carried our sorrows: He was wounded for our transgressions, He was bruised for our iniquities: the chastisement of our peace was upon Him, and with His stripes we are healed."

There are some who deny all real substitution, and say that Christ did not bear human sin except as an *example* or *martyr.* But the Word of God says, "The chastisement of our peace was upon Him;" that is to say, we had lost peace with God; we were in a condition of alienation and rebellion; and there could be no peace between God and rebels; but the chastisement that Christ endured for us restored peace between us and God. And, as though to be still more explicit, "With His stripes we are healed." The word translated "stripes" does not refer to the applying of the scourge to the back of the victim, but to the marks or wales left by the scourge. You look at Christ, and you see the marks of scourging on His back; by those stripes your healing comes. God is a just God. He does not lay your sin on Jesus, and then lay your sin on you too. If you, by faith in Christ, embracing and accepting His mediation, partake of the benefits and blessings of His death, you can look on the very wounds left on His back by the scourge, or the very wounds left in His hands and feet by the nails, and in His side by the spear, and you may say "Bless God, I am healed because He was wounded; His stripes are my healing." So Peter says in the text that He Himself "bare our sins in His own body on the tree, that we, being dead to sins, should live unto righteousness, by whose stripes ye were healed."

That sacrifice of Jesus Christ must be appropriated by faith, to be of any benefit in the salvation of a human soul. If we were left to the testimony of John, that Christ bare the sin of the whole world, we might conceive of universal salvation as the consequence of His death. But Christ Himself, the very Lamb of God, said to the Jews, "If ye believe not that I am He, ye shall die in your sins, and whither I go ye cannot come." The possibility of universal salvation is shut out from our creed by the very words of the atoning Saviour. These are not any theologian's limitations; they are bounds set on His own work by Himself. The very Redeemer, who bowed beneath the weight of human sin and sorrow to lift the intolerable load from you, says, with awful solemnity and pathos, "If ye believe not that I am He, ye shall die in your sins, and whither I go ye cannot come." Let us look back to the thought that met us at the beginning, and see what this means. Sin is a load, an awful load, an indescribable load, a load that sinks the sinner to a hopeless perdition. Jesus Christ says, "If ye believe not that I am He, ye shall die with your sins yet upon you." And what will be the consequence? You will sink, and whither He has gone you cannot come. Where has Christ gone? He has not sunk beneath, as one borne down by a burden of guilt. He has risen above. No load of sin is on Him. He ascended up on high. When the unforgiven sinner dies there can be no ascent; it must be descent. The load of sin is on him, and he gravitates toward perdition, and so it is true of him: "Whither I go ye cannot come." "I go up, ye go down. I go without a load to my Father; you go with a load to your father, the devil." Notwithstanding Christ's sacrifice, guilt, power, penalty yet lie on everyone who does not believe in and accept Him as Saviour. That is the dark and terrible side of this great subject.

How immense is the responsibility of hearing this gospel. Thousands of people gather here within the sound of these four words that tell the simple fact of a provided salvation. It is a tremendous thought that you may hear this gospel message, and yet go down to the depths of perdition like Judas, with the sin of the rejection of Christ added to every other sin to weigh your soul down. In the thirty-third chapter of Ezekiel, it is written: "Son of man, I have set thee a watchman unto the house of Israel; therefore thou shalt hear the word at my mouth and warn them from me. If thou warn the wicked of his way to turn from it; if he do not turn from his way, he shall die in his iniquity; but thou hast delivered thy soul." He who gives you the word of warning and the word of invitation, may solemnly wash His hands clean of your blood. He has no more responsibility for the loss of your soul. The load of your sin rests heavily upon yourself. Whom will you have to bear it? Will you let Him bear it, or will you bear it yourself? If He bears it, released from the load, you rise as He rose, to the presence of the Father, justified and sanctified. If you will bear it, notwithstanding that He offers to bear it for you, you shall die in your sins, and whither He goes you cannot go.

Doubtless many of you have seen that very simple device for the instruction of children, where three crosses are represented. Over one cross are the words, "In, not on." Over another cross are the words, "On, not in." Over a third cross, "On and in." The first cross with the words, "In, not on," represents the penitent thief. Sin was in him, but it was not laid on him, for he trusted in Jesus Christ. The third cross, "On and in," represents the impenitent thief. His sin was in him, and it was also on him. But the other cross, "On, not in," represents Jesus. No sin in Him, but sin laid on Him. What was represented by the three crosses on Calvary is the picture and parable of all history. Jesus was there in the midst, the penitent and believing thief on one side, and the impenitent and scoffing thief on the other. From Christ's right hand went up a soul to Paradise; from Christ's left hand went down a soul to perdition. And it has been so all the way through the annals of the race. Christ is set forth here tonight, crucified for you. On one side there are believing souls that are going to Paradise; on the other side, unbelieving souls that are going to perdition, *for a man may go to hell from the side of a crucified Jesus.*

If his will were still his own, the risk of loss would be his own. But since his will has been handed over to Jesus Christ, he is persuaded that He is able to keep that which has been committed unto him against that day (2 Timothy 1:12).

But there is something more than bare commitment and preservation here. The One to Whom we are returned is *"the Shepherd and Bishop of our souls."* A shepherd not only keeps his sheep, but tends and feeds it. He causes it to lie down in green pastures and leads it beside still waters. He restores it when wounded. He comforts it in danger. He defends it when attacked. He showers his love upon it. His goodness towards it never fails. All this our reconciled God and Saviour is, and does, to us. All this is involved in our being returned to Him; all this is included in the work of the atonement, and all this has been purchased for us by the merits of His shed blood.

Who would not commit himself unto Him to be saved, and to be kept?

BIBLIOGRAPHY

R. Eyton: *The True Life,* London, 1889, pp. 49-60
James M. Gray: *Salvation from Start to Finish,* Chicago, 1911, pp. 35-52
Charles Moinet: *The "Good Cheer" of Jesus* Christ, London, 1893, pp. 35-47
Arthur T. Pierson: *The Hopes of the Gospel,* New York, 1896, pp. 85-98
Charles H. Spurgeon: *Metropolitan Tabernacle Pulpit,* Vol. 19, 1873, No. 1143, pp. 649-660, Vol. 48, 1902, No. 2790, pp. 361-371

ARTHUR T. PIERSON
(1837-1911)

Arthur T. Pierson same from a long line of New England settlers. The first of this line, Abraham Pierson, arrived at Plymouth, Massachusetts, in 1639, and for forty years was the leader of a band of colonists who founded a number of towns in Connecticut and New Jersey. Arthur Tappan was born in New York City, March 6, 1837, and was so thoroughly grounded in the Greek language while attending the Mount Washington Collegiate Institute, that he was able to read the Greek New Testament when ten years old. After four years at Hamilton College, Clinton, New York (1853-1857), he enrolled in Union Theological Seminary, graduating in 1860, during which time he sat under such distinguished professors as Henry Boyton Smith and Thomas H. Skinner. During his first year at Union, the great revival of 1857 was experienced, in which he became earnestly active. Pierson began preaching at the age of twenty-one, and was called to the First Congregational Church of Binghamton, New York, September 5, 1860. During his ministry there, he suffered many hardships, the salary was seldom paid in full, and often the family was reduced to a diet of pea soup. During this time, however, he began to write for various periodicals, and thus began a rich literary career. From August 1863 to 1869 he was the pastor of the church at Waterford, New York. It was during these years that he underwent two experiences that permanently stamped his life. After a rather prolonged period of doubt, he himself, wrote: "My gloom lasted for days, but was then dispersed by a most marked communication of the Holy Spirit, conducting me to a full assurance of faith. It was an uncommon experience of the grace of God." His study of Christian evidences led him to say: "My reason was convinced at that time largely by the argument from prophecy. I came to the conclusion that the Bible is indeed the Word of God and I was prepared to receive it, with all its apparent errors and contradictions, and to wait calmly for their explanation either here or hereafter. It was a great day for me when I learned to stand on the immutable Word of the immutable God, on the inspired Word of the inspiring God. This Word has brought to millions salvation and sanctification and no weapon that has been formed against it shall prosper. . . . I was now prepared to expect some mystery in God's Word, as I saw that otherwise I would be claiming equality with Him. I found that to understand the Bible rightly I must be taught by the Spirit of God and not lean to my own understanding."

It was during this same pastorate that for the first time a missionary fire was kindled in the pastor's heart, leading him to read extensively in missionary history and in the field of comparative religions. He himself said of this period, "I wanted power in my ministry to convert souls at home, but I could get no peace with God until I reconsidered the entire question. I fell on my knees before God and askd Him to forgive me for the superficial manner in which I had considered the claims of the world upon me when I was in the Theological Seminary. I told Him that if He called me now to the foreign field, I would leave my pastorate, and with my family, consecrate myself to this work." But the Lord had other plans for this young man.

In 1869, Mr. Pierson was called to the Fort Street Presbyterian Church, of Detroit, which had suffered such a decline that he could only discover 82 pew holders when he assumed the pastorate here. This was the longest ministry (thirteen years) which he enjoyed. For a little more than a year, he was the pastor of the Second Presbyterian Church of Indianapolis, from which he was called to the great Bethany Presbyterian Church of Philadelphia, where John Wanamaker was the Superintendent of its world-famous Sunday School.

In 1866, Mr. Pierson in his first visit to England, came under the spell of the preaching and ministry of Charles H. Spurgeon, little realizing that some day he himself would be the minister of the great Metropolitan Tabernacle, where he was to labor from October 1891 to June 1893. While at Bethany Church, Pierson in 1881 became editor of the *Missionary Review of the*

World, which soon became, under his brilliant guidance, the outstanding missionary journal of the English speaking world.

His own ideal of what a church ought to be might be of interest to the readers of these pages. While this was in a communication to the Fort Street Church, the principles here set forth were never abandoned in subsequent years.

"With perfect frankness, I wish to lay down plank by plank the platform of Bible principles, as I see them, on this subject:

"1.   The Church of God exists on earth in great part to rescue unsaved souls.

"2.   The more destitute souls are, the greater is the obligation of the church towards them.

"3.   Practical indifference to the salvation of the unevangelized forfeits the claim of the church to God's blessing or even to a place among His Golden Candlesticks.

"4.   The twofold work of evangelization and edification must go on side by side.

"5.   Everything in the church should be adapted to these two ends — the salvation of the unsaved and the building up of believers.

"Now as a church are we reaching the results that God's promises lead us to expect? . . ."

Dr. Pierson's influence over university students was outstanding. His vast knowledge, his ability to interpret the Scriptures, and his almost perfect literary style, together with his own spirit of deep earnestness, commended him to young men, who recognized in him one whom they could well believe and follow. An illustration of this influence was to be seen in the life of that great missionary statesman, Dr. Robert E. Speer. "On the day of Prayer for Colleges, in 1886, Dr. Pierson was asked by President James McCosh, of Princeton, to preach in the College Chapel. In the after-meeting a young man arose, in answer to an appeal, and dedicated his life and his energies to Christ. Twenty-five years later, on the occasion of the preacher's golden wedding aniversary, that young man wrote:

" 'My dear Dr. Pierson:

There are many throughout the world who are under spiritual obligation to you but there are few who can feel towards you the same grateful and filial love which I feel. Although I grew up in a Christian home and was not unidentified with Christian work in school and college it was in my freshman year at Princeton, on the day of prayer for schools and colleges, after your sermon in the afternoon and at the after-meeting which you conducted in the evening, that I first publicly acknowledged Christ and resolved to join myself openly to His Church. During all the years since, I have owed much to your unfailing interest, encouragement and confidence. For all this I thank you and thank God.

'Ever affectionately yours,
Robert E. Speer.' "

It was Dr. Pierson who suggested the appointment of Robert Speer to the position of Secretary of the Presbyterian Board of Foreign Missions.

Dr. Pierson's writings are still eminently worth reading, especially the three volumes relating to Biblical themes: *Many Infallible Proofs; The Bible and Spiritual Criticism;* and *The Bible and Spiritual Life.* His *Biography of George Mueller* was written after years of friendship with this mighty man of prayer, and is still the standard work on this fascinating story of great results of prevailing faith. Dr. Pierson died June 3, 1911. His work as editor of the *Missionary Review of the World* was continued by his gifted son, Delevan Pierson (1867-1934).

THE LAMB AND THE BOOK
by
W. M. Clow

*"Thou art worthy to take the book and to open the seals thereof:
for thou wast slain, and hast redeemed us to God by thy blood."*
— Revelation 5:9

A Scottish midsummer day often dawns in calm, entrancingly
clear and sweet, with mountain and moorland and loch lying in
mystic and enchanting light. Before the sun is far above the
horizon the sky has become overcast, the mists have crept down
and begin to drift up the glens. The storm breaks, and the
tempest is out among the hills. Towards evening the winds are
hushed, the clouds are gathered away, and the sun sets in azure
light, fretting a few bars of mist with gold, and lifting one's
thoughts to the throne of God.

That is the recollection that rises into the memory in the
reading of this Book of Revelation. It opens with a song. It
has its morning of clear and dazzling light. The eye looks out on
a scene of heavenly beauty. Soon the darkness gathers. The
mist of sin falls over the landscape. Then there is heard the
noise of battle, and the cry of pain, as storm after storm passes
over the world. As the book closes the storm ceases, the clouds
drift away, and the light falls upon a scene of splendour, and we
find ourselves looking in through the gates of the city of God.

The central and the larger portion of this book has suffered
from an unjust neglect. Sober minds have been dismayed at
the fantastic theories founded upon its symbols. Reverent believers are shocked at the fast and loose way in which ignorant
interpreters continue to play with its figures. Simple folk are
bewildered by the confident dogmatism of many who unroll its

map of history, and set dates to its events. But the book itself is neither so dark nor so perplexing as many suppose. If men would read it patiently, and be less eager to turn its symbols into realities, and its figures into doctrine; if they would ask only its moral and spiritual significances, and leave its material fulfilment greatly alone, the strangest and most pictorial chapters of the Book of Revelation would be to us, as they were to the early Christian Church, a well of consolation whose waters would never fail.

Look in this light at this scene of the Lamb with the sealed book. We are shown One sitting on a throne. We hear the songs of the angels and the response to them from the living creatures. That is the picture of the power and authority and dominion of God. Then we see a book — a roll — in God's hands. It is sealed with seven seals, simply because seven is the perfect number. No man is able to break these binding seals. The seer who beholds the vision weeps, and weeps much, because the knowledge and the wisdom of the book cannot be disclosed. There rises up the Lamb that was slain, the Lamb with the print of the nails in His hands. He takes the book and breaks seal after seal and unbinds page after page. As He does so the tragic history of the Church is unrolled, and the secret of its travail and sorrow and pain is revealed, and the certainty of its triumph is proclaimed.

The meaning of that scene is unmistakable and instantly clear. It sets forth this truth, that Jesus, the Lamb of God who was slain at Calvary, alone has the power to disclose and to interpret the mind and purpose and ways of God. The marrow of the message is that the unfolding and interpretations of the things of God, which are dark with mystery and strange with sorrow, lie in Christ's Cross. It is not the lion of the tribe of Judah, and not the Lamb in His innocence and undisfigured beauty, but the Lamb which was slain, who takes the fast-closed book and breaks the seals. To rise clear of all symbol and figure it is Christ, in and by His Cross, who opens the book of God, gives the interpretation of its record, and sets the hidden mysteries of providence and grace in clear light. It was when the Lamb had taken the book and was about to break the first seal that they sung the new song, saying, "Thou art worthy to take the book, and to open the seals thereof: for thou wast slain, and hast redeemed us to God by thy blood."

Let me illustrate this great truth that the crucified Christ unseals the book of God. God has more than one book, and yet all His books give us the one revelation. Let us see how Christ breaks the seals, and what He gives us to read on pages which otherwise had been dark to men.

Look, to begin with, at *"the sealed book of Scripture."* It should be a commonplace to us that we cannot tread the Old Testament except in Christ's light. Only by an effort of the imagination can we realise how closely sealed and how dark with mystery the Old Testament would have been if Christ had not died and risen again. What would the Old Testament be if there had been no Cross? It would have been the strange and difficult literature of a small and now scattered Syrian race. The names of its heroes and saints would have been as alien to our ears as those of Persian star-gazers or Buddhist devotees. Its prophets would be dervishes with a saner and nobler note. Its sacrifices and types and emblems would be a study for the Orientalist. Its stories would have been no better known to the mass of men than those of the Talmud. Even the Jew of to-day does not know the Old Testament, and does not understand its spirit. "The veil is still upon their hearts." It was not until Christ hung upon His cross that the secret of the Old Testament was disclosed, pregnant with truth profounder than the Rabbis had discerned, rich with a revelation mightier than Abraham had craved, prophetic of a kingdom wider and more spiritual than David conceived, tender with a message more redeeming than its prophets knew. It is the Lamb which was slain who has broken the seal.

The truth is as clearly illustrated by the New Testament scriptures. There are some today to whom the New Testament is still a sealed book. There are scholars to whom we owe a great debt, who know its sources and its history as an astronomer knows the motions of the planets. There are students who have searched out its literature, canvassed its references, inquired into its customs and times. There are teachers who find no praise too high for the wonder of its parables, the wisdom of its counsels, and the tenderness of its epistles. Yet its secret is hidden from them. For them it is merely the story of the greatest religious movement of the East, the record of a lovely life, and a collection of letters in which the hope and joy of simple hearts are expressed. It is, at most and at best, a golden treasury of moral and spiritual beauty. One has only to take up such a book as Martineau's *Seat of Authority in Religion* to find that so clear, so penetrating, so spiritual a mind cannot read the plainest pages of the book. The depth of its moral wisdom, the divineness of its message, and the power of its appeal to the conscience bear in upon his mind and move him to impassioned praise. But the meaning and purpose of the book are hidden from him. The simplest peasant could be his teacher, and would stand amazed that learning and genius should so miss what lies so plainly revealed. Had Martineau looked up at the Cross and seen the Lamb who was slain to redeem, all would have been clear. Read the Gospels and the Epistles in the light of that death for sin, and every word and deed is translated. The cradle of Bethlehem, the carpenter's shop at Nazareth, the Jordan water at baptism, the wilderness of temptation, the garden of Gethsemane, and all the riches of grace in sermon and parable and miracle, stand out as the life-story that leads to the Cross. It is the Lamb that was slain that unfolds, interprets, and expounds the New Testament.

Look, in the second place, at *the sealed book of nature*. There are times when nature seems wholly beneficent and beautiful. There are days when it is bliss to be alive. In the freshness of the newborn spring, when the love calls of the birds are making every woodland musical; in the early summer, when the trees are radiant with blossom, and every garden is a harbour of fragrance; in the autumn, when harvest is laughing in the valleys, what a ministry of well-being and delight nature gives! But how often do we stand aghast at the pitiless cruelty and the blind savagery of nature! How often have men thought, as they have seen the merciless havoc caused by storm, and the ruthless death wrought by pestilence, that there can be no God behind nature at all? There are times when the beauty of nature seems to be only a hypocrite's mask to hide the ferocity of nature's laws, and to blind us to the pain and anguish and death of the never-ceasing tragedy. The blossoms are wilted by untimely frosts, until not one in a hundred comes to fruit. The tender shoots are bitten and broken by the keen spring winds. The nestlings are swept out of their little homes by the unexpected flood. In every glade and under every brushwood defenceless animals lie paralysed with fear. The soil is stained with the blood of hunted and often harmless creatures. In the depths of the sea millions prey upon each other. The whole world of nature is an arena of struggle and pain and death.

How dark with mystery it seems! Take up any Greek poet, or any singer before Christ came, and listen to their cry as they shudder at the strange ferocity of nature. The Greek chorus is, in many cases, only the medium through which a Greek poet uttered his perplexity and his pain. But let the Lamb that was slain open this long-sealed book. Let His pain, His struggle, His death, throw their light upon the mystery of nature. His struggle that others might have the victory, His pain that others might have peace, His death that others might have life, are all but the willing and conscious experience of what nature passes through blindly and unwillingly. In the light of Christ's Cross we see that life in nature is also sacrificial and redeeming. In the light of Christ's Cross we see that the pain and agony and death, which so abound, are only the inevitable condition that life may continue, the species be perpetuated, and the high and beneficent ends of nature gained. Modern science is reading the purpose and the meaning of nature in the light of the ttruth taught by the death of Christ.

Look, in the third place, at *the sealed book of history*. This was the first seal broken by the Lamb in the roll which the seer saw in the hand of God. This was the page over whose sealing John wept. Plainly what John meant to suggest was that the actual history of his own time, a time of bewildering and heart-shaking trial and persecution and death, had been a mystery to him. That the Christian Church should be so imperilled, and so hopeless in the hands of its foes, troubled many hearts, and shook the faith of humble believers. The historians of the Roman Empire have written the record of those tragic years, through which the early Christian Church passed, when its saints died their martyr deaths, and all the hopes and promises they had surely believed seemed false. It was an age when life was hard and brutal and cruel, when not only shame and loss and contempt, but pitiless torture caught the humblest Christian folk in its grasp. Do you wonder that the seer wept much when no man was able to break the seal, and to read the dark and hidden secret of these years of pain and death?

In every century since our historians stand before the sealed book. In every generation the hearts of Christian people fail them for fear. This twentieth century has only begun. We are scarcely across its threshold, and yet east and west, the red horse of war, the black horse of famine, and the pale horse of death have gone forth. The cries of terror and pain are ascending to God. A great part of the struggle between the nations, and the consequent waste of precious life and pain of tender hearts, is actually due to the advance of the Cross. It is the civilisation of Christendom coming into conflict with the ideals of heathendom. It is the leaven of the thoughts of the gospel fermenting in Eastern minds. Within the Church itself there is also bewilderment and pain. There are questions which find no answer, problems which reach no solution, doctrines that seem to be shaken. Who shall unfold this page of mystery? Who shall break the seal of this secret? The Lamb that was slain.

As we see His wound-prints and remember His tears and cries, as we mark His struggle with ignorance and despotism, with misery and sin, we realise that the history of His Church is but the record of His struggle continued by His people, and that they are filling up in their body what is behind of the afflictions of Christ. This pain is but the pain of progress. This conflict among the peoples is but the conflict of light and darkness. This dying of the bravest and most chivalrous is but the dying of the Lamb. These hours of bewilderment and pain, and seeming loss and defeat, are but the hours of the Cross of Christ. The issue will be a world redeemed.

Look, in the fourth place, at *the sealed book of our own lives.* The book of each individual life is also a sealed roll in the hands of God. It is as difficult to read as the books of Scripture, as full of mystery as the book of nature, as strange with calamity and sorrow and seeming mischance as the book of history. It is not, as they were not, all sad and sombre. It is not all perplexity and bewilderment, all strife and pain. There are years of almost unbroken peace, days of achievement and gain, hours of uplifting joy when life seems altogether lovely, and God's ways with us are full of delight. Yet how strange and how burdened, and how marked with what seemed to us needless sorrow and embittering trials our life seemed to be!

I never see a crowded assembly of men and women, or mark them in some day of popular excitement when they pass through the streets, but I think of the privations and disappointments, the unsatisfied hungers and unalleviated sorrows which make up their lot. I never look out on any Christian congregation such as this, of which I have some knowledge, without recalling how much you have suffered, how much you have lost, how frequent have been your sicknesses and your bereavements, how humbling have been your defeats, how searching have been your mortifications and betrayals, how full of anxiety your out-look on life! I never sit and speak with an old man who opens out the story of his long life, but I realise again how closely sealed the book of life is to a man himself. The story told is one of hope unfulfilled, work unfinished, love baffled, trial upon trial, sorrow upon sorrow, death upon death, impoverishing and shadowing life all the way through.

How dark all human life once was! Before Christ's time men scarce dared face the problem. Even Socrates must die only in a wistful wonder, with a sober jest on his lips. The men of the Old Testament, seers into the way of God though they were, could not break the seal. In the story of Job and the psalms of Asaph they leave the mystery of life unsolved. Even the prophets living nearer the dawn were unable to do more than hope that out of exile and captivity, and pain and death, restoration and joy would yet come. But stand below the Cross, and look up at the Lamb that was slain, and mark the course and issue of His passion and His death, and you will realize why the pages of your book are dark with sorrow and wet with tears. Out of life's battle comes conquest over self. Out of life's dark hours come light and strength and peace. Out of life's meek acceptance of death, there comes life for ourselves and others. When the Lamb that was slain breaks the seal of our book of life, and reads its mystery, we can sing as George Matheson sang, when the light from Christ's death fell across the darkest page of his experience —

> "O Cross that liftest up my head,
> I dare not ask to fly from thee,
> I lay in dust life's glory dead,
> And from the ground there blossoms red
> Life that shall endless be."

There is another book, called in the Scriptures "The Book of Life," whose seal is also to be broken by the hand that bears the print of the nails. That book is not ours to read. Its record will also be unrolled and interpreted by the Cross. Let me rather, as I close, impress upon you the comfort that lies in the truth of the Lamb who was slain opening the book. Why is the Cross the unfolding and the interpretation of the sealed roll? It is because the Cross declares not only God's purpose and God's love, but *God's method of helping and healing.* If sin is to be finally banished from human life, if wrong and shame are to cease, if there is to be no more death, and no more pain, and no more tears, if there is to be a city of God into which nothing shall enter that defileth, and a life within it of purity and of peace, *that* can be attained only by a cross. You yourselves can be brought into the way of it only through the acceptance of Christ's Cross. You can continue in the pathway only by the acceptance and the carrying of your own. You can fulfil the work of Christ only by being crucified as He was. The whole creation shall groan and travail in pain until Christ's Cross has completed its work. The sacred Scriptures shall not yield up the full revelation of their everlasting gospel, until the Cross throws its light upon every page. The long march of history shall reach its goal only as the Cross leads on. Your own life shall attain its triumph over sin and pain and fear as you endure your cross. The Lamb that was slain discloses not only the secret but the method of its victory.

May I be allowed, in one closing word, to point out that the mystery has not wholly passed away? Neither in Scripture nor in nature, nor in history nor in life, are the ways of God all clear and comforting to us. The whole seven seals are not broken at once, but only seal after seal. "What I do thou knowest not now, but thou shalt know hereafter." That hereafter will be fulfilled not in earth but only in heaven. Here to the end we shall see in a glass darkly. Here we shall know only in part. Only when we stand before the throne, and see Him who shall take the book and open the seal, shall we fully know why the Lamb was slain from the foundation of the world, and understand why Christ's Cross is in the interpretation of all God's books, and the mode of His people's victory. Then shall we sing the new song, "Thou art worthy to take the book, and to open the seals thereof: for thou wast slain, and hast redeemed us to God by thy blood out of every kindred, and tongue, and people, and nation; and hast made us unto our God kings and priests: and we shall reign on the earth."

BIBLIOGRAPHY

W. M. Clow: *The Cross in Christian Experience,* London, 1908, pp. 139-151
Andrew Murray: *The Blood of the Cross,* London, 1935, pp. 95-104
W. M. Simcox: *The Cessation of Prophecy,* London, 1891, pp. 158-167

WILLIAM M. CLOW
(1853-1930)

William McCallum Clow was born in Glasgow in 1853, where, after preparatory school, he entered Glasgow University, and after graduating, enrolled in the United Free Church College. He held a number of pastorates, as in the South Church, Aberdeen, 1889-1897, followed by brilliant pastoral and preaching ministries in Edinburgh and Glasgow. In 1911, the United Free Church College of Glasgow called him to be a member of its faculty, and ten years later, he was made principal of this noted theological institution. Dr. Clow was the author of a number of important books, most of them consisting of scholarly addresses and sermons of unusual beauty. Among these were *The Day of the Cross,* 1899; *The Cross in Christian Experience,* a most remarkable work, published in 1908; *The Secret of the Lord,* 1910, for the most part expositions of the Gospel accounts of the Transfiguration; and that exquisite volume, *Idylls of Bethany,* 1919, consisting of studies of the references to events occurring in Bethany in the life of our Lord. Dr. Clow died January 6, 1930.

APPENDICES

A. A CLASSIFIED LIST OF ALL REFERENCES TO THE DEATH OF CHRIST OCCURRING IN THE NEW TESTAMENT

B. AN ALPHABETICAL LIST OF SUBJECTS RELATED TO THE BIBLICAL ACCOUNT OF THE CRUCIFIXION AND DEATH OF CHRIST

C. THE STRANGE ASSERTION OF THE KORAN THAT JESUS DID NOT DIE ON THE CROSS

D. THE TESTIMONY OF SIR WILLIAM M. RAMSAY TO THE PREEMINENT SIGNIFICANCE IN HISTORY OF THE DEATH OF CHRIST

E. BIBLIOGRAPHIES

A CLASSIFIED ARRANGEMENT OF ALL
REFERENCES TO THE DEATH OF CHRIST
OCCURRING IN THE NEW TESTAMENT

As far as I know, the following is the only attempt (in print) to enumerate and classify every reference to the Death of Christ found in the writings of the New Testament. The data is far more extensive than one would think, even if he be a close student of the Bible. The number of *different* verses in which Christ's death is referred to is approximately 255 — occurring in all New Testament books except II Thessalonians, Philemon, II Peter, the Epistle of Jude, and II and III John. (The total number of lines in a Greek Testament of these six books is only one-half the number of lines in First Corinthians).

I have included some passages in which, while the specific nomenclature of *death* does not occur, yet death is clearly implied, e.g., "three days and three nights in the heart of the earth," Matthew 12:40; "depart out of this world" John 12:1; 13:36; 16:5,7; etc. On the other hand I have not included, though they might easily be, such passages as Luke 2:35; 12:50; John 7:33; Galatians 3:13.

I have felt justified in including all passages in which Christ's resurrection *from the dead* is declared, because such statements are direct testimonies in the fact of His having died. On the other hand, I have *not* included passages, affirming only the fact of Christ's resurrection, if the concept of *from the dead* is not also included. I have not felt it necessary to include the thirty-three passages in which the *tomb* (or *sepulchre*) of Joseph of Arimathea is referred to.

Most will be surprised at three truths that such a classification as this so clearly reveals: (1) The number of *different predictions* of Christ that He would die at the hands of His enemies — there are nineteen of them (thirty-one, including parallel accounts). (2) The great number of different Greek words used to describe the putting of Christ to death — there are eleven of them. (3) The vast, profound, and eternal consequences that result from the Death of Christ, and how tragic the present state and eternal doom of all who are not reconciled to God by the death of His Son.

A. *PREDICTIONS OF CHRIST'S DEATH IN THE GOSPELS*

   I. Declared by John the Baptist, John 1:29,36
  II. Discussed by Moses and Elijah at the time of the Transfiguration, Luke 9:31
 III. Predictions by Christ Himself
    A. In the Synoptics
      1. reference to Jonah, Matthew 12:40
      2. suffer many things and be killed, Matthew 16:21; Mark 8:31; Luke 9:22
      3. "till the Son of Man is risen from the dead," Matthew 17:9; Mark 9:9
      4. delivered up and be killed, Matthew 17:22,23; Mark 9:31; Luke 9:44
      5. first He must suffer many things, Luke 17:25
      6. that He would be crucified, Matthew 20:18,19; Mark 10:33, 34; Luke 18:33; cf. John 18:32
      7. He would give His life a ransom, Matthew 20:28; Mark 10:45
      8. the Son of man shall suffer, Matthew 17:12; Mark 9:12
      9. delivered up to be crucified, Matthew 26:2
     10. anointed for burial, Matthew 26:12; Mark 14:8; John 12:8
     11. must eat the Passover before He suffered, Luke 22:15
     12. His words at the Last Supper, (listed under F)
     13. in a parable, Matthew 21:39; Mark 12:7,8
    B. In the Fourth Gospel
      1. "destroy this temple," 2:19,21
      2. concerning eating His flesh, etc. 6:51-56
      3. the good Shepherd to lay down His life, 10:11, 15,17,18
      4. "I, if I be lifted up," 12:32,33

5. "I go away," etc., 13:1,36; 14:28; 16:5,7, etc.
IV. By Caiaphas, John 11:31

B. *DETERMINATION OF THE JEWS TO PUT JESUS TO DEATH*

1. They took counsel together against Him how they might destroy Him, Matthew 12:14; Mark 3:6
2. They sought how they might destroy Him, Mark 11:18; Luke 19:47
3. The Jews sought to kill Him, John 7:1; cf. vv. 20,25
4. They took counsel to put Him to death, John 11:53
5. The chief priests sought how they might kill Him, Luke 22:2; Mark 14:1
6. That they should destroy Jesus, Matthew 27:20
7. "He ought to die," John 19:7
8. "Let Him be crucified," Matthew 27:22,23; Mark 15:13; Luke 23:21,23; John 19:15
9. "His blood be on us," Matthew 27:25

Note: It is very significant that while the verb translated *destroy, apollumi,* (often translated *perish* as in John 3:15,16; 6:27; 10:10,28, etc.), is the verb used to indicate the *purpose* of the enemies of Christ, it is never once used of any aspect of their actually putting Christ to death, i.e., no one ever *destroyed* Jesus.

C. *TESTIMONIES TO THE FACT OF HIS DEATH*

1. The soldiers, Mark 15:44,45; John 19:30
2. The angels, Matthew 28:5,7; Mark 16:6; Luke 24:7
3. The evangelists — all references to the fact that Christ was *crucified* (see below) and John 2:22; 20:9; 21:14
4. St. Luke, Acts 1:3
5. The Jews, Acts 5:28
6. Festus, Acts 25:19
7. Apostle Peter, Acts 2:23,24,32; 3:15; 4:10; 5:30; 7:52; 10:39,41

1 Peter 1:2,3,11,19,21; 2:21,23,24; 3:18; 4:1,13

8. Apostle Paul, Acts 13:28,29,30,34,37; 17:3,31; 26:23
   Romans 1:4; 4:24,25; 5:6,8,9,10; 6:3,4,5,8,9,10;
   7:4; 8:11,32,34; 10:9; 14:9,15
   1 Corinthians 1:18,23; 2:2,8; 5:7, 8:11; 10:16;
   11:25,26,27; 15:3,12,20
   2 Corinthians 4:10; 5:14,15; 13:4
   Galatians 1:1,4; 2:20,21; 3:1; 5:11; 6:12,14
   Ephesians 1:7,20; 2:13,16; 5:2,25
   Philippians 2:8; 3:10,18
   Colossians 1:18,20,22,24; 2:12,14,20; 1 Thessalonians 1:10; 2:15; 4:14; 5:10; 1 Timothy 2:6; 2
   Timothy 2:8,11; Titus 2:14

9. Epistle to the Hebrews, 1:3; 2:9,10,14,17; 5:8; 7:27;
   9:12,14,15,26,28; 10:10,12,14,19,29; 12:2,24; 13:12,
   20.

10. St. James, 5:6

11. St. John, 1 John 1:7; 5:6,8; Revelation 1:5; 5:6

12. Groups in heaven, Revelation 5:9,12; 7:14; 12:11

13. Christ Himself, Luke 24:46; Revelation 1:18; 2:8

D. *VARIOUS TERMS USED TO INDICATE HOW CHRIST DIED*

1. *Crucified — stauroō*
   Matthew 20:19; 26:2; 27:22,23,26,31,35,38; 28:5;
   Mark 15:13,14,15,20,24,25,27; 16:6; Luke 23:21,
   23,33; 24:7,20; John 19:6,10,15,16,18,20,23; Acts
   2:36; 4:10; 1 Corinthians 1:23; 2:2,8; 2 Corinthians
   13:4; Galatians 3:1; Revelation 11:8. also *prospegnumi* — Acts 2:24

2. *On a cross — stauros*
   Matthew 27:32,40,42; Mark 15:21,30,32; Luke 23:
   26; John 19:17,19,25,31; 1 Corinthians 1:17,18;
   Galatians 5:11; 6:12,14; Ephesians 2:16; Philippians
   2:8; 3:18; Colossians 1:20; 2:14; Hebrews 12:2

3. *He was hung on a tree*
    Acts 5:30; 10:39; 13:29; 1 Peter 2:24; cf. Galatians 3:13
4. *He suffered*
    Verb — pascho
        Matthew 16:21; 17:12; Mark 8:31; 9:12; Luke 9:22; 17:25; 22:15; 24:26,46; Acts 1:3; 3:18; 17:3; Hebrews 2:18; 5:8; 9:26; 13:12; 1 Peter 2:21,23; 3:18; 4:1
    Noun — pathema
        2 Corinthians 1:5,6,7; Philippians 3:10; Hebrews 2:9,10; 10:32; 1 Peter 1:11; 4:13; 5:19
5. *He gave up the ghost*
    Matthew 27:50; Mark 15:37; Luke 23:46; John 19:30
6. *His decease — exodos*
    Luke 9:31
7. *He shed His blood — ekkuno*
    Matthew 26:28; 27:4,6,8,24,25; Mark 14:24; Luke 2:22,44; John 6:53,54,55,56; Acts 1:19; 5:28; 18:6; 20:28; Romans 3:25; 5:9; 1 Corinthians 10:16; 11:25,27; Ephesians 1:7; 2:13; Colossians 1:14,20; Hebrews 9:12,14; 10:19,29; 12:24; 13:12,20; 1 Peter 1:2,19; 1 John 1:7; 5:6,8; Revelation 1:5; 5:9; 7:14; 12:11
8. *He was killed (slain)*
    (in the order of frequency — many passages are referred to in other sections, and I have not attempted to repeat all of them).
    (1) *apokteinoo* — to kill, Matthew 16:21; 17:23; 21:38,39; 26:4; Mark 8:31; 9:31; 10:34; 12:7,8; 14:1; Luke 9:22; 18:33; 20:14,15; John 5:16,18; 7:1,19,25; 8:37,40; 11:53; Acts 3:15; 1 Thessalonians 2:15
    (2) *thanatoo* — to put to death, Matthew 26:59;

27:1; Mark 14:55; 1 Peter 3:18. Also, with use of the noun *thanatos*, Matthew 20:18; Mark 10:34; Luke 24:20; Hebrews 2:9,14, etc.

(3) *tithemi* — to lay down, hence to lay down His life, John 10:11,15,17,18; 1 John 3:16

(4) *anaireoo* — to lift up, to slay, Luke 22:2; 23:2; Acts 2:23; 10:39; 13:28

(5) *sphattoo* — to put to death by violence, Revelation 5:6,9,12; 13:8

(6) *phoneuoo* — to murder, James 5:6. The noun form "murderer," occurs in Acts 7:52

(7) *diacheirizamai* — to lay honds on, Acts 5:30

9. Pierced — Revelation 1:7; John 19:34

E. *CHRIST'S DEATH AS A DIVINE TRANSACTION BETWEEN THE FATHER AND THE SON*

1. He was delivered by the determinate counsel and fore-knowledge of God, Acts 2:23

2. The Father loved Him because He laid down His life, John 10:11,15,17,18

3. He gave Himself up, Galatians 2:20

4. He gave Himself up an offering to God, Ephesians 5:2; Hebrews 10:10,14 *prophora*

5. He gave Himself up a sacrifice to God, Ephesians 5:2; Hebrews 9:26; 10:12; 11:4; *thusia*. The verbal form, 1 Corinthians 5:7

6. A propitiation — *hilasmos*, 1 John 2:2; 4:10; *hilasterion*, Romans 3:25; *hilaskomai*, Hebrews 2:17

7. A ransom, Matthew 20:28; Mark 10:45; 1 Timothy 2:6, *lutron*

8. Through the eternal Spirit He offered Himself without blemish unto God, Hebrews 9:14

F. *THE VAST CONSEQUENCES OF CHRIST'S DEATH*

I. Its universality

    1. For all, 2 Corinthians 5:14,15; "for us all" Romans 8:32; 1 Corinthians 8:11
    2. "for every man," Hebrews 2:9
    3. "for many," Hebrews 9:28
    4. "for us," Romans 5:8; Titus 2:14
    5. for those for whom He died, Romans 14:15
    6. "for me," i.e., for Paul, Galatians 2:20

II. In its Relation to Sin
    1. Basically — He died for sin, Romans 4:25; 1 Corinthians 15:3; Galatians 1:4; Hebrews 10:12; 1 Peter 3:18
    2. He shed His blood for the remission of sins, Matthew 26:28; Mark 14:24; Luke 22:20
    3. to bear the sins of many, Hebrews 9:28; He bare our sins in His own body on the tree, 1 Peter 2:24
    4. for the purification of sins, Hebrews 9:14
    5. to put away sin, Hebrews 9:26

III. Two Consequences for Christ Himself
    1. He learned obedience, Hebrews 5:8
    2. He was made perfect through suffering, Hebrews 2:10

IV. For the Redeemed — By His Death
    1. We are redeemed, Ephesians 1:7; 1 Peter 1:19
    2. We are made nigh to God, Ephesians 2:13
    3. We are reconciled to God, Colossians 1:20,21; Romans 5:10
    4. Jew and Gentile are now made one, Ephesians 2:16
    5. We are cleansed, Hebrews 9:14; 1 John 1:7
    6. We are justified, Romans 5:9
    7. We are sanctified, Hebrews 10:10; 13:12
    8. We are perfected forever, Hebrews 10:14
    9. We have been purchased unto God, Revelation 5:9
    10. The bond that was against us has been nailed to the cross, Colossians 2:14
    11. We have boldness to enter into the holy place, Hebrews 10:19
    12. We are loosed from our sins, Revelation 1:5

13. We may overcome by the blood of the Lamb, Revelation 12:11
14. By His cross peace with God has been secured, Colossians 1:20
15. His blood establishes a new covenant, 1 Corinthians 11:25; Hebrews 12:20
16. His death was to redeem us from all iniquity, Titus 2:14

V. In Relation to the Church "which He purchased with His own blood," Acts 20:28
VI. In Relation to Heaven — Purification, Hebrews 9:12
VII. In Relation to Evil Powers
1. On the cross He made an open show of principalities and powers, Colossians 2:15
2. Through His death He brought to nought the Devil, who had the power of death, Hebrews 2:14
VIII. The Finality of Christ's Sacrifice, Romans 6:9,10; Hebrews 10:12; 7:27; 9:26,28
IX. The Death of Christ fulfilled the relevant prophecies of His Death in the Old Testament, Mark 9:12; Luke 18:31; 24:26,46; Acts 3:18; 26:23; 1 Corinthians 15:3; 1 Peter 1:11

G. *OUR RESPONSE TO CHRIST'S DEATH*

1. We have faith in the efficacy of His blood, Romans 3:25
2. We are to glory alone in the Cross of Christ, Galatians 6:14
3. We should determine to know nothing save Jesus Christ and Him crucified, 1 Corinthians 2:2
4. We are to look upon Christ's offering of Himself as an example, and to follow in His steps, 1 Peter 2:21
5. We are to overcome by the blood of the Lamb, Revelation 12:11
6. We are to reckon ourselves crucified with Christ, and continually seek to be made conformable unto His death — Romans 6:3,4,5,8; Galatians 2:20; Philippians 3:10;

Colossians 2:12; 2 Timothy 2:11; 1 Peter 4:13
7. We are to preach Christ crucified, 1 Corinthians 1:23
8. We are to "proclaim the Lord's death till He come," in our observing the Lord's Supper, 1 Corinthians 11:26, cf. "a communion of the blood of Christ," 1 Corinthians 10:16

B. AN ALPHABETICAL LIST OF SUBJECTS RELATED TO THE BIBLICAL ACCOUNT OF THE CRUCIFIXION AND DEATH OF CHRIST

The most extensive series of encyclopedia articles relating to subjects pertaining to the crucifixion and death of Christ will be found in the two volume *Dictionary of Christ and the Gospels* edited by James Hastings. To many of these subjects articles are also assigned in the *Dictionary of the Apostolic Church* edited by James Hastings, and in practically all Biblical and Theological encyclopedias. In the *Dictionary of Christian Antiquities* (London, 1875, 2 volumes), there are to be found articles on these additional subjects: Adoration of the Cross, Finding of the Cross, Sign of the Cross, and Crucifix.

Akeldema	Price of Blood
Atonement	Print
Blood	Propitiation
Blood and Water	Ransom
Burial	Reconciliation
Calvary	Redemption
The Cross	Reviling
Crown of Thorns	Sacrifice
Crucifixion	Scourge
Darkness	Seal
Death of Christ	Sepulchre
Golgotha	Seven Words from the Cross
Grave	Spices
Grave Clothes	Suffering
Linen	Superscription
Lots	Thirst
Mediator	Thorns
Napkin	Title on the Cross
Passion	Tomb
Passion Week	The Tree
Passover	

C. THE STRANGE ASSERTION OF THE KORAN THAT JESUS DID NOT DIE ON THE CROSS

One of the strangest and deeply erroneous misinterpretations of the New Testament records of the life of Jesus Christ to be found in all post-apostolic religious literature, is the statement in the Koran that Jesus Himself did not die on the cross. The most extended assertion of this strange teaching is found in Part VI of the Koran, Chapter IV, Section 22, on "Transgressions of the Jews." Paragraph 157 read as follows:

"And their saying: Surely we have killed the Messiah, Jesus son of Mary, the apostle of Allah; and they did not kill him nor did they crucify him, but (the matter) was made dubious to them, and most surely those who differ therein are only in a doubt about it; they have no knowledge respecting it, but only follow a conjecture, and they *know it* not for sure;"

In the learned edition of the Koran edited by Maulvi Muhammad Ali, published at Lahore in 1935 is a long note attempting to list fourteen different lines of evidence in support of this strange misstatement of the Koran. There is no need to repeat these here, for they are really nothing less than silly, as any Western student, Christian or not, would unhesitatingly admit. One of them reads as follows: "The side of Jesus being pierced, blood rushed out, and this was a certain sign of life." This statement of the Koran makes it exceedingly difficult for missionaries in Mohammedan countries to persuade Mohammedans of the efficacy of the atonement provided by Christ in His death.

D. THE TESTIMONY OF SIR WILLIAM M. RAMSAY TO THE PREEMINENT SIGNIFICANCE IN HISTORY OF THE DEATH OF CHRIST

On the evening of September 30, 1913, the world-famous archaeologist and historian, Sir William Mitchell Ramsay, delivered an address at the Moody Bible Institute in Chicago on "The Central Fact in History," which was printed from a stenographic report in *The Christian Workers Magazine* (now *Moody Monthly*), November 1913 (Volume 14, pp. 140-143). I believe that this remarkable address has never appeared in any of the many volumes relating to New Testament interpretation that came from the pen of this distinguished scholar, and I thought perhaps it should have a place in this volume on messages on the Death of Christ, inasmuch as it is practically unknown to this present generation of Biblical students.

The address follows:

The central fact in history, and in the life of every individual, if he but knew it, is the death of Christ. This is the message of Paul, the salvation he was setting forth to the pagans and the Jews of his time. I attempt in this address to state to you in a very imperfect way, with stammering lips and insufficient tongue, such conceptions as I have been able to form of the books of the New Testament and the message it conveys. I speak as a student of history, and I desire to offer you my experience in the study of history.

In the first place, I want to give you a somewhat clearer idea how this message sounded in the ears of those men and women, nearly nineteen centuries ago, to whom Paul addressed his words. What did they think of it? How were they able to appreciate it? From what education and in what surroundings were they contemplating this new message? In the second place, I want to give you some clearer idea how this message sounds to some who have lived in the center of the busy university life and thought of Europe.

235

The Advance of Science

Science has advanced marvelously during my life time. I have seen it progressing through the studies and the lectures of many great scientific men whom I listened to when I was a boy at college, and with whom I have been in intercourse in my maturer years. What we now call the most fundamental laws and principles of the highest science would have seemed unintelligible probably to those who taught me thirty to forty years ago. The change has been so extraordinary that what now is accepted as the basis of all scientific reasoning, as the highest exposition of the thought to which science has attained, would have seemed absolute silliness, mere verbiage, to my professors. And the progress has been entirely in the direction of the divine truth. It has been from the material, which was the ruling point of view in my early time, to the spiritual. A number of years ago there was a book published, and widely read, which had great influence. It was called "Natural Law in the Spiritual World" but what we now want, and are looking for, is an exposition which shall be entitled "Spiritual Law in the Material World." It is spiritual law which we desire. Matter is now recognized to be mere expression of our ignorance. When we don't understand a thing, it seems to be matter, but that is all the reality of matter. I do not know whether we can see through what we don't understand, but still that marvelous fact, the death of Christ, remains above us and in front of us. It is the most fundamental, and yet in a way the most incomprehensible truth, in the world. It is incomprehensible because it is fundamental. All things rest on it; it rests on nothing deeper or simpler. It is the beginning and the end. The history of the creation centers, culminates, in the death of Christ. From that event history takes a new start, and the modern world begins. From this truth all knowledge begins and in this truth all knowledge culminates. It is the purpose of God from the beginning of the world, conceived in the creation, a fundamental fact in the whole plan of creation, that the world was to move onward towards that event and then to start afresh from it. It was not a device which was struck out in despair at the evil of the world; it was the plan of the world, conceived by the divine will in the beginning, and by this will planned out.

Paul's Deepest and Loftiest Thought

We have viewed this central event, and now I want to set before you certain considerations connected with the epistle to the Ephesians, in which more than in any other of Paul's epistles, we have his deepest and his loftiest thoughts on the nature of God and of man. It is the most glorious, the most glittering, the most splendid of all the letters. In all ages of the world, at the present time, and in the remote past, there have been people, there are many people, who do not see the real truth but who judge only from superficial fancy. People who have been filled with the thought that this world is all awry, and "the times are out of joint," and fate is hard and cruel, that the lot of man is naught but misery. Such has been the experience, such was the general opinion of the pagan world which Paul was addressing. He speaks always with that knowledge in his mind. And to that pagan world, to its statesmen, its philosophers, its writers, the common people, who were discouraged and hopeless and had resigned themselves to the conclusion that we should "eat and drink for tomorrow we die," he came with his message of hope, joy, love, peace — the message of salvation. They were, all those pagans, praying and making vows for salvation. That was the very word that Paul used, but in a different, more spiritual sense. They had no conception of the spiritual meaning which Jesus, first, and then Paul put into it. They were natural. They had something in their minds which they prayed and longed for, and that idea they called salvation. Now, in contrast with the despair which filled the pagan world, Paul is always transported, and especially in this letter to the Ephesians. He is transported with a lively perception of the beauty, the love, the kindness — in one word, the grace of God in all His dealings with men. That was the message he had to give. It was not a message of sorrow, of apprehension for the future; it was not a message of terror. What he seems always to be saying is, "What an abundantly happy lot is that of mankind! What perfect and indescribable grace is that of God's!" That was the message that the pagan world needed. Melancholy runs through all pagan literature in Greece and Rome, characterizes every book, and appears as an undertone in almost every poem however gay and joyous on the surface. It had so deeply affected the whole thought of the pagan world, that it was necessary for Paul to arouse in them love and faith, which had become almost extinct. He had to give them something worth living for and something worth dying for. Now, before a world like that it was useless to set forth a picture of the misfortune of those who did not understand the message Paul was giving. It was useless to set before them the terrors of a future world. No misfortune could be worse than what they were enduring. Take a picture drawn by a pagan writer who lived just the century before Paul, or scarcely that. He depicts the lot of a wealthy, prosperous, powerful noble in the mighty city of Rome. He says of this Roman noble, a representative of the most powerful aristocracy of that time, "sick of home, he goes forth from it and as suddenly comes back, finding that he is no better off. He races to his country house from the town, driving his carriage furiously. He yawns the moment he has reached the door, or sinks heavily into sleep, or hurries back again to town." In this way, says the poet, each man flees from himself or hides himself, because he is sick of life.

Pagan Despair and Christian Hope

This was the frame of mind in which the pagans dwelt and in which they were praying and making their vows for salvation. Such a people had no faith in the present and no hope for the future. They were filled with fear as to the world around them and with utter despair as to that which was to come. Threats of terror meant nothing more to them in the future than they were already suffering in the present. Paul had to recreate these men and he did this in the only way possible, by awakening their belief in the goodness of God, and along with this, their hope and their power of loving and serving Him. Those to whom he spoke did not want a message of philosophy. They did not want a mere learned, or skillful or highly wrought exposition of the principles of philosophy or arguments as to the being and nature of God in the abstract. They wanted life and hope and it was this that Paul declared to them, and hence it is that Paul says so little in his letters about the lot of the wicked.

What he had to urge upon people he addressed was the happiness which was offered to them; and he rises to the loftiest heights of enthusiasm. He expresses himself almost in a kind of lyrical, poetical prose when he contemplates the grace of God as planned before He created the foundation of the world, and worked out stage by stage to its perfection in the death of Christ. Words almost fail him to picture the exceeding riches of God's grace in kindness towards us in Christ Jesus, or in picturing the unsearchable riches of Christ. And it is not merely that we receive from Christ. Our lot is even more blessed, more splendid than that. We, he says, are the riches of Christ; we are the inheritance of Christ: His body, the saints. Christ is the head of the church but a head without a body is nothing. We are necessary to Him. To that honor have we been exalted by the grace of God. The purpose of God from the creation has been to create and complete this body, the glory of Christ's inheritance in the saints. Thus we are necessary to God and to Christ. What an honor! What a happiness for man! The glory of God and the splendor of Christ cannot be made real and established definitely in the universe except through the completion of the salvation of man, in the congregation of saints. Our bliss is His glory, and he heaps up words upon words to blazon before the eyes of those Ephesian Christians the glitter of their lot in being made the completion and the perfection of the eternal purpose of God, the riches and the glory of the inheritance of Christ. Now we have become so familiarized from infancy with this and other expressions, that we need to fear and hold them in thought, as it were, apart from ourselves, and gaze upon their true meaning so as to realize the dazzling beauty of that which they describe.

A Practical Lesson for Us

But from that thought on which one might enlarge, I pass on to draw a lesson which we have to gain from this epistle to the Ephesians.

Paul had seen in revelation — those revelations constitute his highest glory, his exaltation in trouble and difficulty, his strength for the future — he had seen in those revelations the glory of God, and the glory of God is the completion of His purpose in the perfection of His creation. That idea lay in Paul's heart and gave passion to his life, and power to his words: but that idea must not be given, not be declared fully at any time to men. It was not lawful to mention all that he had seen and known. It was the sort of knowledge which can never be comprehended except by those who have risen to the same level. And who is there among us that can say he has as yet done that? Now this knowledge is the mystery of God and it is also the knowledge of God. The mystery of God is that supreme knowledge which was previously hidden from the world but which is being revealed, which is in the process of being revealed to us through our faith in Christ. Our life is the process of acquiring the knowledge of God which is from Christ, and which, to use Paul's words, seizes and takes possession of us. And just in proportion as the saints in Ephesus had reached this knowledge, so it became possible for Paul to declare it more and more fully to them.

But there is just one point in conclusion on which I hardly dare to speak. A point in treating about which it is necessary to use the utmost reverence and reticence. Is it not the case that in what I have been saying there lies the way towards understanding better, in some small degree, that greatest of all mysteries, and most fundamental and yet incomprehensible of all truths — the death of Christ? It is the law of the universe — it is the will of God, that the sin of man makes the suffering of God. If our righteousness, if our salvation, makes the happiness of God, then the sin of man makes the suffering of God. This is the divine purpose and plan existent from the beginning. Deliberately intended and contemplated in the beginning of the world. It is part of the nature of God. The death of Christ was looked forward to before the foundation of the world as the completion of His gradually unfolding purpose. He summed up all things in Christ, all things in the heavens and all things on the earth, according to the purpose of Him Who worketh all things after the counsel of His will. Now the supreme blessing which Paul invokes for the Ephesians is that they may be granted that insight into the purpose and the knowledge of God, so that they may understand how and why God has called them, and may appreciate what His inheritance is. It is achieved through the triumphant death and resurrection of Christ. The death of Christ pays in full the penalty of the sin of the creature. The man who through the sin had died, gains life through the payment of the penalty of Jesus Christ, and is inheritor along with Him of all that He has gained. It is no longer we that live but it is Christ that lives in us.

E. BIBLIOGRAPHIES

In the following bibliographies, I have felt it was not necessary to undertake lists of a number of rich subjects that bear upon the death of our Lord, confining myself for the most part here to volumes that interpret the atoning values of His death. I have, therefore, omitted volumes on the following subjects: (1) Typical foreshadowings and prophecies of Christ's death in the Old Testament; (2) The crowded events of Holy Week leading up to the death of Christ, as for example, His agony, the betrayal, the trials, etc.; (3) Character studies of those involved in Christ's crucifixion; (4) The seven last words; (5) Volumes of sermons relating to our Lord's death which are for the most part included in the separate preceding bibliographies; (6) The extensive treatment of our Lord's death in the great systematic theologies.

I. THE DEATH OF CHRIST AS AN HISTORICAL EVENT

F. W. Krummacher, *The Suffering Saviour,* 1854. Edinburgh, 1856. 8th ed. 1875, Chicago, 1953, pp. xxviii.444.

K. Schilder: *Christ Crucified,* Grand Rapids, 1940, pp. 561

II. THE CROSS AS AN INSTRUMENT OF PUTTING CHRIST TO DEATH

W. H. Aslam: *The Cross and the Serpent, being a Brief History of the Triumph of the Cross through a long series of ages, in Prophecy, Types, and Fulfillment,* Oxford, 1849, pp. 273

William C. Prime: *A History of the Invention, Preservation, and Disappearance of the Wood known as the True Cross,* New York, 1877, pp. 143.

William Wood Seymour: *The Cross in Tradition, History, and Art,* New York, 1898, pp. xxx.489. A superb work of quarto size, with some 270 illustrations, and a bibliography of over 300 titles.

Charles H. Spurgeon: *Sermons on the Blood and Cross of Christ,* Grand Rapids, 1961, John 12:32, pp. 155-160; Romans 5:8, pp. 18-28; Galatians 6:14, pp. 244-256; Ephesians 1:7, pp. 203-215.

James Stalker: *The Trial and Death of Jesus Christ,* London, 1894, pp. 321

Otto Zoeckler: *The Cross of Christ,* London, 1877, pp. xxvi.447. This is a work of great learning, not often seen, with chapters on such subjects as Constantine's Vision of the Cross; The Cross in the Church of the Middle Ages; the Cross in the Theology and Church of the Reformation; The Sign of the Returning Son of Man, etc., together with an extensive bibliography.

III. THE BIBLICAL DOCTRINE OF SACRIFICE

Horace Bushnell: *Vicarious Sacrifice*. New York, 1865, pp. 552
Alfred Cave: *The Scriptural Doctrine of Sacrifice*, 1877. new ed., Edinburgh, 1890, pp. 546
Thomas J. Crawford: *The Doctrine of Holy Scripture respecting the Atonement*, Edinburgh, 1871, 3rd ed., 1880, pp, 538
G. B. Gray: *Sacrifice in the Old Testament*, Oxford, 1925, pp, 434
F. C. N. Hicks: *The Fulness of Sacrifice*, 3rd ed., 1946, pp. 388
Archibald W. Magee: *Discourses and Dissertations of Atonement and Sacrifice*, 4th ed., London, 1816, 3 vols. 1 vol. ed., New York, 1813, pp. 541
Frederick Dennison Maurice: *The Doctrine of Sacrifice Deduced from the Scriptures*, new ed., London, 1893, pp. 315
James G. Murphy: *Sacrifice as set forth in Scripture*, London, 1889, pp. 252
Archibald Scott: *Sacrifice; Its Prophecy and Its Fulfillment*, Baird Lecture, 1892-1893. Edinburgh, 1894, pp. 372

IV. THE ATONEMENT ACCOMPLISHED BY THE DEATH OF CHRIST

The Atonement in Modern Religious Thought. A Theological Symposium. London, 1900, pp. 380
The Atonement. A Clerical Symposium, by Archdeacon Farrar, Principal Rainy, and others. London, 1883, 1935, pp. 179
L. Berkhof: *Vicarious Atonement through Christ*, Grand Rapids, 1936, pp. 184
Loraine Boettner: *The Atonement*, Grand Rapids, 1941, pp. 136
Emil Brunner: *The Mediator*, Philadelphia, 1947, pp. 623
John McLeod Campbell: *The Nature of the Atonement*, Cambridge, 1856. 3rd ed. London, 1869, 4th ed. 1873, pp. 390
Robert S. Candlish: *The Atonement*, London, 1861, pp. 400
R. W. Dale: *The Atonement*, London, 1875, 17th ed. 1896, pp. 560
James Denney: *The Atonement and the Modern Mind.* New York, 1903, pp. 159
—————: *The Christian Doctrine of Reconciliation*, London, New York, 1918, pp. 339
—————: *The Death of Christ: Its Place and Interpretation in the New Testament*, London, 1902. pp. 354
Daniel Dewar: *The Atonement, Its Nature, Reality and Efficacy*, Edinburgh, 1831, London, 3rd ed., 1860, pp. 562
Nathaniel Dimock: *The Doctrine of the Death of Christ*, 2nd ed., London, 1903, pp. 136, XCVIII. (The appendix of over 90 pages consists of Extracts from Christian Writers from the Second Century to the Fifteenth Century inclusive).
Robert McCheyne Edgar: *The Philosophy of the Cross*, London, 1874. 2nd ed. 1878, pp. 368
F. W. Dillistone: *The Significance of the Cross*, Philadelphia, 1944, pp. 247
J. T. Ferrier: *Sacrifice A Necessity of the Atonement*, etc. London, 1888, pp. 196
P. T. Forsyth: *The Cruciality of the Cross*, London, 1910, pp. 218
Joseph Gilbert: *The Christian Atonement*, London, 1836, pp. 477
L. W. Grensted (ed.) *The Atonement in History and in Life*, New York, 1929, pp. 340
H. E. Guilleband: *Why the Cross*, London, 1937, pp. 267
Roswell Dwight Hitchcock: *Eternal Atonement*, New York, 1888, pp. 306
A. A. Hodge: *The Atonement*, Philadelphia, 1867, pp. 440

244

Leonard Hodgson: *The Doctrine of the Atonement*, London, 1951, pp. 159

John Knox: *The Death of Christ*, New York, 1958, pp. 190

J. J. Lias: *The Atonement Viewed in the Light of Certain Moral Difficulties*, Hulsean Lectures, 1883-1884. London, 2nd ed. 1888, pp. 166

John Scott Lidgett: *The Spiritual Principle of the Atonement*, etc., London, 1897, pp. 522, 3rd ed., 1901

Alexander B. Macaulay: *The Death of Jesus*, London, 1938, pp. 181

A. B. Mackay: *The Glory of the Cross*. 2nd ed. London, 1877

John Miley: *The Atonement in Christ*. New York, 1879, pp. 351

R. C. Moberly: *Atonement and Personality*, New York, 1901, pp. 418

Leon Morris: *The Apostolic Preaching of the Cross*, Grand Rapids, 1955, pp. 280

Hastings Rashdall: *The Idea of the Atonement in Christian Theology*, London, 1919, pp. 502

Julius B. Remensnyder: *The Atonement and Modern Thought*, Philadelphia, 1905, pp. xxx.223

D. M. Ross: *The Cross of Christ*, Garden City, N.Y. 1928, pp. 288

George Smeaton: *The Doctrine of the Atonement as Taught by Christ Himself*, Edinburgh, 1868, Grand Rapids, 1953, pp. 460

——————: *The Doctrine of the Atonement as taught by the Apostles*, Edinburgh, 1870, Grand Rapids, 1957, pp. 540

C. Ryder Smith: *The Bible Doctrine of Salvation. A Study of the Atonement*, London, 1941, rev. ed. 1946, pp. 270

David Smith: *The Atonement in the Light of History and the Modern Spirit*, London, 1919, pp. 226

John Pye Smith: *Four Discourses on the Sacrifice and Priesthood of Jesus Christ*, etc , 3rd ed., London, 1847, pp. 375

George B. Stevens: *The Christian Doctrine of Salvation*, New York, 1905, pp. 546

Vernon F. Storr: *The Problem of the Cross*, London, 1919, pp. 137

Wm. Symington: *The Atonement and Intercession of Jesus Christ*, London, 1863, pp. 308

Vincent Taylor: *The Christian Doctrine of Atonement in New Testament Teaching*, London, 1940, 2nd ed., 1945, pp. 219

——————: *The Cross of Christ*, London, 1956, pp. 108

——————: *Forgiveness and Reconciliation*, London, 1952, pp. 242

——————: *Jesus and His Sacrifice*, London, 1948, pp. 335

R. W. Wardlaw: *Discourses on the Nature and Extent of the Atonement in Christ*, 2nd ed. Glasgow, 1844, pp. 289

What the Cross Means to Me. A Theological Symposium, London, 1943, pp. 177